WITHD

D0077105

Collin College Library
SPRING CREEK CAMPUS
Plano, Texas 75074

Policing Terrorism

Research Studies into
Police Counterterrorism
Investigations

Advances in Police Theory and Practice Series

Series Editor: Dilip K. Das

Policing Terrorism: Research Studies into Police Counterterrorism Investigations
David Lowe

Policing in Hong Kong: History and Reform
Kam C. Wong

Cold Cases: Evaluation Models with Follow-up Strategies for Investigators, Second Edition
James M. Adcock and Sarah L. Stein

Crime Linkage: Theory, Research, and Practice
Jessica Woodhams and Craig Bennell

Police Investigative Interviews and Interpreting: Context, Challenges, and Strategies
Sedat Mulayim, Miranda Lai, and Caroline Norma

Policing White Collar Crime: Characteristics of White Collar Criminals
Petter Gottschalk

Honor-Based Violence: Policing and Prevention
Karl Anton Roberts, Gerry Campbell, and Glen Lloyd

Policing and the Mentally Ill: International Perspectives
Duncan Chappell

Security Governance, Policing, and Local Capacity
Jan Froestad with Clifford D. Shearing

Policing in Hong Kong: History and Reform
Kam C. Wong

Police Performance Appraisals: A Comparative Perspective
Serdar Kenan Gul and Paul O'Connell

Los Angeles Police Department Meltdown: The Fall of the Professional-Reform Model of Policing
James Lasley

Financial Crimes: A Global Threat
Maximillian Edelbacher, Peter Kratcoski, and Michael Theil

Police Integrity Management in Australia: Global Lessons for Combating Police Misconduct
Louise Porter and Tim Prenzler

FORTHCOMING

Policing Terrorism

Research Studies into Police Counterterrorism Investigations

David Lowe
Liverpool John Moores University
School of Law
UK

CRC Press
Taylor & Francis Group
Boca Raton London New York

CRC Press is an imprint of the
Taylor & Francis Group, an **informa** business

CRC Press
Taylor & Francis Group
6000 Broken Sound Parkway NW, Suite 300
Boca Raton, FL 33487-2742

© 2016 by Taylor & Francis Group, LLC
CRC Press is an imprint of Taylor & Francis Group, an Informa business

No claim to original U.S. Government works

Printed on acid-free paper
Version Date: 20150616

International Standard Book Number-13: 978-1-4822-2683-6 (Hardback)

This book contains information obtained from authentic and highly regarded sources. Reasonable efforts have been made to publish reliable data and information, but the author and publisher cannot assume responsibility for the validity of all materials or the consequences of their use. The authors and publishers have attempted to trace the copyright holders of all material reproduced in this publication and apologize to copyright holders if permission to publish in this form has not been obtained. If any copyright material has not been acknowledged please write and let us know so we may rectify in any future reprint.

Except as permitted under U.S. Copyright Law, no part of this book may be reprinted, reproduced, transmitted, or utilized in any form by any electronic, mechanical, or other means, now known or hereafter invented, including photocopying, microfilming, and recording, or in any information storage or retrieval system, without written permission from the publishers.

For permission to photocopy or use material electronically from this work, please access www.copyright.com (http://www.copyright.com/) or contact the Copyright Clearance Center, Inc. (CCC), 222 Rosewood Drive, Danvers, MA 01923, 978-750-8400. CCC is a not-for-profit organization that provides licenses and registration for a variety of users. For organizations that have been granted a photocopy license by the CCC, a separate system of payment has been arranged.

Trademark Notice: Product or corporate names may be trademarks or registered trademarks, and are used only for identification and explanation without intent to infringe.

Visit the Taylor & Francis Web site at
http://www.taylorandfrancis.com

and the CRC Press Web site at
http://www.crcpress.com

This book is dedicated to my wife Kathleen, who tolerated the long hours I spent as a detective investigating terrorism and who is now tolerating similar absences while I research the topic. Her support for me has been unswerving and I would not be where I am now if it were not for her encouragement and instillment of a belief in me. The book is also written in memory of two inspirational academics whose work at a global level transformed and shaped the study of policing: Jean-Paul Brodeur and Daniel Koenig.

Jean-Paul Brodeur died in 2010. He was a professor at the University of Montreal, Canada. A former editor of the international journal Police Practice and Research, *Jean-Paul developed theoretical contexts to aid the study of policing, including his theory of high and low policing roles. His expertise was revered by academic and practitioner alike and he headed several research projects commissioned by the Law Reform Commission of Canada.*

Daniel Koenig was a professor of criminology at the University of Victoria, Canada, and was an IPES (International Police Executive Symposium) book editor. Daniel died in 2001. During his academic career he had the ability to combine theoretical approaches to policing with practical applications to his work. As a result he was regularly consulted by the police in the State of Victoria and the Royal Canadian Mounted Police on policing methods. This is exemplified in the book he coedited with the current editor-in-chief of the Police Practice and Research Series, *Professor Dilip Das,* International Police Cooperation: A World Perspective. *Published in 2001, the book was an original and key text in bringing together work from academics and practitioners in policing from around the world into one book from which policing scholars and practitioners could distinguish not just differences in policing between nation states, but, importantly, the many areas of similarities that exist.*

It is academics' pioneering work like Jean-Paul and Daniel's that have been inspirational to me and behind my development as both an academic and practitioner.

Contents

Section II

INVESTIGATING TERRORISM

5 Lack of Discretion in High Policing   97

6 Radicalization of Terrorist Causes: A Study of the 32CSM/IRA Threat to UK Security   115

Series Editor's Preface

While the literature on police and allied subjects is growing exponentially, its impact upon day-to-day policing remains small. The two worlds of research and practice of policing remain disconnected even though cooperation between the two is growing. A major reason is that the two groups speak in different languages. The research work is published in hard-to-access journals and presented in a manner that is difficult to comprehend for a layperson. On the other hand, the police practitioners tend not to mix with researchers and remain secretive about their work. Consequently, there is little dialog between the two and almost no attempt to learn from one another. Dialog across the globe, among researchers and practitioners situated in different continents, is of course even more limited.

I attempted to address this problem by starting the International Police Executive Symposium (IPES), www.ipes.info, where a common platform has brought the two together. IPES is now in its 17th year. The annual meetings, which constitute most of the organization's major annual events, have been hosted in all parts of the world. Several publications have come out of these deliberations, and a new collaborative community of scholars and police officers has been created whose membership runs into several hundreds.

Another attempt was to begin a new journal, aptly called *Police Practice and Research: An International Journal* (*PPR*), which has opened the gate for practitioners to share their work and experiences. The journal has attempted to focus upon issues that help bring the two on a single platform. *PPR* completed its 16th year in 2015. It is certainly evidence of the growing collaboration between police research and practice that *PPR*, which began with four issues a year, expanded to five issues in its fourth year and now is issued six times a year.

Clearly, these attempts, despite their success, remain limited. Conferences and journal publications do help create a body of knowledge and an association of police activists but cannot address substantial issues in depth. The limitations of time and space preclude larger discussions and more authoritative expositions that can provide stronger and broader linkages between the two worlds.

It is this realization of the increasing dialog between police research and practice that has encouraged many of us—my close colleagues and I, connected closely with IPES and *PPR* across the world—to conceive and implement a new attempt in this direction. I am now embarking on a book series, Advances in Police Theory and Practice, that seeks to attract writers from all parts of the world. Further, the attempt is to find practitioner contributors. The objective is to make the series a serious contribution to our knowledge of the police, as well as to improve police practices. The focus is not only in work that describes the best and most successful police practices, but also one that challenges current paradigms and breaks new ground to prepare police for the twenty-first century. The series seeks comparative analysis that highlights achievements in distant parts of the world as well as that which encourages an in-depth examination of specific problems confronting particular police forces.

It is hoped that, through this series, it will be possible to accelerate the process of building knowledge about policing and helping to bridge the gap between the two worlds—the world of police research and police practice. This is an invitation to police scholars and practitioners across the world to come and join in this venture.

Dilip K. Das, PhD
Founding President,
International Police Executive Symposium, IPES, www.ipes.info

Founding editor-in-chief, Police Practice and Research:
An International Journal,
PPR, www.tandf.co.uk/journals

Prologue

As part of the Advances in Police Theory and Practice Series, this is a socio-legal study of terrorism investigations. The research conducted for this book is a combination of legal and empirical research. As the law should guide police investigators' actions during investigations and with legal definitions determining the boundaries of various categories of criminal activity, it is important that the law surrounding aspects of terrorism is researched and examined. The legal research carried out for this book examined both terrorism-related statutes and relevant case reports (predominantly in the United Kingdom, the United States, Canada, and Australia). In addition to the legal research, this book also includes empirical research covering aspects of counterterrorism investigations.

As a former counterterrorism detective, I wrote the book with practitioners in mind as well as academic scholars and students studying the areas of security and terrorism. Investigating terrorist activity is one of the most challenging roles in policing, and the most challenging factor in counterterrorism investigations is the pressure placed on investigators to prevent terrorist acts from occurring. The impact and fallout of a terrorist attack are devastating, not just the deaths and serious injuries sustained but the terror effect it leaves in people's minds. The terror effect leaves a sense of vulnerability in people's minds, ranging from those who may be at the scene and who are not physically injured but who have to recover from the effects of conditions such as posttraumatic stress disorder, to those who see the reports of the attack in the media. In terrorist attacks there is no direct relationship between the attacker and the victim, with most attacks occurring in locations where people are literally going about their daily business, from going to work or simply shopping; part of the terror effect is that some may no longer feel safe. As a terrorist act has some form of ideological cause motivating it, normally a cause that opposes the government of a state, governments become an important stakeholder in ensuring that counterterrorism investigations result in acts being prevented. A consequence of this is that, compared to other policing roles and responsibilities in terrorism investigations, the political oversight is more intensive. As a result, this adds further pressure on investigating officers to ensure terror acts do not occur. It also explains why states have introduced statutes and policies widening police powers in relation to terrorism investigations.

By analyzing terrorism, the laws underpinning counterterrorism and the approaches taken by investigators, the contribution this book makes to the Advances in Police Theory and Practice Series is significant in the study of policing. The recent terrorist attacks at the Canadian government buildings in Ottawa in October 2014 and in Paris on January 7–9, 2015, highlight the devastating threat many Western states face, in particular from the threat of low-level attacks involving the use of small arms fire. At the time of writing, the tragic events of the attack at the Charlie Hebdo offices, the Paris Metro, and the Jewish Supermarket in Paris are so recent that actual facts as pertaining to these events have yet to be released. What has already come out is that the Kouachi brothers who carried out the attack on the Charlie Hebdo offices, despite being known in the French authorities' intelligence systems as potential terrorist suspects, by operating in a relatively small cell and carrying out a low-level attack, the authorities struggled to pick up details of when this attack was to be carried out and prevent it from happening. This demonstrates how important intelligence gathering and analysis of that intelligence are in counterterrorism. In this current period, where many states are at a high threat level, it is imperative that there is increased international cooperation between states' counterterrorism agencies, especially to counter the threat international groups pose to national security, in particular Islamic State and Al Qaeda affiliates, such as the Jabhat al-Nusra Front. To aid this cooperation there is an argument concerning the relevance of nation states having compatible antiterrorism laws to ensure that evidence obtained in one state's jurisdiction is admissible in another. By examining issues surrounding the legal definition of terrorism, statutory preventative measures, surveillance, and the recruitment and handling of informants, this book addresses some of the issues related to the events that occurred in Paris. As a result this book complements other policing studies in the Advances in Police Theory and Practice Series, enabling policing scholars to have a more rounded understanding of issues and problems facing policing agencies' functions and duties in the twenty-first century.

To aid this understanding, this book is broken down into two sections. The chapters in Section I are based predominantly on legal research examining the law governing terrorism investigations and is a comparative study of the law among a number of states. Section II contains mainly empirical studies into aspects of terrorism investigations that include the level of operational officers' discretion in using the powers given to them, the radicalization of individuals to terrorist causes, and the recruiting and handling of informants. The law covered in Section I includes the legal definition of terrorism, statutory preventative measures, surveillance, and the funding of terrorism. With the threat international terrorist groups pose to national security—especially jihadist groups such as Al Qaeda, which pose a threat to a number of Western states' security, including the United Kingdom, the

United States, Canada, and Australia—Section I covers a comparative study of the law. This comparative study allows the reader not only the opportunity to see where there are similarities in the respective legal jurisdictions, but also to see where gaps exist within the states' laws that can make compatibility in cooperation difficult. Section II continues with a comparative study in the practices of counterterrorism agencies. The coverage of the use of informants is an example that highlights not just where there are similarities but also where differences exist between states' agencies.

Author

David Lowe is a principal lecturer at Liverpool John Moores University Law School. Prior to becoming an academic, he was a police officer for 27 years with the UK's Merseyside Police. Except for a few years performing uniform police duties, the majority of Lowe's police service was as a detective, where he mostly served in the United Kingdom's Special Branch Counterterrorism Unit. His research in the area of policing, terrorism, and security has been published in several books and journals, including his last book on terrorism, *Examining Political Violence: Studies in Terrorism, Counterterrorism, and Internal War.* He also coedited (with Dilip Das) the second volume of *Trends in the Judiciary: Interviews with Judges from across the Globe,* which was published in 2014. He is a regular contributor to the Westlaw® legal encyclopedia, *Insight*, on legal issues related to terrorism. In addition to his recent publications, he regularly provides commentary in these areas for television, radio, and print media (particularly the BBC and LBC) in the United Kingdom and the rest of Europe and for US print media (including *Wall Street Journal, Washington Post,* and *The New York Times*).

Introduction

Terrorism imbues a number of emotions and responses that, depending upon the situation and a person's standpoint, can range from horror at the outcome of an attack to support and understanding of a terrorist group's cause. For officers investigating terrorism, these emotions have to be put to one side as they work toward the main aim of any terrorism investigation: prevention. Prevention is also the main aim of governments as they not only try to keep their citizens safe, but also attempt to show that they have the capability to do so, thereby nullifying the effects of terrorism on their populations. To assist in ensuring this is the case, state governments have legislated or introduced policies giving investigators wider powers to intrude upon the lives of those suspected to be involved in acts of terrorism. This in turn has resulted in further debates on the necessity of such powers, argued between those in favor of the needs of national security and those who are more in favor of protecting an individual's rights or liberty. Terrorism has never been a topic of discussion drawing passive views; any discussion on the topic draws polarized views. At the time of this writing, this was evident with the actions of the Islamic State in Syria and Iraq, especially in the West when the Islamic State beheaded US and UK citizens whom it held hostage in 2014. A sociolegal study that contains both legal and empirical research, this book considers some of those views by examining the legal debates that have been carried out in cases brought before the courts. Added to these criminological explanations and opinions are consideration of the ongoing debate between balancing the needs of national security and protecting the rights and liberties of the individual.

Section I examines the law governing terrorism investigations. Focusing predominantly on the UK, European Union, US, and Canadian jurisdictions, Chapter 1 examines the legal definition of terrorism. While the respective governments of the Commonwealth countries of the United Kingdom, Canada, and Australia have incorporated a legal definition of terrorism into their statutes, it is somewhat surprising that the United States has not done so, even if the US government introduced a legal definition solely for its federal agencies to work from. While definitions of what actions amount to an act of international terrorism can be found in the US Code 18, Part 1, Chapter 113B, the US government has left it to respective agencies to derive their own definition of what amounts to an act of terrorism. While the US government may be reluctant to have a single legal definition due to the conflict that can

arise when trying to create a consensus, Canada and Australia are also federal states, yet they have achieved this task. Even though it is not a federal
government, the European Union has drafted into its legislation a definition that all of its 28 member states (including the United Kingdom) should
include in their legislative process. It appears that the threat international
terrorism poses from groups such as Al Qaeda has resulted in a similarity of
the definitions of terrorism, including between those drawn up by US federal
agencies. This is important, as an international terrorist threat has resulted in
the requirement for a coherent and agreed international response. As counterterrorism agencies in a number of states work in close cooperation, it is
necessary that investigators can readily identify actions construed as terrorist acts defined in the respective states' legal instruments. This is especially
important where investigators obtain evidence that subsequently could be
used in a criminal trial in another state's jurisdiction.

Retaining focus on the importance the international jihadist threat
poses to many states, mainly through researching case reports, Chapter 1
concludes with an examination of how the courts have interpreted what
amounts to a religious cause that motivates acts of terrorism, along with the
evidence they require to prove a person was motivated toward committing
terrorist offenses through a religious cause. This examination considers what
amounts to a religious cause in the legal definitions of terrorism. This section
studies a number of activities ranging from the collecting and possessing of
information that may be useful to a terrorist to distributing or circulating
terrorist publications. A final activity this section examines under a religious
cause is how the judiciary has considered the factors necessary to differentiate between a legitimate war and acts of terrorism where armed conflict
exists in states around the world carried out in the name of a religious cause.
The chapter concludes with an examination of whether a religious cause
should be included in the definition of terrorism. The argument is that by
doing so it widens the definition, thereby bringing certain communities in
society under the state's gaze, which could result in the identification of a
disproportionate risk or threat to national security.

Since the main objective in any terrorism investigation is to prevent acts
of terrorism from occurring, Chapter 2 examines government policies that
underpin terrorism legislation and the statutory preventative measures that
they have introduced. The two main preventative areas examined are the
possession of articles that could be of use to a person preparing or committing acts of terrorism and those related to proscribed/banned organizations. As statutory preventative measures are introduced to prevent acts of
terrorism, the width of the powers granted to investigating officers to interfere with people's lives has been criticized. The examination looks at how
the courts have interpreted the powers and have, to a degree, fettered any
overenthusiastic application of these powers by investigators and prosecuting

counsel. There has been criticism of terrorism preventative measures, with most of that criticism vented toward what is termed as "quasi-criminal" measures. The chapter concludes with an examination of the UK's control orders, known as Terrorism Prevention Investigatory Measures (TPIM), and how they compare with other jurisdictions. Also included in this chapter is a discussion on how stop and search powers were used on a person believed to be carrying secret files taken by the former US National Security Agency (NSA) employee Edward Snowden in 2013. Underpinning the analysis is how a balance has to be drawn between the needs of national security and the protection of an individual's liberty.

Surveillance is an important tool for any investigator and none more so than those involved in counterterrorism investigations. Chapter 3 examines the legislation governing surveillance in the United Kingdom and the United States. Underpinning this examination is how, following the Edward Snowden revelations, the UK and US authorities cooperated under the rule of law. Included throughout the analysis is how the courts have applied the legal principle of proportionality when balancing the interests of national security and individual liberty. This is an important process, as surveillance into the private lives of citizens is intrusive. In the current e-communication age, in which state agencies have access to a plethora of private transactions that range from telephone to social media usage, it has never been more appropriate or important for the courts to draw a fair balance between these interests. It is also an important and onerous role for the courts to ensure these agencies can access such sources of communication under the rule of law and how the agencies use the personal data obtained. On this theme the chapter assesses how, on a legal footing, the US NSA could use the services of the UK General Communications Headquarters (GCHQ) during its surveillance of suspected terrorist targets.

Although carrying out some terrorist attacks is relatively inexpensive, running a terrorist group can be an expensive operation, especially when the group plans to carry out prolonged periods of conflict. Chapter 4 examines the legal provisions introduced to freeze assets of those suspected of involvement in acts of terrorism. Focusing mainly on the United Kingdom and the United States, the chapter examines orders issued that allow their respective treasuries to issue asset-freezing direction measures in response to the United Nations' Security Council Resolutions (SCR). The examination includes the judicial decisions made in both jurisdictions, as well as coverage of the Canadian judiciary's concerns regarding asset-freezing orders. All three states' judiciary concerns center on the points that in quasi-criminal procedures there is no right to a trial and a lack of judicial supervision and involvement in the issuing of the orders. Among the rationale of the judiciary's concern is the impact these measures can have, not just on the financial position of the person named within the measure, but also upon their families who live with them. One of those judiciary concerns is how these measures can result in families being forced to live a parsimonious lifestyle.

Section II is a series of empirical pieces of research examining aspects of terrorist investigations. As a former UK special branch counterterrorism officer and with consequent access obtained, all of the primary data are obtained from the United Kingdom. Chapter 5 examines the amount of discretion operational counterterrorism officers have during an investigation. Underpinned by Brodeur's concept of separating policing into two distinct categories of high and low policing, the chapter demonstrates how, unlike their uniform colleagues, counterterrorism detectives have very little discretion as to when and where they can carry out arrests or searches of individuals and premises. One of the reasons for this is the number of stakeholders, including government departments and national security agencies in counterterrorism investigations. Even though, as seen in Section I, wider powers giving a greater breadth of discretion against suspected terrorists have been granted to counterterrorism officers, unlike low policing activity such as uniform patrol duties, it is the senior investigating officers who make the decisions, not the junior-ranking officers who are out in the field.

A concern for many states is how terrorist groups utilize and exploit both social conditions and social media to radicalize individuals to their cause. Most states have policies and initiatives to prevent successful radicalization of individuals to terrorist causes and to encourage citizenship and inclusivity into society. In examining the impact terrorist groups' radicalization has on individuals and groups in society, Chapter 6 uses the primary data from empirical research to examine a variety of radicalization processes used by the Irish Republican Army (IRA) and its political wing, the 32 County Sovereignty Movement (32CSM). In addition to examining how the IRA/32CSM use traditional forms of radicalization through fund-raising and the use of symbols, the chapter discusses how terrorist groups effectively utilize e-sources available on the Internet, from websites to the use of the various forms of social media such as Facebook or YouTube. Disconcerting is how, through the use of social media in particular, the terrorists' message can reach millions and influence thousands to have sympathy for the cause, resulting in hundreds of people taking the next step and becoming actively involved in terrorist acts.

As discussed in Chapter 3, intelligence gathering is a vital tool in policing, especially for officers investigating organized crime and terrorism. As it is difficult to penetrate the inner working of terrorist groups, using informants who have association with terrorists can provide vital intelligence to an investigation. Chapter 7 discusses the recruitment of informants in counterterrorism investigations. Using primary data obtained from informants I handled as a detective, underpinning the analysis is Cooper's role theory (Cooper 2012) to assess if noble cause corruption is present during the recruitment of informants, especially when they are recruited whilst under arrest and in police custody. As the analysis examines whether officers' integrity is compromised in the recruitment of informants who are in police custody, the pressure those officers are under to prevent acts of terrorism occurring is considered in the tactics used to recruit informants. The argument contained in the chapter concludes that if there is any loss of integrity, it is in the use of mind games by officers on vulnerable suspects in police custody.

Once recruited, informants have to be handled by officers in the operational field. Chapter 8 examines the law and policy governing the use of informants in the United Kingdom, Australia, the United States, and Canada. While there are some statutory provisions in Australia, it is only in the United Kingdom where all aspects of informant use are governed by statute (Regulation of Investigatory Powers Act 2000—RIPA) with the other states being governed by policy directives. US policy directives, in particular the attorney general's guidelines regarding the use of confidential informants, apply mainly to federal agencies. In some US states and counties there is not even a policy guiding officers in the use of informants. This is a cause for concern, as the chapter examines the ethical issues in handling informants, covering topics ranging from the motives and incentives for individuals to inform to issues that can arise in handling informants who are involved in criminal activity. In demonstrating how the handling of informants in terrorism investigations can become unethical, the 1968–1997 Irish Troubles is used as a case study when it got to the stage that informant handlers were turning a blind eye to their informants committing murder. The chapter also examines the inclusion of informants' evidence in criminal trials that can result in the informants obtaining immunity from prosecution and a reduction in sentence. This includes a discussion on how an informant's anonymity can be maintained during any criminal trial. This is an important issue as on the one hand a defendant has his or her right to a fair trial and to be given the opportunity to face his or her accuser. On the other hand, once an informant's identity is known he or she is no longer any use as an informant and importantly, there is the potential for violent retribution on the informant and his or her family.

The Law
Governing
Terrorism
Investigations

I

Legal Definition of Terrorism

1

Introduction

This chapter examines the legal definition of terrorism that policing agencies use during investigations to assess if an act is one of terrorism. The main focus of this chapter is an examination of the United Kingdom, European Union (EU), Canadian and US legal definition. This chapter also demonstrates how much of a catalyst the Al Qaeda attack on the United States on September 11, 2001, has been on Western states introducing legislation that on the whole is comparable between the respective states. Comparability in the law is important in relation to intelligence exchange and cooperation between the states' counterterrorism agencies. While minor differences exist regarding the rules of evidence in the judicial process of the respective jurisdictions, compatibility in the law allows the information obtained and used by the agencies' officers in one state, a degree of admissibility in the trial in a different state's court.

As the main threat to most states' security is from jihadist-based terrorism, the chapter also examines how the courts have interpreted what amounts to a religious cause that motivates acts of terrorism. The examination looks at what evidence must be present for the courts to determine if actions come under a religious cause in the legal definition of terrorism. The evidence considered comes from a range of activities ranging from collecting or possessing information that may be useful to a terrorist to distributing or circulating terrorist publications. Another action that is considered is when individuals leave their state of birth to fight in a conflict in another state that is for a religious cause. This section examines how the courts determine whether the conflict is a legitimate war or an act of terrorism. The chapter concludes with an examination of whether a religious cause should be included in legal definitions of terrorism by raising the issue that by doing so it allows state agencies to bring in communities under their gaze and by doing so it could result in the identification of disproportionate risk tor threat to national security.

Legal Definitions of Terrorism

Defining what actions amount to an act of terrorism has been problematic for many scholars, as there are so many categories of terrorism ranging from geopolitical groups such as the Irish Republican Army (IRA) in Ireland, Eta in Spain, and Chechen fighters in Russia, to terrorism by the state (Laqueur 1987, pp. 142–145; Weinberg et al. 2004, pp. 777–778; Martin 2013, p. 35). While Martin notes there is a degree of consensus in defining terrorism, there is no unanimity on the kind of violence or causes that constitute terrorism (Martin 2013, p. 35). This issue has existed from the earliest studies on terrorism as seen from what Laqueur states:

> There will be no agreement on whether terrorism is violence in general or some specific form of violence; on whether the stress should be put on its political character, on its methods of combat, or on the extra-normal character of its strategy … (Laqueur 1987, p. 143).

Although reaching a consensus in law that produces a legal definition capable of covering all aspects of terrorism has been equally problematic, it is this definition counterterrorism agencies use in their investigations to ascertain if actions of targets under surveillance amount to acts of terrorism. Another consideration in examining the legal definition is because it is equally important to establish that counterterrorism agencies operate within the legal principle of the rule of law. It is a rudimentary principle in democratic states that in granting its clandestine agencies-wide powers to interfere with citizens' human rights they operate within the law and remain accountable to their state's judiciary and parliamentary standing committees that act as a watchdog on the agencies' activities (Government of Canada 2013, p. 10; Council of Europe 2005a, p. 12). This section examines the United Kingdom, the EU, Canadian statutory definition, and the definitions developed and applied by US Federal agencies.

UK Definition of Terrorism

Till the introduction of the Terrorism Act of 2000, the UK's legal definition of terrorism was in section 20 Prevention of Terrorism (Temporary Provisions) Act (PTA) 1989 that stated terrorism occurs when violence was used:

> … for political ends and includes any use of violence for the purpose of putting the public or any section of the public in fear.

Apart from this definition being narrow as regards what actions amount to an act of terrorism, the PTA was limited as the act was drafted to deal solely with Irish terrorist groups such as the IRA during the period referred to as the Irish Troubles (1968–1997) (Punch 2012). The legislators had no intention for it to be used for international terror activity, mainly because at the time of drafting the act it was not recognized as a threat in the United Kingdom. After the signing of the Good Friday Agreement between the British government and Irish republican and loyalist groups in Belfast in 1998, which brought about the cessation of a violent conflict (Nolan 2012, pp. 19–22) that tore the province of Northern Ireland apart (Punch 2012, pp. 1–2), the United Kingdom turned its attention toward international terrorism. This shift was brought in part by persuasion from the UK's European neighbors.

By 1998, political events moved on within the European Union of which the United Kingdom is a member state. The 1992 Treaty of Union (TEU) transformed the European Union from being a "common market" used for free trade as agreed under its founding document, the Treaty of Rome 1957, into a union that conferred fundamental freedoms for its citizens. The TEU also created the Justice and Home Affairs Council and Commission (JHA) to deal with criminal matters affecting the EU, along with the Common Foreign Policy Council and Commission (Kaczorowska 2011, pp. 17–21). Since 1999, the JHA has been implementing the principle of mutual recognition in criminal matters to ensure effective prosecutions by balancing a defendant's rights within an EU-wide harmonization of member state domestic criminal procedural law (Peers 2011, pp. 655–656). This harmonization of procedural law included terrorism-related offenses (Murphy 2012, pp. 27–28). EU member states, in particular France, in spite of its connections with its former northern African colonies (as well as the immigration of citizens from those countries to France), raised the threat international jihadist-based terror activity posed not just to individual member states but potentially to the EU as a whole (Joffe 2008, p. 154). This was aggravated by the number of supporters of jihadist causes, who were granted asylum by the UK government in the late 1980s and 1990s. At the time their asylum was granted, scrutiny of these jihadist supporters was not as strict because the UK government's focus was on the threat Irish terrorist groups posed to the security of the British mainland as well as the north of Ireland. As a result, London became a hub for international jihadist causes in conflicts around the world where supporters were openly fundraising for these causes, which resulted in French intelligence giving London the nickname "Londonistan" (Pantucci 2010, p. 254). While distracted by events in the north of Ireland, under the nose of the UK government, the number of disaffected home-grown and non-UK citizen Muslims had developed as a major terrorist threat not just to the United Kingdom but to all Western states (Bamford 2004, p. 740). Pantucci sums up the development of this danger saying:

> What appeared at the time to be marginal and irrelevant was in fact a very active effort to attract young men and women from the UK's broad base of disaffected and detached Muslim youth to quite a specific globalist Islamist cause, and in some cases to drive them to go and participate in the global jihad (Pantucci 2010, p. 253).

At the 1999 Tampere Conference, such threats along with problem of organized crime posed to the EU member states resulted in the JHA Council (containing all the representatives of the member states' justice ministries) creating within the EU an area of "… citizenship, freedom, security and justice" (Council of European Communities 2005, p. 2). The UK's "Inquiry into Legislation Against Terrorism" led by the then House of Lords' judges who recommended the US FBI definition (see below) be adopted (Douglas 2010, p. 295) along with the multilateral agreements between the UK and EU member states brought about the change of the UK's legal definition of terrorism that took into account France's and Germany's concerns regarding the threat international jihadist groups posed to European Security (Joffe 2008, p. 155). As a result, section 1 of the Terrorism Act 2000 was introduced defining an act of terrorism occurring when there is

1. … The use or threat of action where
   a. The action falls within subsection (2).
   b. The use or threat is designed to influence the government or an international governmental organization,* or to intimidate the public or a section of the public.
   c. The use or threat is made for the purpose of advancing a political, religious, racial,† or ideological cause.
2. Action falls within this subsection if it
   a. Involves serious violence against a person.
   b. Involves serious damage to property.
   c. Endangers a person's life, other than that of the person committing the action.
   d. Causes a serious risk to the health or safety of the public or a section of the public.
   e. Is designed seriously to interfere with or seriously to disrupt an electronic system.
3. The use or threat of action falling within subsection (2) which involves the use of firearms or explosives is terrorism whether subsection (1)(b) is satisfied.
4. In this section
   a. "Action" includes action outside the United Kingdom.
   b. A reference to any person or to property is a reference to any person, or to property, wherever situated.
   c. A reference to the public includes a reference to the public of a country other than the United Kingdom.
   d. "The government" means the government of the United Kingdom, of a Part of the United Kingdom or of a country other than the United Kingdom.

---

* An amendment brought in by section 34(a) Terrorism Act 2006.
† An amendment brought in by section 75(1) Counter-Terrorism Act 2008.

5. In this Act, a reference to action taken for the purposes of terrorism includes a reference to action taken for the benefit of a proscribed organization.

One main change between the PTA and the 2000 Act is the scope of activity under the 2000 Act's definition amounting to an act of terrorism that has the potential for widening the number of communities or groups in society coming under the gaze of the counterterrorism agencies. This definition has been amended by subsequent terrorism legislation since 2000. The significant amendments are the action to be deemed terrorist action that must be for the purpose of advancing a political, religious, racial, or ideological cause, and, the action is aimed at influencing a government or international government organization (such as the EU, United Nations, and potentially organizations like the G8 nations). Regarding the term "ideological," when the act was a Bill going through its passage in the UK Parliament, the nation's fire-fighters were on national strike. A House of Commons Member of Parliament questioned the then Home Secretary whether industrial action would amount to an act of terrorism as by being on strike the fire-fighters' action could be perceived as having the intention of influencing the government to change its policy on pay and working conditions and by withdrawing their labor they were endangering peoples' lives. It was made clear by the Home Secretary that industrial action did not amount an act of terrorism but ideological causes such as ecoterrorism, antiabortion groups, and animal liberation groups' actions that fall in with the definition could be seen as ideological for the purposes of section of the act (Walker 2009, p. 10).

Section 1(4) incorporates the international terrorist threat by stating that an act of terrorism applies not solely to one committed or planned for the United Kingdom but to include any state in the world. It was held that one reason for section 1 being reflective of the international nature of terrorism was to ensure the United Kingdom did not become or appear to be a safe haven for terrorists of any nationality.[*] The UK's Court of Appeal explained that this part is intentionally comprehensive in its scope as

> … acts by insurgents against the armed forces of a state anywhere in the world which seek to influence a government and are made for political purposes are terrorism. There is no exemption for those engaged in an armed insurrection and an armed struggle against a government.[†]

In defining what factors amount to the meaning of a government, under section 1(4) the English Court of Appeal held a democratic government is

---

[*] England & Wales Court of Appeal *R v F* [2007] EWCA Crim 243, paragraph 16.
[†] *R v Mohammed Gul* [2012] EWCA Crim 280, paragraph 16.

one based on the consent of the people that is subject to the rule of law should be the "lodestar" for modern civilized communities, and those states that adhere to the European Convention on Human Rights or adhere to a human rights convention would also amount to a government. The Court added that even where there is an infringement by states on freedoms, provided the infringements were proportionate they too would be seen under section 1 as a government but, "… it did not extend to the tyrants under whose yoke [citizens] were forced to live."* As Saul points out, the conception of democracy is radically contested in both theory and practice. He raises the question that if terrorism is a crime against democracy, does that mean terrorism against nondemocratic states or those that trample over human rights are permissible (Saul 2010, p. 37)? From UN resolutions, including human rights resolutions, no form of terrorism is permissible as all the resolutions' preamble clearly states that all forms of terrorism are criminal and unjustifiable, even against authoritarian regimes, adding that terrorism cannot be used as a means to protect human rights.† This contradicts the UK courts' findings of the type of government such as tyrannical despotic regimes against whom violent politically motivated acts are directed against are seen as legitimate and outside actions that amount to an act of terrorism. In finding compatibility between the UK courts' findings and the UN resolutions, it could be that the UK courts included states infringing on human rights only where it is proportionate and legitimate for that state to do so.

Comparability between states' laws on terrorism is important as it eases potential hurdles. Although at macro level it is important that states' leading figures do work in cooperation, the importance in the comparability in law lies at the micro level, which is in effect the coalface of operations as those states' respective counterterrorism agencies work in cooperation with each other. This point was raised by the English Court of Appeal in *R v Mohammed Gul*,‡ which held it was common ground that international law has developed so that international terrorism can be recognized in a time of peace§ with international law developing to enable the crime of terrorism to be recognized in situations where there is no armed conflict.¶

EU Definition of Terrorism

To enable and ease cooperation between the respective counterterrorism agencies among its member states, the EU has introduced legislation that

---

* *R v Mohammed Gul* [2012] EWCA Crim 280, paragraph 23.
† UNComHR preambles to 1998/47, 1999/27, 2000/30, 2001/31, 2002/35.
‡ [2012] EWCA Crim 280.
§ [2012] EWCA Crim 280, paragraph 32.
¶ [2012] EWCA Crim 280, paragraph 35.

those member states incorporate into their own legislative process, supported by EU policy programs. In creating an area of citizenship, freedom, security, and justice, the EU's Justice and Home Affairs Council gave its rationale for introducing antiterrorism legislation along with the domestic antiterror provisions at member state level, saying:

> The protection of the life and property of citizens is a core task giving legitimacy to public power and public polices and citizens expect the threats to their health and safety will also be countered at European level (Council of European Communities 2005, p. 2).

Prior to the September 11th, 2001, Al Qaeda attack on the United States, there was no antiterrorism legislation at EU level. What did exist was solely at member state level with some Members States having no specific antiterror legislation in place as those states dealt with terrorist violence through their ordinary justice systems and legal provisions (Murphy 2012, p. 17). The attack was the catalyst for the EU introducing antiterror legislation that came in the form of a Framework Decision (EC Commission 2007, p. 10).*

Article 1 of the Council Framework Decision on combating terrorism (2002/475/JHA) defines what actions amount to an act of terrorism, which are

a. Attacks on a person's life which may cause death.
b. Attacks on the physical integrity of a person.
c. Kidnapping or hostage taking.
d. Causing extensive destruction to a Government or public facility, a transport system, an infrastructure facility, including an information system, a fixed platform located on the continental shelf, a public place or private property likely to endanger human life, or result in major economic loss.
e. Seizure of aircraft, ships, or other means of public or goods transport.
f. Manufacture, possession, acquisition, transport, supply, or use of weapons, explosives, or of nuclear, biological, or chemical weapons, as well as research into, and development of, biological and chemical weapons.
g. Release of dangerous substances, or causing fires, floods, or explosions, the effect of which is to endanger human life.

---

* An EU Framework Decision is a piece of legislation that does not have to be scrutinized by the European Parliament and to be passed and active requires a unanimous vote by all the members of the Council, which in this case is the EU Justice and Home Affairs Council. Once passed, it is down to the individual member states to incorporate the provisions contained in a Framework Decisions into their domestic law.

h. Interfering with or disrupting the supply of water, power, or any other fundamental natural resource the effect of which is to endanger human life.
i. Threatening to commit any of the acts listed in (a)–(h).

Article 1 adds that the nature of the occurrence of these actions must be aimed at seriously damaging a country or an international organization which is committed with the aim of

1. Seriously intimidating a population.
2. Unduly compelling a government or international organization to perform or abstain from performing any act.
3. Seriously destabilizing or destroying the fundamental political, constitutional, economic, or social structures of a country or an international organization.

One can see the similarity between the framework decision's terrorism definition to section 1 of the UK's Terrorism Act 2000 regarding what the aim must be and to whom the action must be directed. Where the framework decision is different, it is in specifying the criminal acts that, along with the presence of the other provisions, amounts to an act of terrorism.

Canadian Definition of Terrorism

Section 83.01(b) of the Canadian Criminal Code defines terrorism as an act or omission, in or outside Canada, that is committed

A. In whole or in part for a political, religious, or ideological purpose, objective or cause.
B. In whole or in part with the intention of intimidating the public, or a segment of the public, with regard to its security, including its economic security, or compelling a person, a government, or a domestic or an international organization to do or to refrain from doing any act, whether the public or the person, government or organization is inside or outside Canada.

That intentionally:

A. Causes death or serious bodily harm to a person by the use of violence.
B. Endangers a person's life.
C. Causes a serious risk to the health or safety of the public or any segment of the public.

    D. Causes substantial property damage, whether to public or private property, if causing such damage is likely to result in the conduct or harm referred to in any of clauses (A) to (C).

    E. Causes serious interference with or serious disruption of an essential service, facility or system, whether public or private, other than as a result of advocacy, protest, dissent, or stoppage of work that is not intended to result in conduct referred to in any of clauses (A) to (C), and includes a conspiracy, attempt, or threat to commit any such act or omission, or being an accessory after the fact or counseling in relation to any such act or omission, but, for greater certainty, does not include an act or omission that is committed during an armed conflict and that, at the time and in the place of its commission, is in accordance with customary international law or conventional law applicable to the conflict, or the activities undertaken by military forces or a state in the exercise of their official duties, to the extent that those activities are governed by other rules of intentional law.*

The impact of international terror groups in formulating legal definitions of terrorism by states can be seen again as the Canadian definition includes similarities in the aim of the act (political, ideological, or religious cause), whom the act is targeted at, and the intent of the act. However, the Canadian definition clearly differentiates between industrial dispute and protest which may not amount to an act of terrorism as well as expanding on not applying to an individual's actions that occurred during an armed conflict that was carried out in accordance with international law. What is interesting is how the Commonwealth countries such as Canada and the United Kingdom have similar phrasing in their antiterrorism legislation (Douglas 2010, p. 295) as seen in Australia, where the Security Legislation Amendment (Terrorism) Act 2002 amended the Criminal Code 1995 states for action to be classed as terrorism, the action taken must be for advancing a political, religious, or ideological cause[†] with the act aimed at influencing or intimidating a government be it Australian or foreign[‡] or intimidating the public or a section of the public.[§] The Australian law also makes it clear that such action does not apply to a protest, dissent, or industrial action.[¶]

In Canada, what amounts to an individual's actions that occur during an armed conflict carried out in accordance with international law was tested in *R v Khawaja*,** where K claimed that the situation in Afghanistan since 2002

---

* Criminal Code R.S.C.1985, c. C-46.
† Section 100.1(b) Criminal Code 1995 (Australia).
‡ Section 100.1(c)(i).
§ Section 100.1(c)(ii).
¶ Section 100.3(a).
** 2012 SCC69 [2012] 3 S.C.R. 555.

was a war within the definition. The Canadian Supreme Court held that K's actions went beyond Afghanistan to include acts of violence in the United Kingdom and in Pakistan based on a violent jihadist ideology and that the conflict in Afghanistan was an insurrection against an Afghan government by groups whose "... credo was to take arms against whoever supports non-Islamic regimes and that recognized that suicide attacks on civilians may sometimes be justified by the ends of jihad."[*] The Court held that the purpose of the armed conflict exemption is "... to exempt conduct taken during an armed conflict win accordance with applicable international law."[†]

US Definition of Terrorism Investigation

What may come as a surprise to many is that in the United States, there is no single legal definitive definition of terrorism. The closest is the definition, which differentiates between international and domestic terrorism, found in the US Code 18 Part 1 Chapter 113B section 2331:

1. The term "international terrorism" means activities that
   A. Involves violent acts or acts dangerous to human life that are a violation of the criminal laws of the United States or of any state, or that would be a criminal violation if committed within the jurisdiction of the United States or of any state
   B. Appear to be intended
      i. To intimidate or coerce a civilian population
      ii. To influence the policy of a government by intimidation or coercion
      iii. To affect the conduct of a government by mass destruction, assassination, or kidnapping
   C. Occur primarily outside the territorial jurisdiction of the United States, or transcend national boundaries in terms of the means by which they are accomplished, the persons they appear intended to intimidate or coerce, or the locale in which their perpetrators operate or seek asylum; ...
2. The term "domestic terrorism" means activities that
   A. Involve acts dangerous to human life that are a violation of the criminal laws of the United States or of any State
   B. Appear to be intended
      i. To intimidate or coerce a civilian population
      ii. To influence the policy of a government by intimidation or coercion

---

[*] 2012 SCC69 [2012] 3 S.C.R. 555, paragraph 102.
[†] 2012 SCC69 [2012] 3 S.C.R. 555, paragraph 100.

    iii. To affect the conduct of a government by mass destruction, assassination, or kidnapping
  C. Occur primarily within the territorial jurisdiction of the United States

When compared with the United Kingdom and the EU definitions, we see the similarities reading the scale of the dangerousness of the actions and the intention to be achieved through those actions. However, in the United States, section 2331 of US Code 18 is not the only definition that counterterrorism policing agencies work from. Jacobson explains why there is no single legal definition of terrorism in the United States as "… the US government is as conflicted as anyone" adding that even US federal agencies such as the FBI, Department of Homeland Security, and the Defenses Department operate from their own definition of terrorism.[*] The FBI defines terrorism as

> … the unlawful use of force or violence against persons or property to intimidate or coerce a Government, the civilian population, or any segment thereof, in furtherance of political or social objectives. (Staniforth 2010, p. 5)

This is a very wide definition, as it is open to question what actions amount to a "social objective" for the purposes of terrorism. There has been some guidance from FBI documentation as what actions are sufficient to meet social objectives in the definition such as attacks against abortion clinics, medical research facilities (normally by animal rights campaigners), and business accused of harming the environment (ecoterrorists).[†] While these activities have the potential to come under most definitions of terrorism, the FBI is specific in stating, attacks on private property can be acts of terrorism provided the attack is motivated by ideology.[*] Such actions would also come under the UK, EU, Canadian, and Australian definitions if the action on private property was owned by a member of a community that is constantly targeted by a terrorist group as that would amount a section of the public. There is a danger that this category of objective could broaden and go beyond what actions terrorism definitions were intended to include.

To rein in policing agencies from applying terrorism law to conventional criminal activity investigations, the US courts have given some direction as to the extent a definition of terrorism can be applied, especially where a

[*] Jacobson, L. (2013) "What's the definition of terrorism" *Tampa Bay Times Politifact* July 9, 2013 retrieved from http://www.politifact.com/truth-o-meter/article/2013/jul/09/whats-definition-terrorism/ [accessed August 22, 2013].

[†] FBI (Counterterrorism Division) "Terrorism 2002–2005" retrieved from http://www.fbi.gov/stats-services/publications/terrorism-2002–2005 [accessed September 4, 2013].

person commits a specified offense with the intent to intimidate or coerce a civilian population.* In *The People v Edgar Morales*,† a member of a street gang in the Bronx, the "St. James Boys" (SJB) was involved in a fight between the SJB and a Mexican gang that resulted in a number of murders. As their actions were seen by the investigating officers as being designed to intimidate or coerce a civilian population, the offenders were charged with terrorism. This situation appears to have occurred due to the fact that there is no specific and tight legal definition of what actions amount to an act of terrorism in the United States like that found in the United Kingdom, EU, and Canada, thereby allowing respective agencies to apply a very liberal interpretation of what actions amount to an act of terrorism. However, the New York State Court of Appeals adopted a pragmatic interpretation of what in law amounts to an act of terrorism designed to intimidate or coerce a civilian population. The court held that if it was to apply a broad definition of intent to intimidate or coerce a civilian population, it would invoke the specter of terrorism every time an organized crime group orchestrates murder, saying:

> … the concept of terrorism has a unique meaning and its implications risk being trivialised if the terminology is applied loosely in situations that do not match our collective understanding of what constitutes a terrorist act.‡

Defining and Ascertaining Evidence That Amounts to a Religious Cause

Out of the four main categories of a political, religious, racial, or ideological cause that has increased the number of activities that can be defined as acts of terrorism, the most contentious and difficult for the courts has been to ascertain is what factors amount to a religious cause.

Why Ascertaining the Motivations of a Cause in the Definition Is Important

Section 1 of the UK's Terrorism Act of 2000 definition is the basis on which a number of offenses and preventive measures contained in the UK's terrorism Acts are assessed as to whether certain actions amount to acts of terrorism. Section 20, Terrorism Act of 2006 states that the section 1 definition in the 2000 Act applies to the offense of the encouragement of acts of terrorism (section 1 Terrorism Act 2006). As this is a factor taken into account by

---

* Penal Law article 490.25[1].
† No.186, NYLJ 1202581035138 at *1 (Ct. of App., Decided December 11, 2012).
‡ No.186, NYLJ 1202581035138 at *1 (Ct. of App., Decided December 11, 2012), paragraph 10.

the UK courts while sentencing,[*] it is important in assessing whether individuals connected to such actions should be classified as terrorists. Equally important is the Terrorism Act 2000 definition that determines actions that amount to an act of terrorism outside the United Kingdom.[†]

What Is a Religious Cause?

Blackstone's *Counter-Terrorism Handbook* describes a religious cause as terrorist action motivated by an interpretation of religion (2010 paragraph 1.1.3) and that motivation is driven by a belief in another worldly power which sanctions and commands behavior (Martin 2013, p. 188). Perhaps the most prominent religious-based terrorist organization is Al Qaeda that seeks to unite Muslims throughout the world in a holy war. It is important to differentiate between causes where religion is secondary to the principal cause. Examples include the 1968–1997 Irish Troubles where members of the republican movement were predominantly Roman Catholics and the members of the Loyalist movement were Protestants. It was a political cause not a religious one motivating their actions as the republicans wanted the six northern Irish counties to be united with the 26 southern counties and come under the rule of the Dial in Dublin, whereas the Loyalists wanted the six counties to remain under British rule. There are Islamic-based groups where religion is secondary to their main cause such as that seen in the Russian Caucasian states such as Ingushetia and Dagestan, where the cause is political as they want independence from Russian rule or Boko Haram in Nigeria where their primary cause is self-governance of three northeastern Nigerian states. It has been problematic for the law and academics to show a clear delineation between a political, religious, racial, or ideological cause. This is seen in groups such as Al Qaeda and its various associated groups such as Al Qaeda in the Maghreb and those affiliated to it such as Al Shabab in Somalia and the Al-Nusra Front in Syria. They may appear to have some political objectives, but they are distinctively religious as they make use of well-established, mainstream religious concepts (Sedgwick 2004, p. 808).

Evidence of a Religious Cause

Differentiating what amounts to a religious cause from a political, ideological, or racial cause has been an issue the courts have had to deliberate over with great care. Examples how the UK courts approached the issue are described below.

---

[*] R v Abu Baker Mansha [2006] EWCA Crim 2051.
[†] Terrorism Act 2000 s.1(4).

A Religious Cause in Collecting or Possessing Information That May Be Useful to a Terrorist

One preventative terrorist measure in the UK's Terrorism Act of 2000 is section 58 that is concerned with the collection of information of a kind that is likely to be useful to a person committing or preparing an act of terrorism[*] or possessing a document or record containing information of that kind.[†] The word "likely" widens the scope of what constitutes "material" and has the potential to be interpreted subjectively by investigators. This is seen in *K v R*,[‡] where K possessed copy of the Al Qaeda training manual on a CD rom along with a copy of publication of *Zaad-e-Mujahid* and *The Absent Obligation*. *Zaad-e-Mujahid* is a text directed to the formation and organization of jihad movements and *The Absent Obligation* is a text arguing that a Muslim is under an obligation to work for the establishment of an Islamic state. K claimed the material was theological or propagandist material that section 58 was never intended to criminalize.[§]

In their examination of section 58, the Court of Appeal held that the material has to be of a kind to provide practical assistance to a person committing or preparing an act of terrorism, adding that a document that simply encourages the commission of acts of terrorism does not fall within section 58.[¶] Acknowledging section 58 was not intended to cover propaganda material; the Court dismissed K's appeal and was held for the purposes of section 58, it is important to ascertain whether the material actively assists a person committing or preparing a terrorist act and this should be resolved before a jury is empanelled.[**] In *R v G and R v J*,[††] the House of Lords examined section 58 in relation to J who possessed on recorded digital files an Al Qaeda training manual, a copy of the *Terrorist's Handbook*, a file of *Military Training* and a document *How Can I Train Myself for Jihad?* The House of Lords held that a key requirement for a conviction under section 58 is the defendant must be aware of the nature of the information the material contains.[‡‡] The House held that three criteria are required for a conviction under section 58: (1) the defendant has control of the record containing information that is likely to provide practical assistance to a person committing or preparing an act of terrorism, (2) the

---

[*] Terrorism Act 2000 s.58(1)(a).
[†] Terrorism Act 2000 s.58(1)(b).
[‡] [2008] EWCA Crim 185.
[§] *K v R* [2008] EWCA Crim 185, paragraph 5.
[¶] *K v R* [2008] EWCA Crim 185, paragraph 13.
[**] *K v R* [2008] EWCA Crim 185, paragraph 16.
[††] [2009] UKHL 13.
[‡‡] In *R v G, R v J* [2009] UKHL 13, paragraph 47.

defendant knew they had the record, and (3) the defendant also knew of the information that material contained.[*]

A Religious Cause in Distributing or Circulating Terrorist Publications

A religious cause is also considered under section 2 of the UK's Terrorism Act 2006. Among the provisions contained within the section, it applies to a person who distributes or circulates a terrorist publication, gives, sells, or lends such a publication, or offers such a publication for sale or loan or provides a service enabling others to obtain, read, listen, or look at such a publication,[†] when a person does so they commit an offense if they intend such conduct to be a direct or indirect encouragement of other inducement to the commission, preparation, or instigation of acts of terrorism,[‡] or intend that such conduct be the provision of assistance in the commission or preparation of such acts[§] or is reckless as to whether their conduct has such an effect.[¶] Section 20 of the 2006 Act clearly states that an act of terrorism is anything constituting that which comes within the meaning of section 1 Terrorism Act 2000,[**] this includes where such action is for a religious cause.

In *Ahmed Raza Faraz v R*,[††] the Court of Appeal deliberated on this issue in relation to Islamic publications. Faraz was the manager of an Islamic bookshop that traded from a bookshop as well as through an on-line website along with publishing for sale books, articles, videos, and DVD's that supported the case for militant Islam.[‡‡] Included among the material submitted as evidence of a religious cause was *Milestones—a special edition* written by Sayid Qutb, a leading member of the Muslim Brotherhood containing appendices of works by other authors that, when taken as a whole, the book was perceived as a polemic in favor of the Jihadist movement encouraging violence toward nonbelievers. Also submitted as evidence by the prosecution was *21st Century Crusaders*, a DVD purported to be a documentary focusing on the suffering of Muslims throughout the world that included an interview with a masked man who defended terrorist attacks by or on behalf of Al Qaeda, a number of texts that supported Bin Laden's role and texts of the other mujahidin and Islamic groups against Russia, a DVD, *Malcolm X*, that

---

[*] In *R v G, R v J* [2009] UKHL 13, paragraph 50.
[†] Terrorism Act 2006 section 2(a)–(d).
[‡] Terrorism Act 2006 section 1(a).
[§] Terrorism Act 2006 section 1(b).
[¶] Terrorism Act 2006 section 1(c).
[**] Terrorism Act 2006 section 20(2).
[††] [2012] EWCA Crim 2820.
[‡‡] *Ahmed Raza Faraz v R* [2012] EWCA Crim 2820, paragraph 6.

included trailers and other recordings of interviews with the families of men who died fighting US forces in Afghanistan and Israeli forces in the occupied Palestinian territory, and the book *The Absent Obligation*. The prosecution's case centered on the fact the publications sought to encourage the followers of Islam to attack nonbelievers and to seek martyrdom in the pursuit of jihad. The prosecution claimed it was achieving encouragement under section 2 by providing a theological justification of attacks on non-believers and in celebrating the achievements of militant and terrorist followers of Islam.[*] The Court of Appeal dismissed this as evidence of a religious cause in relation to terrorism. Crucial in the Court coming to this finding was the question whether the publications would be understood by a significant number of its readers as directly or indirectly encouraging terrorism. The Court could find no probative value that these publications were likely to encourage the commission of terrorist acts.

In *R v Gul*,[†] Gul was found to be in possession of videos uploaded onto various sites on his computer that showed attacks by Al Qaeda and the Taliban on Coalition forces in Iraq and Afghanistan, the use of improvised explosive devices on Coalition forces, and excerpts from jihadist martyrdom. The Supreme Court adopted a similar position as the Court of Appeal in *Faraz* in their findings of Gul's involvement in relation to section 2 Terrorism Act 2006. While acknowledging the need by the state to grant police and security officers wide powers to intrude on the lives of citizens in connection with preventing acts for terrorism, the Supreme Court stated what is a cause for concern is that such powers are so wide as to add to prosecutorial powers Acts such as the 2006 give rise to.[‡]

Consideration of article 10 European Convention on Human Rights (right to freedom of expression) is also a factor the courts will consider in relation to a religious cause. For example, in *Faraz* the Court of Appeal made it clear that a jury cannot convict a defendant and offend their article 10 right to freedom of expression simply because materials express a religious view. In *Faraz*, the Court also stated that in establishing a religious cause there has to be evidence the material would be understood by a significant number of readers as encouraging of the unlawful commission of terrorist offenses.[§] The courts appear to recognize the need for wide powers to enable police and security officers to examine and determine if the contents of materials can potentially breach terrorism-related legislation. However, when taking the next stage in determining if there is sufficient evidence to charge and for a prosecution to succeed, evidence related to a religious cause must be shown

---

[*] *Ahmed Raza Faraz v R* [2012] EWCA Crim 2820, paragraph 17.
[†] [2013] UKSC 64.
[‡] *R v Gul* [2013] UKSC 64, paragraph 63.
[§] *Ahmed Raza Faraz v R* [2012] EWCA Crim 2820, paragraph 54.

SPRING CREEK CAMPUS

to have a significant impact on encouraging or influencing others to a terrorist cause, or, that any material possessed by a person will significantly assist a person committing or preparing acts of terrorism.

Armed Conflict in the Name of a Religious Cause

Under section 1(4), Terrorism Act 2000, UK, antiterrorism legislation also applies to acts of terrorism that occur outside the United Kingdom. Again, consideration has to be given as to the cause terrorist action is taken under. In *CF v SSHD** (a judicial review on a Terrorism Prevention and Investigation Measures (TPIM) order issued by the Home Secretary under the TPIM Act 2011) CF was a British citizen of Somali descent. In 2008, he was prosecuted for attempting to travel to Afghanistan for the purposes of engaging in acts of terrorism, where he was acquitted after a trial, and in 2009 he travelled to Somalia where he attended a terrorist training camp. Between 2009 and 2011, he became involved in the jihadist terror group Al Shabaab (which is affiliated to Al Qaeda), returning to the United Kingdom in 2011. A factor the Court found important was that in his association with a religious cause, CF had more than a mere association with Al Shabaab, he had a substantial role in their cause by training and fighting with them.[†]

The nature of the conflict in a country outside the United Kingdom is also an important issue for the courts to consider when assessing if the action falls under section 1(4) Terrorism Act 2000. In *R v F*,[‡] F, a native of Libya, was in possession of a handwritten document detailing how a terrorist cell can be formed that was intended to be a "blueprint" for support of groups in Libya opposed to the former Colonel Gaddafi regime that governed the country at that time. The document pointed to taking a jihadist route of action against the then Libyan government.[§] The jihadist substance of the document was not seen as sufficient to warrant a religious cause, but it was for a political cause where under section 1(4) Terrorism Act 2000 the Court of Appeal held that

> … given the random impact of the protection of terrorist activities, the citizens of Libya should be protected from such activities by those residents in this country … (paragraph 26).

Commenting on how broad the definition of terrorism is under section 1 Terrorism Act 2000, the Court of Appeal expressed concern that it makes no exemption in creating a defense or exculpation from describing the act of terrorism as a just cause. This is because section 1(4) does not specify that this provision

---

[*] [2013] EWHC 843 (Admin).
[†] *CF v SSHD* [2013] EWHC 843 (Admin), paragraph 44.
[‡] [2007] EWCA Crim 243.
[§] *R v F* [2007] EWCA Crim 243, paragraphs 5 and 6.

only applies to governments of particular type that the United Kingdom would regard as the desirable characteristics of a representative government. In *R v F*, the Court said, "… terrorism is terrorism, whatever the motives of the perpetrators" and that appears to include where there is a religious cause.[*]

The problem in separating and defining what amounts to a religious cause from other causes given in statutory provisions is not unique to the United Kingdom; similar issues have arisen in Canada. In *Khawaja v R*,[†] the Supreme Court of Canada had to deliberate on what amounts to a religious cause. After becoming obsessed with Osama Bin Laden and his cause, Khawaja began communicating with other people committed to violence in the name of Islam (including the leader of a terrorist cell in London).[‡] Among the evidence found in Khawaja's possession was instructional literature on bomb making, military books, and jihad-related books.[§] There was also evidence that he had participated in a terrorist group by taking weapons training at a camp in northern Pakistan for the purpose of enhancing the ability of a terrorist group to facilitate or carry out a terrorist attack anywhere in the world.[¶] section 83 of the Canadian Criminal Code has a very similar definition of terrorism to that in the UK's Terrorism Act 2000, including the statutory provision to include terrorist activity carried outside Canada, which if committed inside Canada would be an act of terrorism (section 83.01(1)(a)(i) Canadian Criminal Code).

In examining what amounts to a religious cause under section 83.01(1.1), the Canadian Supreme Court made it clear that terrorist activity does not include a nonviolent expression of a religious thought, belief, or opinion,[**] adding that criminal liability should not be based on persons' religious views and that the police should not target people as suspects nor should a justice system prosecute persons because of their views. In *Khawaja*, there was strong evidence that his religious belief and motive was linked to a violent jihad and therefore amounted to a religious cause.[††]

Should a Religious Cause Be Included in the Statutory Definition of Terrorism?

In his report, the former independent reviewer of the UK's terrorism legislation, Lord Carlile, concluded, that a religious cause should be included in section 1 Terrorism Act of 2000 as it was consistent with the provisions in a

---

[*] *R v F* [2007] EWCA Crim 243, paragraph 27.
[†] [2012] 3 SCR 555.
[‡] *Khawaja v R* [2012] 3 SCR 555, paragraph 4.
[§] *Khawaja v R* [2012] 3 SCR 555, paragraph 7.
[¶] *Khawaja v R* [2012] 3 SCR 555, paragraph 12.
[**] *Khawaja v R* [2012] 3 SCR 555, paragraph 82.
[††] *Khawaja v R* [2012] 3 SCR 555, paragraph 89.

number of other states (2007 paragraph 54) and international comparators and treaties thereby making the category of a religious cause as broadly fit for purpose as a category of a cause action is taken for the purposes of the legal definition of terrorism (2007 paragraph 86(4)). It has been reported that more than any other European country, the United Kingdom is facing its biggest threat from "home-grown" Islamic violent extremism with more people having been arrested for terrorism-related activities motivated by a religious cause in the United Kingdom than elsewhere in Europe (Vermeulen 2014, p. 293). The UK's current independent reviewer of terrorism legislation, David Anderson QC discusses the objections to having a religious cause in the section 1 Terrorism Act 2000 definition. He has taken the view that it would be premature to currently make any changes (2013 paragraph 4.9) saying that evidence of a religious cause will emerge as a matter of course during terrorism trials. He is confident that scrupulous care is taken by all concerned in the trial process to emphasize during terrorist trials that whatever the purported justification is, it has "… nothing to do with the peaceful practice of religion" (2013 paragraph 4.13). As highlighted in the above cases, the judiciary has made it clear that for a prosecution to succeed in a terrorist offense trial where a religious cause is claimed to be the motive behind the actions, the person's action has to go beyond nonviolent, passive behavior and must be significantly related to the use of violence in the name of religious cause.

Is a Wide Legal Definition of Terrorism Assisting Agencies in Identifying a Disproportionate Risk in Society?

In the three national state jurisdictions as well as the EU's, we see a very wide legal definition of terrorism, with the United States going even wider allowing their federal agencies to develop their own working definition of what actions amount to terrorism. Although this was reined back a little by the New York Appeal Court in *The People v Edgar Morales*, not only do we see a degree of compatibility that assists states in drawing up international agreements on international agency cooperation, there is also the potential for these agencies to target wider communities, groups, and individuals in their attempt to eliminate the terrorist risk. Giving state agencies powers of investigation, especially powers to assist in the prevention of crime, has long been a cause of concern. Studying the increased UK's police targeting of young Black males seen as responsible for street robberies in the 1970s, Hall et al. looked at the "control-culture" they saw as pervasive in the state. In their analysis, they examined the application of the law by the police whereby referring to the UK's Special Branch, they claim the application of laws by the police that are liberally interpreted by the courts is an extension of the arm of the law. They add that this produces a bias in favor of the police that allows

for the widening and toughening of the law as seen in the increased surveillance and information gathering by Special Branch (Hall et al. 1978, p. 85).
Underpinned by a Marxist analysis, their rationale as to why this is the case
centers on hegemony, the hegemony of the ruling economic class in a capital-
ist state where the law, which they see as the legal system, the police, courts,
and prison system, are instruments to assist in maintaining that hegemony
over those in society that dare to challenge the state by their difference (Hall
et al. 1978, p. 194). The result of this is the state uses the law as an instrument
of class domination (Hall et al. 1978, p. 196).

Cohen's concern in the 1980s was how law was simply an instrument of
social control where surveillance, target hardening, and proactive policing
were all forms of intervention at hard forms of deviance (which today would
include the threat of international terrorism, in particular jihadist-based terror activity) (Cohen 1985, p. 232). Cohen sees the surveillance and targeting
of individuals being at the "hard end" of state action where, although these
methods are recognized crime control methods, in reality social control creates scapegoats who are perceived as a threat to the safety of the state and its
citizens, which in turns reinforces social solidarity among the wider population (Cohen 1985, p. 233). By being seen as a threat to society, it allows the
wider citizenry to give their legitimacy to state agencies to take punitive and
intrusive action on these scapegoats to keep the wider public safe.

One apparent impact in having a wide definition of terrorism is that the
pervasive use for surveillance centers on eliminating the risk terrorism poses
to the security of citizens as well as the state structure. Intelligence is crucial
in helping counterterrorism agencies to eliminate risk, which Ericson and
Haggerty recognize can overwhelm policing agencies through the sheer volume of knowledge work as policing and security agencies:

> ... have a strong sense of organisational risk and insecurity because of exter-
> nal demands of knowledge; a perpetual feeling of having insufficient knowl-
> edge; and a reflexive awareness that there are always systematic faults that can
> be corrected through better communication rules, formats and technologies.
> (Ericson and Haggerty 1997, p. 295).

For Ericson and Haggerty, a risk society is a regulatory society (Ericson
and Haggerty 1997, p. 48). By trying to identify the risk entails agencies having to maintain surveillance not just on individuals, but on communities
that are perceived as a threat. Garland sees wider surveillance as a form of
social order involving realignment and integration of diverse social routines
and institutions that compose modern society saying it is "... a problem of
ensuring coordination ... not of building normative consensus" (Garland
2001, p. 183). Terrorism and crime is a staple of political discourse and of
electoral politics (Newburn 2006, p. 232) that can be seen in how individuals
or groups within communities can be used to demonize entire communities

in the society. In the United Kingdom, one example of the politicization of terrorism and a willingness to curry favor with the UK electorate comes to mind. Following the outcry at the UK government's numerous attempts to extradite the Islamic radical cleric Abu Qatada to Jordan to face charges of being involved in terrorism that cost the United Kingdom £1.7 million of taxpayers' money led to the UK's Home Secretary saying that terror suspect's state benefits should be cut, where the imagery of Jihadist terror was used which, in turn pointed an accusatory finger at the UK's Muslim community.* When contextualizing a terrorist threat like this, Loader and Walker state that these type of events have a marked impact on Muslim populations. In the clamor to erode Muslims' democratic rights and freedoms, the symbolic resonance lays in enmity toward minority groups where, albeit dispropor-tionately, it is perceived that such rights are used to protect terrorists, which in turn imperils public safety (Loader and Walker 2007, p. 87).

This observation can be applied to the point Pantucci raises in his examination of government policies related to preventing terrorism. He argues that by aligning a religious cause into the legal definition of terror-ism, governments choose to engage only with those they see "… as 'good Muslims', suggesting by default that those who have not been engaged with are 'bad Muslims'" (Pantucci 2010, p. 262). In the debate regarding whether a religious cause should be included within the legal definitions, Fenwick argues the legal definition of terrorism does not create a criminal offense of being a terrorist. She makes the point it allows for the application of special terrorism sanctions to be applied on persons or communities whose behav-ior causes them to be suspected of activity linked to terrorism where the state agencies are not dependent on charging those within that community of specific offenses (Fenwick 2008, pp. 260–261). As a consequence, it gives state agencies the potential to encourage racial or religious profiling of per-sons. This was a cause of concern for a number of Canadian parliamentari-ans when the Canadian terrorist legislation was going through its legislative passage. The parliamentarians felt it could lead to state agencies being able to discriminate against constitutionally protected activities and as a result wanted to have a religious case dropped from the definition (Douglas 2010, p. 305). In the debate in differentiating between a political and religious or ideological cause Sedgwick makes a valid point. Referring to the most demonized jihadist terror group in by Western states, Al Qaeda, he states the group's ultimate aims may be defined as religious, adding that Al Qaeda is distinctively religious in that it makes use of well-established, mainstream religious concepts, but Al Qaeda's objectives are as much political as those of any other terrorist groups (Sedgwick 2004, p. 808). This suggests that any

---

* BBC News July 8, 2013 "Terror suspect benefits could be cut—Theresa May" retrieved from http://www.bbc.co.uk/news/uk-23230421 [accessed September 12, 2013].

differences between causes is only paper thin, but from the legal definitions and the wide powers granted to counterterrorism agencies has allowed for the net widening of surveillance on communities enabling those agencies to discipline those whose behavior deviates from the norm.

Conclusion

When examining the legal definitions of terrorism in the respective states' jurisdictions, there is no doubt that specifying actions and increasing the causes that underpin acts of terrorism have enabled state agencies to widen the categories of individuals' and groups' activities that can come under the gaze of the state. As seen in the cases where there is an armed conflict in overseas territories that is legitimate this does not amount to an act of terrorism. At the time of writing, the civil war in Syria shows no signs of abating and Iraq is heading toward a civil war with the Sunni jihadists, ISIS claiming a caliphate in the North West area of Iraq and the Kurds having control of the Northeast.[*] Under the legal definition, as clarified by the relevant cases, a person going to Syria or Iraq to fight or to support parties not part of the Syrian or Iraqi government would be deemed to be terrorists as has already occurred in the United Kingdom[†] and in France's response in banning travel to persons suspected to be terrorists to Syria and Iraq under an "individual terrorist enterprise" offense.[‡] While it is clear the intention of the respective states' legal definitions contained in the respective statutory instruments a religious cause is aimed at jihadist-based groups such a Al Qaeda and its affiliates such as Al Qaeda in the Maghreb or the Al-Nusra Front in Syria, deliberating as to what evidence is required to prove a religious cause has not been a simple task for the courts to determine. What the courts have decided is the action behind a religious cause must go beyond a nonviolent, passive behavior and must be significantly related to the use of violence carried out in the name of a religious cause.

[*] BBC News 2014 "Iraq rebels seize nuclear materials" retrieved from http://www.bbc. co.uk/news/world-middle-east-28240140 [accessed July 10, 2014].
[†] BBC News 2014 "Three arrested in Syria terrorism probe" retrieved from http://www. bbc.co.uk/news/uk-england-berkshire-28227003 [accessed July 10, 2014].
[‡] BBC News 2014 "France proposes anti-terrorist travel ban" retrieved from http://www. bbc.co.uk/news/uk-england-berkshire-28227003 [accessed July 10, 2014].

Government Policies and Statutory Preventative Measures

2

I am not prepared to be a prime minister who has to address the people after a terrorist incident and explain that I could have done more to *prevent* it. [emphasis added]

David Cameron
UK Prime Minister, July 14, 2014

This quote from David Cameron sums up what most state leaders feel, a feeling that echoes with most states' citizens as well as those investigating acts of terrorism. Due to the catastrophic results terrorist acts have, the primary aim of counterterrorism is to prevent terrorism acts from occurring, not to detect them. This chapter begins with an examination of government policies related to terrorism, in particular the pursue arm of policies as this is the arm of the policy that covers how terrorism is investigated with the focus being on prevention.

One measure states can take to enable this is to grant counterterrorism agencies' officers wider powers, allowing them to become more intrusive into the lives of those who are suspected to be involved in terrorist activity, no matter how peripheral that activity may be to a terrorist cause. This chapter examines some of those provisions and the court cases associated with them. The statutory preventative measures the chapter looks at includes offenses related to the possession of and providing materials that may be useful to persons committing or preparing acts of terrorism to offenses related to groups that are proscribed or banned by the state because they are seen as terrorist groups that pose a threat to national security.

The chapter also examines quasi-criminal measures. These have been controversial measures as they are issued by politicians, not the judiciary, where there is intelligence to suggest that a person is linked to terrorist groups or causes but there is insufficient evidence to charge these individuals with offenses and bring them before a court for trial. The chapter concludes with a case study of port and border controls during an investigation that involved agencies form the United Kingdom and the United States related to

---

* BBC News 2014 "Emergency phone and internet data laws to be passed" retrieved from http://www.bbc.co.uk/news/uk-politics-28237111 [accessed July 11, 2014].

the Edward Snowden affair. The study is based in the United Kingdom where counterterrorism officers stopped the partner of a newspaper journalist who was suspected to be in possession of documents taken by the former US national Security Agency (NSA) employee, Edward Snowden and released to the UK newspaper *The Guardian.*

Government Policies Related to Preventing or Preempting Acts of Terrorism: The Risk Is Not Disproportionate, the Risk Is Real

In addition to anti-terror legislation, states have also introduced governmental counterterrorism policies providing a strategic response to the terrorist threat they face. The UK's CONTEST policy is based on four p's: pursue, prevent, protect, and prepare. Prepare is concerned with ensuring facilities are in place to deal with the occurrence of a terrorist attacks (HM Government 2011, p. 93), with protect being concerned with strengthening protection against a terrorist attack such as strengthening border security reducing vulnerability of the transport network and improving security for crowded places (HM Government 2011, p. 79). The prevent and pursue strands are concerned with preventing terrorist acts with the prevent strand aimed at addressing radicalization (HM Government 2011, p. 59) and pursue aimed at arresting and the prosecution of terrorist suspects (HM Government 2011, p. 45). The policy emphasizes that terrorist threats must be detected and investigated at the earliest possible stage to disrupt terrorist activity before it can endanger the public and this is achieved by increasing

> ... intelligence coverage of people engaged in terrorist related activity in or against this country, here and overseas ... [improving] the effectiveness of our prosecution process ... [developing] more effective non-prosecution actions ... [disrupting] terrorist activity overseas where there is no alternative course of action (HM Government 2011, p. 46).

This echoes closely the EU counterterrorism strategy that also has four strands to it. The EU policies' prevent and protect strands are exactly the same as that of the UK's whereas the respond strand of the EU strategy corresponds to the UK's prepare strand. Both the pursue elements of the respective strategies are the same (Council of the European Union 2005). The Canadian government has also produced a counterterrorism strategy containing four strands. While its prevent strand is very similar to the UK and EU's strategy, it has given the other three strands different titles, but they are not dissimilar to those found in the UK or EU strategies. The Canadian respond strand is the same as the UK's prepare strand, the deny strand is the same as the UK or

EU's prevent strand with the Canadian detect strand being focused on investigating terrorism (Government of Canada 2013, pp. 4–5). We see a similar outline in the Australian government's counterterrorism strategy where its four strands are preparedness, prevention, response, and recovery. However, these four strands are not so easy to align with those found in the United Kingdom, EU, and Canadian strategy as there is little on preventing radicalization with the main focus being on preventing acts of terrorism (apart from recovery that focuses on dealing with an incident) (Commonwealth of Australia 2012).

While the United States has no single policy document like the UK's CONTEST policy, the US's policy can be found in the National Strategy for Counterterrorism that contains similar information to the four strands found in the UK's, EU's, and Canada's strategies. The National Strategy document discusses the measures related to the pursue element of the CONTEST policy that states, "… every lawful tool and authority is available" to investigators and that intelligence procedures have been strengthened to "improve" the US's capabilities in countering terrorism especially by preventing acts occurring (National Strategy for Counterterrorism 2011).

There is a degree of criticism and concern over the effectiveness of governmental counterterrorism policies. Examining the US strategy, Arreguin-Toft believes there is little reason to believe the US strategy can help win a war against international terrorism as this type of terrorism is primarily a political not a military problem (Arreguin-Toft 2002, p. 550). Regarding the UK's CONTEST strategy, Pantucci found conflicting roles between the agencies involved where those agencies operating at the harder end of the scale had a natural skepticism with those at the softer end with whom they were obliged to share information, saying, "Spooks and social workers are an awkward mix" (Pantucci 2010, p. 257). Another problem his study identified with CONTEST was that those at the softer end involved in community work became part of the securitization process as long-standing community workers were effectively turned into outposts for the security agencies (Pantucci 2010, pp. 257–258). This can be understood in terms of disciplinary power and governmentality in the net widening of social control (Cohen 1985, pp. 56–58). What we are seeing is a truly varied multi-agency approach to preventing terrorism where behavior of individuals within communities is compared, differentiated, hierarchized, homogenized, and excluded in the normalizing process (Foucault 1978, p. 183).

In determining the "normalization process" what is seen in these governmental policies is a broad brush approach to dealing with terrorism. In the pursue or detect strand of the policies, the main agencies it applies to are the policing or national security agencies, not the wider community. Yet, when it comes to the prevent strand of the policies, it is a natural and logical consequence that a number of nonpolicing agencies and communities are involved. Preventing acts of terrorism is not the sole responsibility of the state and its policing and national security agencies. Preventing terrorism starts within communities, be it either supporting individuals who are susceptible to being radicalized into terror causes or in passing information of activity that could be related to terrorist activities of the relevant bodies. Involving bodies or agencies whose work is a nonpolicing role, especially those on the periphery of terrorist activity may appear to be an awkward mix, but it is a necessary mix to include agencies that work at what Pantucci sees as operating at the softer end of societal problems.

Examples of Statutory Preventative Measures

This section examines two terrorism preventative measures related to the legal definition of terrorism, collecting or possession of articles that can be used in terrorist activity, and preventative measures linked to proscribed or banned terrorist organizations.

Possessing and Providing Materials Supporting Terrorism

This section looks at the offenses in the United Kingdom and the United States linked to possessing or providing materials that are likely to provide support to those involved in acts of terrorism. These offenses are concerned with the preparatory stages of terrorist acts and are relatively wide sweeping in the activity a person does in relation to supporting acts of terrorism. This section compares the UK and the US statutory provisions that are part of the pursue or detect strand of governmental policy.

United Kingdom: Possessing, Collecting Information for Terrorist Purposes

In the United Kingdom, two offenses were introduced to assist policing agencies in preventing acts of terrorism. Section 57 Terrorism Act of 2000 created the offense of possession of articles for the purpose of committing or preparing an act of terrorism and section 58, which is merely possession of articles of a kind that could be useful to persons involved in terrorism.

Section 57 Terrorism Act 2000: Possession for Terrorist Purposes
1. A person commits an offense if he possesses an article in circumstances which give rise to a reasonable suspicion that his possession is for a purpose connected with the commission, preparation, or instigation of an act of terrorism.
2. It is a defense for a person charged with an offense under this section to prove that his possession of the article was not for a purpose

connected with the commission, preparation, or instigation of an act of terrorism.

3. In proceedings for an offense under this section, if it is proved that an article
   a. Was on any premises at the same time as the accused.
   b. Was on premises of which the accused was the occupier or which he habitually used otherwise than as a member of the public, the court may assume that the accused possessed the article, unless he proves that he did not know of its presence on the premises or that he had no control over it.

Section 58: Collection of Information

1. A person commits an offense if
   a. He collects or makes a record of information of a kind likely to be useful to a person committing or preparing an act of terrorism.
   b. He possesses a document or record containing information of that kind.
2. In this section "record" includes a photographic or electronic record.
3. It is a defense for a person charged with an offense under this section to prove that he had a reasonable excuse for his action or possession.

Judicial Interpretation of Sections 57 and 58 Terrorism Act 2000

As seen with the definitions of terrorism, by having such a wide definition of what can amount to an article that could be useful to a person involved in terrorism, section 58 also has the capability of bringing citizens not normally associated with terrorist activity under the gaze of counterterrorism agencies. As a result, there have been a number of legal challenges as to what amounts to an article for the purposes of section 58. In *R v K*,[*] the Court of Appeal held that section 58 was never intended to criminalize the possession of theological or propagandist material[†] adding that

> A document or record will only fall within section 58 if it is of the kind that is likely to provide practical assistance to a person committing or preparing an act of terrorism. A document that simply encourages the commission of acts of terrorism does not fall within section 58.[‡]

In *R v G* and *R v J*,[§] the House of Lords examined section 58 and, building on the K judgment, the House held that for a conviction under section 58

---

[*] [2008] EWCA Crim 185 (England & Wales Court for Appeal).
[†] [2008] EWCA Crim 185 (England & Wales Court for Appeal), paragraph 5.
[‡] [2008] EWCA Crim 185 (England & Wales Court for Appeal), paragraph 13.
[§] [2009] UKHL 13.

it is a requirement that the defendant not only possessed the document that may be of use to a terrorist, but they must also be aware of the nature of the information contained therein.* The House stressed that this did not mean the prosecution had to show that the defendant knew everything that was contained in the document, only that the defendant knew of the nature of the material it contained.† For a conviction under section 58 the prosecution must prove that the defendant

1. Had control of the record which contained information that was likely to provide practical assistance to a terrorist.
2. Knew that he had the record.
3. Knew the kind of information which it contained.‡

J challenged this decision and went to the European Court of Human Rights (ECtHR), where the case was *Jobe v UK*.§ J claimed that section 58 violated article 7 European Convention on Human Rights (ECHR) where there can be no punishment without law. The premise of J's claim was that section 58 was so vague it was not law and if the court agreed with this argument his article 10 ECHR rights (freedom of expression) was also violated because section 58 would not be deemed to be an act prescribed by law. The ECtHR held there was no violation of article 7 and stated the House of Lords decision was fully and clearly reasoned. Key to the ECtHR reaching this decision was the guidance the House of Lords gave in their decision regarding the three points cited above that have to be proved for a conviction under section 58 to stand.¶ Likewise, the ECtHR found there to be no violation of article 10 saying it was justified under the legitimate aims of the interests of national security and that it did not criminalize in a blanket manner the collection or possession of material likely to be useful to a terrorist.**

United States: Providing Material Support to Terrorists

The United States has similar legislation regarding materials to assist in a terrorist attack. Again, we see more similarities than differences between the US and UK legislation as regards what actions amount to an offense in providing material and documentation that may assist terrorists. The key defenses are due to the different judicial process of the jurisdictions of the respective countries. The main piece of US legislation governing the provision of

---

* [2009] UKHL 13, paragraph 47.
† [2009] UKHL 13, paragraph 48.
‡ [2009] UKHL 13, paragraph 50.
§ [2011] Application number 48278/09.
¶ [2011] Application number 48278/09, paragraph A.
** [2011] Application number 48278/09, paragraph B.

materials to assist terrorists is 18 USC section 2339A, Providing Material Support to Terrorists that states the following:

a. Offense—Whoever provides material support or resources or conceals or disguises the nature, location, source, or ownership of material support or resources, knowing or intending that they are to be used in preparation for ... [List of specific crimes linked to terrorist activity] ... or in preparation for, or in carrying out, the concealment of an escape from the commission of any such violation, or attempts or conspires to do such an act, shall be fined under this title, imprisoned not more than 15 years, or both, and, if the death of any person results, shall be imprisoned for any term of years or for life. A violation of this section may be prosecuted in any Federal judicial district in which the underlying offense was committed, or in any other Federal judicial district as provided by law.
b. Definitions ...
   1. The term "material support or resources" means any property, tangible or intangible, or service, including currency or monetary instruments or financial securities, financial services, lodging, training, expert advice or assistance, safe-houses, false documentation or identification, communications equipment, facilities, weapons, lethal substances, explosives, personnel (1 or more individuals who may be or include oneself), and transportation, except medicine or religious materials.
   2. The term "training" means instruction or teaching designed to impart a specific skill, as opposed to general knowledge.
   3. The term "expert advice or assistance" means advice or assistance derived from scientific, technical, or other specialized knowledge.

Summary of Statutory Preventative Measures

The US definition clarifies the type of material related to being used in the preparation of acts of terrorism compared with the UK definitions, especially in section 57 Terrorism Act 2000 that simply refers to an "article." The UK provisions, in particular section 58, where a person commits an offense by merely possessing information where the mens rea threshold is very low having only to be "likely" to be of use to a terrorist gives policing agencies wide powers. The rationale behind this is by having such wide powers, it grants those agencies correlative powers of entry and search, and, arrest and detention of persons suspected to be involved in acts of terrorism. Underpinning these powers is the states' aim of preventing acts of terrorism as they allow the policing agencies to move at an early stage on targets they have under

investigation. As seen in the decisions of the UK courts in relation to sections 57 and 58, the judiciary has to some extent put a brake on the policing
agencies' application of these statutory provisions. In regard to preventing
acts of terrorism, it allows the investigating agencies wide leverage to obtain
the likes of search warrants and to arrest individuals. However, such actions
are still part of the investigative stage and when applying the guidance from
the courts it results in there being insufficient evidence to charge and for a
prosecution to succeed, that person knows they are in the agencies' intelligence systems and possibly under surveillance. This potentially can curtail
a person's involvement with persons or groups involved in acts of terrorism.

Proscribed Organizations/Listed Foreign Terrorist Organizations

The lists of proscribed organizations (United Kingdom), terrorist organizations (United States), and banned terror groups (Canada) are useful regarding
surveillance gathering stages of investigations as they can act as trigger words.
This is certainly useful to national agencies carrying out electronic surveillance in particular the UK's Government Communications Headquarters
(GCHQ) and the US's NSA. Another advantage of having a list of proscribed
or banned groups is it creates a degree of certainty for investigations if a person's associations or activities come under actions related or concerned with
acts of terrorism. Another objective in proscribing or banning groups is it
deters terrorists from operating in the state they are proscribed or banned as
well as supporting countries disrupted by terrorist activity by sending a sig-
nal that the groups' claims to legitimacy are rejected (Anderson 2013, p. 61).

UK Proscribed Organizations (Section 3 and Schedule 2 Terrorism Act 2000)

UK terrorism legislation allows for the Home Secretary to proscribe organizations if they believe the organization is concerned in acts of terrorism.*
Under Schedule 2 Terrorism Act 2000, 65 organizations are listed as proscribed and they include international terrorist organizations and terrorist
organizations based in Northern Ireland. Generic titles are used for some
groups such as the IRA as this title covers emanations of the IRA. This was
decided by the House of Lords in *R v Z (On Appeal from the Court of Appeal
in Northern Ireland)*,† where a breakaway group "the Real IRA" claimed
they were not proscribed as they were not listed. Lord Bingham stated that

---

* Section 3(4) Terrorism Act 2000.
† [2005] UKHL 35.

"... all manifestations of the IRA should be proscribed."[*] This would apply to Al Qaeda, where in July 2013 the UK Government Order stated that al-Nusra Front and Jabhat al-Nusrah li-ahl al Sham were alternative names for Al Qaeda.[†] This would apply to the groups such as Al Qaeda in the Maghreb, Al Qaeda in Iraq, and Al Qaeda in the Arabian Peninsula. For an organization to be concerned in terrorism it must

1. Commit or participate in acts of terrorism.
2. Prepare for acts of terrorism.
3. Promote or encourage acts of terrorism.
4. Is "otherwise" concerned in terrorism.[‡]

Section 32 Terrorism Act of 2006 expanded the scope of organizations that can be proscribed under section 3 of the 2000 Act by expanding the definition of what is meant by promoting or encouraging acts of terrorism that includes groups that unlawfully glorify the commission or preparation of acts of terrorism or their activities are carried out in a manner that ensures the organization is associated with statements containing any such glorification.[§] Glorification includes any form of praise or celebration.[¶] This offense was added in the 2006 Act, as section 1 of the act created the offense of encouragement of terrorism that is committed when a person publishes a statement intended for members of the public to be directly or indirectly encouraged to be induced by the statement to commit, prepare, or instigate acts of terrorism[**] or they are reckless as to whether members of the public will be directly or indirectly encouraged to commit, prepare, or instigate acts of terrorism.[††] There are three offenses-related proscribed organizations:

1. Membership—where a person belongs or professes to belong membership of a proscribed organization.[‡‡]
2. Support for proscribed organizations—where a person invites support for a proscribed organization[§§] where support is not restricted to the provision of money[¶¶] but also includes where a person arranges, manages, or assists in arranging or managing a meeting that will

---

[*] *R v Z* [2005] 35, paragraph 14.
[†] BBC News 2013 "Profile: Syria's al-Nusra Front" retrieved from http://www.bbc.co.uk/news/world-middle-east-18048033 [accessed June 20, 2014].
[‡] Section 3(5) Terrorism Act 2000.
[§] Section (5A) Terrorism Act 2000.
[¶] Section (5C) Terrorism Act 2000.
[**] Section 1(2)(b)(i) Terrorism Act 2006.
[††] Section 1(2)(b)(ii) Terrorism Act 2006.
[‡‡] Section 11 Terrorism Act 2000.
[§§] Section 12(1)(a) Terrorism Act 2000.
[¶¶] Section 12(1)(b) Terrorism Act 2000.

support a proscribed organization* or will be addressed by a person
from a proscribed organization.[†]

3. Uniform—an offense is committed where in a public place a person wears an item of clothing or wears, carries, or displays an article
in such circumstances as to arouse reasonable suspicion they are a
member or supporter of a proscribed organization.[‡]

US Department of State Foreign Terrorist Organizations

The United States has a list of Foreign Terrorist Organizations that are des-
ignations by the Secretary of State under section 219 of the Immigration and
Nationality Act 1952 (as amended in September 2012) that are considered to
be a danger to the United States.[§] There are more similarities than differences
between the UK and the US lists. The significant differences are that the Al
Qaeda groups are listed as separate entities and there are only two Irish groups,
the Real IRA and Continuity IRA, listed with none of the other Irish republican groups or any of the Irish Loyalist groups listed in Schedule 2 Terrorism
Act 2000. However, while not listed in the United Kingdom as a proscribed
organization, the political wing of the current IRA, the 32 County Sovereignty
Movement is listed as a Foreign Terrorist Organization.[¶] These lists and the
fact there are virtually the same groups is important as this allows for greater
ease in intelligence sharing and cooperation between states like the United
States and the United Kingdom, the process of which is discussed below.

Canada: Banned Terror Groups

Again, we see a similar list in Canada's Listed Entities** that contains 46 proscribed groups that are mainly jihadist groups. While the list includes the
Basque separatists, Euskadi Ta Askatasuna (ETA), it does not contain any
of the Irish republican dissident groups. This could be in part explained by
the fact that the list was introduced after the 9/11 Al Qaeda attacks on the
United States with the Anti-Terrorism Act 2001.[††] Legislative authority for

---

* Section 12(2) Terrorism Act 2000.
† Section 12(3) Terrorism Act 2000.
‡ Section 13 Terrorism Act 2000.
§ US Department of State Foreign Terrorist Organization as at September 28, 2012 retrieved
  form http://www.state.gov/j/ct/rls/other/des/123085.htm [accessed August 29, 2013].
¶ US Department of State Archive retrieved from http://2001-2009.state.gov/r/pa/prs/
  ps/2001/2922.htm [accessed September 4, 2013].
** Public Safety Canada—Currently Listed Entities retrieved from http://www.publicsafety.
  gc.ca/cnt/ntnl-scrt/cntr-trrrsm/lstd-ntts/crrnt-lstd-ntts-eng.aspx [accessed October 20,
  2013].
†† RSC 2001, c 41.

proscribing terror groups comes under PtII.1 Criminal Code.[*] In July 2013, Canada was trying to persuade the EU member states to proscribe Hezbollah (Bell 2013). While the EU did not proscribe Hezbollah per se, it did proscribe its military wing, the Party of God.

Summary on Proscribed/Banned Groups

What is clear from the three states' lists is the degree of similarity between the groups listed as being proscribed or banned. The lists are not fixed; each year the respective states revisit them. Groups can request to come off lists, for example, in the United Kingdom the Proscribed Organizations (Applications for Deproscription) Regulations 2001[†] allow either a person or a group to apply to the UK's Home Office in writing to have their group deproscribed. The group must show the grounds why they should be deproscribed.[‡] The conditions are strict. In the *SSHD v Lord Alton of Liverpool and others*[§] the People's Mojahadeen Organization of Iran (PMOI) made such an application that was refused by the Home Office and the PMOI appealed this decision to the UK Court of Appeal. Founded in Iran in 1965 following the overthrow of the Shah of Iran in 1979, the PMOI came into conflict with the Iranian government led by the Ayatollah Khomeini. During the Iraq–Iran war, the PMOI moved to Iraq and gave military assistance to Iraq.[¶] From 2002, the PMOI was not only a proscribed organization in the United Kingdom, but it was also on the EU's list of terrorist organization and subject to an EU asset-freeze and had been designated by the US government as a Foreign terrorist Organization.[**] The PMOI's claim was that post 2001, it had a permanent cessation of violence and was using political will as a means of bringing about freedom and democracy in Iran.[††] The important issue for the Court of Appeal in deciding the PMOI should remain a proscribed organization was not in the fact, there had been a cessation of violence but that the group was otherwise involved in terrorism as it retained a military capacity for the purpose of carrying out terrorist attacks.[‡‡] As Anderson points out, it takes "eccentric courage" by government minister to deproscribe a group that was once proscribed and the difficulties this can present should the group become active again (Anderson 2013, p. 67). This is why groups remain listed and it

[*] RSC 1985, c 41.
[†] Statutory Instrument 2001 no 107.
[‡] Statutory Instrument 2001 no 107, paragraph 3(2)(c).
[§] [2008] EWCA Civ 443.
[¶] *SSHD v Lord Alton of Liverpool and others* [2008] EWCA Civ 443, paragraphs 7–9.
[**] *SSHD v Lord Alton of Liverpool and others* [2008] EWCA Civ 443, paragraph 10.
[††] *SSHD v Lord Alton of Liverpool and others* [2008] EWCA Civ 443, paragraph 16.
[‡‡] *SSHD v Lord Alton of Liverpool and others* [2008] EWCA Civ 443, paragraph 36.

is important for investigators to utilize their resources effectively by focusing on groups and individuals associated with those groups as they can disrupt their activities to achieve the aim of preventing terrorist attacks.

Quasi-Criminal Preventative Measures: Example of the UK's Terrorism Prevention and Investigative Measures Act 2011

One development in anti-terrorism legislation that has emerged and is subject to criticism is the development of quasi-criminal statutory measures. These are measures used where there is insufficient evidence to arrest, charge, and bring a person before the court for terrorism-related offenses. One such example of this is the UK's terrorism prevention and investigation measure (TPIM) orders granted under the Terrorism Prevention and Investigation Measures Act 2011. As Walker observes, a TPIM is a tool to be used when for the time being an investigation and prosecution can go no further (Walker 2012, p. 429). As Walker points out, TPIMs are special executive measures that go beyond the criminal justice system as they offer a level of risk management which a criminal prosecution cannot (Walker 2012, p. 430). One such measure in a TPIM is it allows the state to keep a person under constant surveillance to prevent them from carrying out activities that are related or connected to acts of terrorism.

Legal Development of TPIMs

The TPIM Act of 2011 repealed the control orders issued under the Prevention of Terrorism Act 2005 and introduced a new order, the TPIM. The legal genealogy of TPIMs can be traced back to Part IV of the Anti-Terrorism, Crime, and Security Act 2001 that allowed a Home Secretary to order the indefinite detention of foreign nationals suspected to be involved in acts of terrorism. Following the House of Lords decision in *A and others v SSHD*,[*] it was held this provision violated article 5 (right to liberty and security of the person), article 6 (right to fair trial), and article 14 (right to freedom from discrimination) ECHR as there was no judicial scrutiny of the detention. The decision was solely the Home Secretary's based on intelligence received from various sources regarding the person detained and it only applied to non-UK citizens. This was replaced by control orders issued under the Prevention of Terrorism Act of 2005, that following judicial scrutiny, applied to both UK and non-UK

[*] [2005] 2 AC 68.

citizens and placed very restrictive conditions on that citizen's movements. Following criticism of control orders, in his 2011 review of counterterrorism and security powers, Lord MacDonald said that if such orders were replaced by those linked to criminal investigations, to maintain public safety and not hinder a route to prosecution of an individual, any replacement orders should contain conditions close to those issued in traditional bail conditions in criminal investigations (Lord MacDonald 2011, paragraph 15). Due to Lord MacDonald's recommendation, the decision in *SSHD v AP** where the UK's Supreme Court held control orders violated article 8 (right to privacy and family life) ECHR, the UK government replaced control orders with less restrictive TPIMs.

Overview of the Operation of TPIMs

The A–E conditions under which a TPIM can be authorized and prior permission of the court.

Issued by the Secretary of State (Home Secretary) under section 2 TPIM, a TPIM has to be granted if conditions A to E outlined in section 3 TPIM are met. These are conditions necessary for a person subject of a TPIM order and they are

1. The Home Secretary reasonably believes the individual is or has been involved in terrorism-related activity.
2. That some or all of the relevant activity is new terrorism-related activity.
3. The Home Secretary reasonably believes that it is necessary for purposes with protecting members of the public from a risk of terrorism, for terrorism prevention and investigation measures to be imposed on the individual.
4. The Home Secretary reasonably considers that it is necessary, for the purposes connected with preventing or restricting the individual's involvement in terrorism-related activity for the specified terrorism prevention and investigation measures to be imposed on the individual.
5. The Home Secretary requires the permission of the court before issuing a TPIM (section 3(5)(a)).

Under section 6 TPIM, the court's function in granting permission is to determine if the Secretary of State's decisions are "obviously flawed"† and to determine whether to give permission to impose TPIM measures on

---

* [2010] 3 WLR 51.
† Terrorism Prevention and Investigation Measures Act 2011 section 6(3)(a).

the individual* as well as considering where the court determines that the Secretary of State's decision is flawed to give the Secretary of State directions in relation to the measures to be imposed on the individual† (section 6(9)). Under condition E, the Secretary of State can issue a TPIM without a court authority if they reasonably consider it is urgent that a TPIM needs to be imposed on an individual without such permission for the court.‡

Terrorism-Related Activity (TRA)

Under section 30(1) TPIM the term "terrorism" has the same meaning as that under s.1 Terrorism Act 2000 (section 30(1) TPIM).§ However, TRA under TPIM is wider than the Terrorism Act 2000 provision under section 40(1).¶ section 4 TPIM states that TAC occurs when a person is

a. Involved in the commission, preparation, or instigation of acts of terrorism.
b. Conduct facilitating the commission, preparation, or instigation of acts of terrorism or is intended to do so.
c. Conduct which gives encouragement to the commission, preparation, or instigation of acts of terrorism or is intended to do so.
d. Conduct which supports or assists individuals who are known or believed by the individual to be involved in the commission, preparation, or instigation of acts of terrorism.

Certainly, by adding to section 4(1) TPIM, the fact it is immaterial whether the acts of terrorism are specific acts or acts of terrorism in general along with (d) above, one can see why in *SSHD v BM* Collins J stated this activity is wider than section 40 in the 2000 Act.** On assessing if an act is one that applies to section 4 TPIM, Collins J emphasized the point that for a TPIM it is not necessary to establish the actions to a specific TRA to any higher standard than that which can properly give rise to such a belief, saying:

No doubt some facts which go to forming belief will be clearly established, others may be based on an assessment of the various pieces of evidence available. But there is certainly no requirement that particular TRA needs to be established to the standard of at least more probable than not.††

---

* Terrorism Prevention and Investigation Measures Act 2011 section 6(3)(b).
† Terrorism Prevention and Investigation Measures Act 2011 section 6(9).
‡ Terrorism Prevention and Investigation Measures Act 2011 section 3(5)(b).
§ As per Lloyd Jones LJ in *SSHD v CC and CF* [2012] EWHC 2837 (Admin), paragraph 4.
¶ Collins J, *SSHD v BM* [2012] EWHC 714, paragraph 5.
** Collins J, *SSHD v BM* [2012] EWHC 714, paragraph 5.
†† *SSHD v BM* [2012], paragraph 34.

Offenses

If, without reasonable excuse, an individual on whom a TPIM is granted and is in force contravenes any measure specified in the TPIM, they commit an offense.* Because those on whom a TPIM is granted have not been convicted of a terrorist-related offense, their identity is protected. However, since the inception of TPIMs there have been 10 individuals subject to a TPIM and two of them have broken the conditions of the TPIM. As a result they have been named (BX–Ibrahim Mgag and CC–Mohammed Mohamed) who, at the time of writing, are still at large.

Schedule 1 Measures That Can Be Imposed in a TPIM

TPIM measures that can be imposed by the UK's Home Secretary on an individual are

1. Overnight resident measure (Schedule 1 paragraph 1)—This is a major change brought about following the Supreme Court's decision in *AP* and states this can be premises that are the individual's own residence or one provided by the Secretary of State that is situated in an appropriate locality or agreed locality.† An agreed locality is simply one agreed between the Secretary of State and the individual.‡ An appropriate locality has been defined under Schedule 1 in the act as one in which the individual has a residence or, where they have no residence in the UK, the locality is one in which the individual has a connection such as family connections. If neither of these conditions applies, the appropriate locality is one that appears to the Secretary of State to be appropriate.§

2. Travel measure (Schedule 1 paragraph 2)—travel restrictions can be imposed by the Secretary of State on the individual leaving or travelling outside a specified area with the specified area being the United Kingdom or Great Britain or Northern Ireland.

3. Exclusion measure (Schedule 1 paragraph 3)—the Secretary of State can impose restriction on an individual entering a specified area or place.

4. Movement direction measure (Schedule 1 paragraph 4)—the Secretary of State can impose a requirement for an individual to comply with the direction given by a constable in respect of the individual's movements.

---

* Section 23(1) TPIM.
† Schedule 1 paragraph 1(3).
‡ Schedule 1 paragraph 1(5).
§ Schedule 1 paragraph 1(4).

5. Financial services measure (Schedule 1 paragraph 5)—the Secretary of State can impose restrictions on the individual's use or access to financial services. These include only allowing the person to hold an account nominated by the Secretary of State, to close or cease to have an interest in certain accounts or to comply with specified conditions in relation to the holding of an account or a requirement not to possess or control cash over a total value specified by the Secretary of State.*

6. Property measure (Schedule 1 paragraph 6)—this includes restrictions on the transfer of property, be it money or other property to a person or a place outside the United Kingdom.

7. Electronic communication device measure (Schedule 1 paragraph 7)—the Secretary of State can impose restrictions on the possession or use of electronic communication devices owned by the individual or other person's at the individual's residence. This includes a telephone fixed to landline, a computer, a mobile phone,† or any device that is capable of storing, transmitting, or receiving images, sounds, or information by electronic means and includes any component part of any such device.‡

8. Association measure (Schedule 1 paragraph 8)—the Secretary of State can impose restrictions on an individual's association or communication with any other person.

9. Work or studies measure (Schedule 1 paragraph 9)—an individual can only carry out work or studies as those specified by the Secretary of State.

10. Reporting measure (Schedule paragraph 10)—this measure includes a requirement by the Secretary of State to report to a police station at such times in such a manner so requested and to comply with a constable direction made in relation to such reporting.

11. Photography measure (Schedule 1 paragraph 11)—the Secretary of State can require the individual to allow photographs to be taken of them in locations and at times specified in the TPIM.

12. Monitoring measure (Schedule 1 paragraph 12)—the Secretary of State can impose a measure that the individual's movements, communications, or other activities are monitored by electronic means (this includes the wearing of an electronic tag on their person).

---

* Schedule 1 paragraph 5(2).
† Schedule 1 paragraph 7(3).
‡ Schedule 1 paragraph 7(5).

Proportionality

All the measures that can be imposed on an individual in a TPIM must be applied under the legal principle of proportionality. In *CF v SSHD*,* Wilkie J provided the test that is to be applied by the court when examining the measures outlined by the Secretary of States in the TPIM, saying the test should be applied in the following terms:

> 1. The objective must be sufficiently important to justify limiting a fundamental right; 2. The measures must be designed to meet the objective and must be rationally connected to it; and 3. The means used to impair the right or freedom must be no more than that is necessary to accomplish the objective. Furthermore, the graver the impact of the measure, the more compelling the justification will need to be, and the greater the care with which it must be examined … the term "necessity" is not to be equated with "useful," "reasonable," or "desirable." In addition, the court must examine each measure individually and should not too readily accept claims to be deferential … †

The Controversy over TPIMs

The main controversy over TPIMs and its predecessor, control orders, is that they are quasi-criminal procedures (Gearty 2013, p. 46) that Fenwick describes as new methods to protect national security. While acknowledging them some measure of procedural fairness is present, her criticism is these types of measures are aimed at suspected terrorists who the UK government cannot deport or cannot prosecute in a criminal court for terrorist-related offenses (2011, p. 130). In effect, their argument is where there is insufficient evidence to charge and bring before a criminal court for a successful prosecution, the United Kingdom has introduced measures widening the scope of criminalizing individuals and labeling them as terrorists. During its passage as Bill through the UK Parliament, TPIMs were criticized as being no more than a "political fudge" in the UK government's desire to show the electorate they are taking a tough stance against those suspected to be involved in terrorist activity, as the measure did not secure substantive changes from TPIM's predecessor, control orders (Hansard 2011).

Also questioned has been the usefulness of TPIMs. In his speech to the Royal United Services Institute in 2013, the current director of MI5, Andrew Parker, said that individuals being on the security service's radar does not mean they are under their microscope as the security services only focus on their most intrusive attention on a small number of cases at any one time (Parker 2013, paragraphs 37–38). This is evidenced by the fact that since their

---

* [2013] EWHC 843 (Admin).
† *CF v SSHD* [2013] EWHC 843 (Admin), paragraphs 25 and 26.

introduction TPIMs have only been applied to 11 individuals. From the four TPIM's cases, we can see how each individual has had or got some form of direct connection with acts of terrorism. In *CC and CF*, both individuals had travelled to Somalia and had close connections with the terror group Al Shabab,* where both their activities included training and fighting in terrorist conflicts that were so severe it led to Lloyd Jones LJ stating that they had a substantial role in terrorist activity, and as a result he found the national security case against them as "overwhelming."[†] In *BF v SSHD*, it was documented that BF held extreme, radical Islamic views to such an extent that Silber J held it was likely he would engage in terrorism activity overseas if he ceased to be subject to a TPIM.[‡]

One issue that is a cause for concern in the ordering of TPIM measures on individuals is the lack of judicial scrutiny when the applications are being made. In his review of the UK's counterterrorism and security powers, Lord Macdonald argued that a TPIM order should be made initially by the High Court to allow for judicial scrutiny to ensure the order is necessary and, if so, the conditions are proportionate to the risk posed (Lord Macdonald 2011, p. 16). While a mechanism for keeping TPIMs under a formal and audited review has been established with the TPIM Review Group (TRG) comprising of civil servants, police officers, MI5 case handlers, and the Crown Prosecution Service, as the TRG only meet quarterly, this can result in time delays in assessing the validity of a TPIM application (Middleton 2013, p. 577). Another critique of this process is with the TRG comprising of investigators and prosecutors, these agencies cannot be said to be truly independent. They can be said to have a vested interest in the issuing of TPIM on an individual suspected of being involved in terrorist activity. This could be one reason why in Middleton's assessment of TPIM's he said the role of the UK's Independent Reviewer of terrorism legislation should be strengthened further as the reviewer's report could form part of the required consultation process (Middleton 2013, p. 577). Neither this move nor the role of the TRG can replace a truer independent review than that provided by judicial scrutiny. As Walker points out, in the United Kingdom a model of court issuance is applied to similar orders issued under the Serious Crime Act 2007 and risk of sexual harm orders under the Sexual Offenses Act 2003 as there are no logistical problems of a court issuance of an order as the applications are normally issued ex parte (Walker 2012, p. 431). The UK government has resisted such moves claiming consistency is required for TPIMs to be in line with other national security measures such as financial restrictions, deportation or those issued under the UK's Terrorist Asset-Freezing Act 2010.

---

* *SSHD v CC and CF* [2012] EWHC 2837 (Admin), paragraphs 31–36.
† *SSHD v CC and CF* [2012] EWHC 2837 (Admin), paragraph 38.
‡ *BF v SSHD* [2013] EWHC 2329 (Admin), paragraph 35.

Having judicial scrutiny of applications of orders such as TPIMs is not unique. Section 104.4 of Australia's Criminal Code confers powers onto the courts when satisfied on balance of probabilities and to assist in preventing an act of terrorism to issue a control order on a person where the control order, like TPIM measures, impose restrictions on the movements of that person. In *Thomas v Mowbray*,[*] the Australian High Court considered the validity of the courts to impose control orders where the majority was that this power of the court was not a violation of the separation of powers. What was noticeable in the decision was Kirby J's dissenting judgment, where his concerns were that the courts issuing orders to prevent future behavior he did not see as the true exercise of judicial power. For Kirby J, such a role that was expected the courts perform under section 104.4 of Australia's Criminal Code was in essence the creation of future rights and obligations, a role that is more akin to that the legislative or the executive performs.[†] His concern was that in making such orders, the courts were becoming "rubber stamps" for the decisions of the executive government.[‡] Underpinning this concern, Kirby J stressed the importance the court's duty being that of guarding against unwarranted departures from fundamental rights and freedoms.[§]

By having to examine every condition in detail contained in orders controlling the movement of suspected terrorists, Kirby J noted in *Thomas*, this legal duty has also been applied by UK courts where in protecting individuals' rights and freedoms, they have either restricted or removed the conditions imposed by the Secretary of State contained within TPIMs.[¶] This returns to the principle of proportionality and necessity regarding whether a measure contained in a TPIM is appropriate and relevant. In relation to proportionality, in *Guzzardi v Italy*[**] the European Court of Human Rights held the difference between deprivation of and restriction of liberty is one of degree or intensity and not that of nature or substance.[††] In the challenges made in the four TPIM cases by the applicants to the measures contained in their respective TPIM, this issue has been at the heart of the courts' decision making as Wilkie J in *CF v SSHD* stated, an inconvenience is not of such severity to make a measure lack proportionality. The courts have also taken into account the evidence of the applicant's actions prior to an order being commenced. In *SSHD v AM*[‡‡] AM was on a control order under the 2005 Act and he challenged his TPIM measure claiming the imposition of the order was *ultra vires* as he had not

---

[*] [2007] HCA 33.
[†] *Thomas v Mowbray* [2007] HCA 33, paragraph 304.
[‡] *Thomas v Mowbray* [2007] HCA 33, paragraph 329.
[§] *Thomas v Mowbray* [2007] HCA 33, paragraph.
[¶] For example, *BF v SSHD* [2013] EWHC 2329 (Admin), paragraph 42.
[**] (Application no. 7367/76).
[††] (Application no. 7367/76), paragraph 93.
[‡‡] [2012] EWHC 1854 (Admin).

been involved in terrorism-related activity since 2007. In upholding the imposition of the specified measures by the TPIM, the High Court said due to the
terrorist activities AM was involved in, it was an unavoidable consequence
an order would be issued that restricted his movements.[*] While a TPIM may
be a diluted version of the Prevention of Terrorism Act 2005's control order,
it has provided a lighter touch regarding the restrictive measure imposed on
an individual (Cochrane 2013, p. 43). The question is whether there is a need
for them. As the UK government's 2011 Counterterrorism Review reported,
surveillance by the police and the security services on suspected individuals
does not provide control.[†] One possible consideration is to repeal these orders
and let the police and security services maintain surveillance on persons suspected to be involved in terrorist activity under the powers already in place.
This would not only ensure the states' agencies actions are compliant with
the due respect they must show toward an individual's rights, it would also
remove any accusation during the application process of political arbitrariness in the use of a senior politician's powers.

NSA, PRISM Project, Journalistic Material, and Schedule 7 Powers: A Case Study of a Terrorism Preventative Stop and Search Measure Used at the National Level in Response to an International Incident

Another accusation of how anti-terror preventative legislative provisions
have been used for political purposes occurred in the United Kingdom on
August 18, 2013. In June 2013, former NSA employee, Edward Snowden took
and passed on a large quantity of secret and classified documents relating to
surveillance practices by the NSA and its UK counterpart, GCHQ, to the UK's
national newspaper *The Guardian*. In passing on these documents and secrets
relating to the surveillance operation known as the PRISM project, Snowdon
had breached official secrets laws. Not only were US authorities keen to arrest
and speak to Snowden, both the US and UK authorities were keen to regain
the documentation Snowden had taken. While carrying materials Snowden
passed onto *The Guardian* journalist Glenn Greenwald, when catching a
connecting flight to Brazil, Greenwald's partner David Miranda was stopped
by Special Branch Counterterrorism officers at London's Heathrow Airport
using a stop and search power under Schedule 7 Terrorism Act 2000. From
checking the flight lists 2 days earlier, the UK's national security service, MI5

---

[*] SSHD v AM [2012] EWHC 1854 (Admin), paragraph 24.
[†] SSHD v AM [2012] EWHC 1854 (Admin), paragraph 13.

saw that Miranda was arriving at Heathrow on the August 18th and sent a request to Special Branch for him to be stopped. The request read:

> We assess that MIRANDA is knowingly carrying material, the release of which would endanger people's lives. Additionally the disclosure, or threat of disclosure, is designed to influence a government, and is made for the purpose of promoting a political or ideological cause. This therefore falls within the definition of terrorism and as such we request that the subject is examined under Schedule 7 (Anderson 2014, p. 29).

Due to the nature of the Snowden revelations, there was global interest in what up to then had been a little-known UK police power. Miranda was detained for 9 hours where his electronic possessions were seized and examined, and he was interviewed.[*] The electronic devices examined included Miranda's laptop, mobile phone, memory sticks, and DVD's (O'Carroll and Norton-Taylor 2013).

Schedule 7 Terrorism Act 2000 Powers

Schedule 7 allows officers in relation to terrorist activity to collect intelligence on the movements of persons of interest to the police and the Security Service.[†] Schedule 7 powers can only be used by police officers[‡] at ports and airports to stop and question persons who are or may be concerned in the commission, preparation, or instigation of acts of terrorism.[§] The officers are permitted to search that person and examine any property they have with them[¶] and can detain that person's property for up to 7 days.[**] The media's concern was they saw Miranda being stopped as nothing more than the use of arbitrary police powers, with the most vitriolic critic being Greenwald who wrote

> This is obviously a rather profound escalation of their attacks on the news-gathering process and journalism. It's bad enough to prosecute and imprison sources. It's worse still to imprison journalists who report the truth. But to start detaining the family members and loved ones of journalists is simply despotic (Greenwald 2013).

---

[*] BBC News August 19, 2013 "Heathrow detention: 'They asked me about my whole life'" retrieved from http://www.bbc.co.uk/news/world-latin-america-23760966 [accessed September 2, 2013].
[†] Collins J *CC v The Commissioner of Police of the Metropolis and Secretary of State for the Home Department* [2011] EWHCX 3316 (Admin), paragraph 11.
[‡] This applies to immigration officers and customs officers as well as police officers.
[§] Schedule 7 Terrorism Act 2000, paragraph 2(2)(b).
[¶] Schedule 7 Terrorism Act 2000, paragraph 8.
[**] Schedule 7 Terrorism Act 2000, paragraph 11.

Although the UK Home Secretary justified the use of Schedule 7 powers on Miranda stressing that his detention of 9 h was exceptional, there were still protestations from *The Guardian* and other media outlets. Their main claim was that Miranda was solely in possession of journalistic material and the powers were used to fetter the freedom of the press. In their protestations, they *omitted* to point out that what Snowden passed on were stolen secret state documents, property of the US and UK governments.

Judicial Response to Schedule 7 Powers

The question the courts have had to address was whether Schedule 7 powers are proportionate. With coincidental timing, in August 2013 *Sylvie Beghal v Director of Public Prosecutions*[*] went before the UK's High Court where Beghal was challenging Schedule 7 powers regarding their potential violation of related articles contained in the ECHR. A French national and the wife of a convicted terrorist, Beghal arrived at England's East Midlands Airport and was detained under Schedule 7. The police did not suspect her of being a terrorist, but they wanted to speak to her to establish whether she may be a person concerned in the commission, preparation, or instigation of terrorism.[†] As a result of *Beghal* and other cases related to Schedule 7 powers the courts have examined the following provisions contained in those powers.

Purpose of the Stop

Schedule 7 terrorism Act 2000 paragraph 2 states the officer can question a person for the purposes of determining whether he or she is a person who is or has been connected in the commission, preparation, or instigation of acts of terrorism.[‡] As Mr Justice Collins pointed out in *CC v The Commissioner of the Police of the Metropolis and Secretary of State for the Home Department*,[§] the Courts have had to consider if the purpose of the stop is proportionate and falls within the requirements of the ECHR. In *CC*, Mr Justice Collins said the wording of section 40(1)(b) is important. As well as being able to identify acts that constitute terrorism, he said it must be open to an officer to act under Schedule 7 to determine whether a person appears to be or has been concerned in acts of terrorism.[¶] He added:

---

[*] [2013] EWHC 2573 (Admin).
[†] [2013] EWHC 2573 (Admin), paragraph 8.
[‡] Terrorism Act 2000, s. 40(1)(b).
[§] [2011] EWHC 3316 (Admin).
[¶] *CC v The Commissioner of the Police of the Metropolis and Secretary of State for the Home Department* [2011] EWHC 3316 (Admin), paragraph 15.

... the language of s. 40(1)(b) is wide enough to allow for examination not only of whether he appears to be a terrorist but also of the way in which or the act by which he so appears. The officer is not, unless the powers are to be ineffective in their purpose to protect from terrorism, prevented from examining a person even if it appears he is a terrorist in particular respects, for example if in the past or by acts only affecting a foreign government.*

This was an even more contentious issue when David Miranda was stopped at Heathrow Airport in August 2013 as Miranda claimed the purpose of the stop was not to determine his potential involvement in acts of terrorism but to assist the UK Security Service in accessing the material Miranda had in his possession that Snowden had passed on, albeit indirectly, to him.[†] In *Miranda*, Laws LJ held the purpose of the stop was legitimate and proportionate saying:

... it appears to me that the Schedule 7 power is given in order to provide a reasonable but limited opportunity for the ascertainment of a possibility: the possibility that a traveller may be involved ... *directly or indirectly* in any of a range of activities enumerated in s. 1(2) [that defines an act of terrorism][‡] [My emphasis].

This is an important decision as the High Court is recognizing the short window of opportunity officers at ports and border controls have in stopping persons in transit to allow them to question those persons to ascertain their potential involvement in terrorist acts. In both *CC* and *Miranda*, the High Court held that Schedule 7 paragraph 2 does not violate the ECHR.

No Requirement for Reasonable Suspicion

When carrying out a stop under Schedule 7, an officer does not require reasonable grounds to suspect a person is involved in the preparation or commission of acts of terrorism.[§] On the face of it, this provision appears to violate article 5 (right to liberty and security of the person) ECHR that states where a person is detained there must be reasonable suspicion that a person has committed an offense, which in this case is concerning their involvement in an act of terrorism.[¶] This issue was addressed by the High Court in *Sylvie Beghal v Director of Public Prosecutions*[**] that held this provision in paragraph 2(4) is a necessary and rational purpose related to port and border control as with

* *CC v The Commissioner of the Police of the Metropolis and Secretary of State for the Home Department* [2011] EWHC 3316 (Admin), paragraph 16.
† *David Miranda v The Secretary of State for the Home Department and The Commissioner of the Police of the Metropolis* [2014] EWHC 255.
‡ *David Miranda v The Secretary of State for the Home Department and The Commissioner of the Police of the Metropolis* [2014] EWHC 255, paragraph 32.
§ Schedule 7 terrorism Act 2000, paragraph 2(4).
¶ European Convention on Human Rights article 5(1)(c).
** [2013] EWHC 2573 (Admin).

the purpose of Schedule 7 being to inhibit or deter the travel of someone otherwise engaged in the commission of acts of terrorism. The ability of officers to question widely is necessary so they can build up a picture of the travel in question and its connection (if there be one) to acts of terrorism.[*] In his role as Independent Reviewer of UK terrorism legislation, David Anderson's report into the operation of UK terrorism legislation found the police applied Schedule 7 powers proportionately and found no evidence of the powers being exercised in a racially discriminatory manner.[†] (Anderson 2012, paragraph 10.17). Although his findings were positive in the application for Schedule 7 powers, he stressed the point that Schedule 7 powers should not be exercised at random but on the basis of intelligence and other factors that might indicate the presence of a terrorist (Anderson 2012, paragraph 10.15).

Access to Legal Advice

Prior to the Anti-Social Behavior, Crime, and Policing Act 2014 amendments, under Schedule 7 the right to access to consult a solicitor by persons detained was a cause for concern and the main legal point brought to the High Court in *Abderlrazag Elosta v Commissioner of Police of the Metropolis and The Secretary of State for the Home Department*.[‡] In *Elosta* the High Court recognized the changes the Home Secretary brought about through the Home Office circular 07/2011 regarding the mistakes contained in Schedule 7. This included the Codes of Practice accompanying the Schedule 7 provisions and the TACT notification forms issued by examining officers to detained persons regarding their right of access to a solicitor under Schedule 7. *Elosta* confirmed that there was a right to consult with a lawyer in private at public expense and it is expected the consultation with a lawyer at a port will normally be by a private telephone conversation. Under Schedule 9 of the Anti-Social Behavior, Crime and Policing Act 2014, both Schedules 7 and 8 Terrorism Act 2000 were amended regarding the right of access to a solicitor. There is no longer a requirement that a request for a solicitor be made where a person is detained at a police station only. Schedule 8 now reads that where a person is detained simply at a place they can make such a request.[§] This now applies to the place persons are stopped and detained under Schedule 7. The person is entitled to consult a solicitor in person[¶] and an examining officer cannot question that person until they have consulted a solicitor. The only occasion a detained person cannot consult a solicitor and be questioned

---

[*] [2013] EWHC 2573 (Admin), Gross LJ, paragraph 106.
[†] David Anderson QC, *The Terrorism Acts in 2012* (The Stationary Office 2013), 100.
[‡] [2013] EWHC 3397 (Admin).
[§] Terrorism Act 2000 Schedule 8 paragraph 6.
[¶] Terrorism Act 2000 Schedule 7 paragraph 7A(5).

without one having been consulted is when they are not detained at a police station and the examining officer reasonably believes both the time it would take to consult a solicitor and to postpone the questioning are likely to prejudice the determination of relevant matters.[*]

Right to Silence

Persons detained and questioned under Schedule 7 must give the examining officer any information in their possession which that officer requests.[†] In effect, this means that detained persons do not have a right to silence when questioned by the police, which again may seem strange in a police power used today, especially when public bodies must act in a manner that is compatible with the ECHR.[‡] Regarding this provision article 6 (Right to a Fair Trial), ECHR is the relevant article concerning the privilege against self-incrimination. This point was examined in *Beghal*, where comparison was drawn to the decision the European Court of Human Rights held in *Allen v United Kingdom*.[§] Allen was under arrest in a tax case where there was a compulsory power requiring a person being interviewed to provide information about their financial or company affairs. In *Allen*, the European Court held the privilege against self-incrimination does not prohibit the use of compulsory questioning of a person.[¶] Gross LJ clearly established that the privilege against self-incrimination is not absolute and does not apply to Schedule 7 as Beghal was simply stopped by the police, she was not under suspicion and neither was she arrested. In addition to this, Gross LJ stated that the Schedule 7 examination was not carried out for the purpose of obtaining evidence or admissions for use in criminal proceedings (albeit any answers might yield information of potentially evidential value),[**] and importantly, a Schedule 7 examination is not an inquiry preparatory to criminal proceedings.[††]

Search and Seizure of Property under Schedule 7: Can Journalistic Material Be Related to Terrorist Activities?

Under Schedule 7, officers are permitted to search that person and anything he or she has with him or her[‡‡] and can detain that person's property for up to

---

[*] Terrorism Act 2000 Schedule 7 paragraph 7A(6) and 7A(3).
[†] Terrorism Act 2000 Schedule 7 paragraph 5(a).
[‡] Human Rights Act 1998 section 6.
[§] Application no. 7657/01.
[¶] Application no. 7657/01, paragraph 119.
[**] *Sylvie Beghal v Director of Public Prosecutions* [2013] EWHC 2573 (Admin), paragraphs 127–128.
[††] *Sylvie Beghal v Director of Public Prosecutions* [2013] EWHC 2573 (Admin), paragraph 129.
[‡‡] Terrorism Act 2000 Schedule 7 paragraph 8.

7 days to examine the property that person has with him or her.[*] An important point the court in *Miranda* centered on was the nature of the property Miranda was carrying at the time of his stop and examination. Miranda's argument was these documents were not related to terrorism, but were items of journalistic material. This resulted in the outrage shown by the world's media centered on the documents Miranda had in his possession. If there was an element in the facts of the case in relation to his stop and examination that could have resulted in the court finding in his favor it was this particular point. This raised questions over what legally amounts to journalistic material, which traditionally cannot be searched by the police in a democratic state. In England, the Police and Criminal Act 1984 (PACE) provides a wide definition of what amounts to journalistic material by simply stating it is material acquired and created for the purposes of journalism.[†] PACE also classifies journalistic material as "excluded material" which is material a person holds in confidence and which consists of documents or records other than documents.[‡] In the United Kingdom, officers can search for and seize excluded material in terrorism investigations under a search warrant issued under Schedule 5 Terrorism Act 2000. In *Miranda*, the search and seizure was not carried out under a Schedule 5 search warrant, it was conducted under the Schedule 7 power. As a result, the court in *Miranda* did not discuss the conditions of a search and seizure granted under Schedule 5 and consequently the powers of police officers to search journalistic material under that Schedule. *The Guardian*'s editor, Rusbridger maintained that Miranda was in possession of journalistic material saying:

> The state is building such a formidable apparatus of surveillance it will do its best to prevent journalists from reporting on it. … I wonder how many have truly understood the absolute threat to journalism implicit in the idea of total surveillance, when or if it comes—and, increasingly, it looks like when (Rusbridger 2013).

Regarding the incident, one issue omitted by Rusbridger is that Miranda was not carrying the usual journalistic material as it had the potential to be stolen state secrets.

Laws LJ held the stopping of Miranda was proportionate as the material Miranda was suspected to have at the time was not media reporting on terrorism. He added the officers used Schedule 7 powers on Miranda to ascertain the nature of the material he was carrying and therefore their actions fell properly with the construction of Schedule 7.[§] Regarding whether the

---

[*] Terrorism Act 2000 Schedule 7 paragraph 11.
[†] Police and Criminal Evidence Act 1984 section 13(2).
[‡] Police and Criminal Evidence Act 1984 section 11(1)(c).
[§] *David Miranda v The Secretary of State for the Home Department and The Commissioner of the Police of the Metropolis* [2014] EWHC 255, paragraphs 35 and 36.

material in Miranda's possession was journalistic material, the High Court decided this was not the case as the police believed that Miranda was potentially in possession of a substantial number of the 58,000 documents stolen by Snowden.[*] How the materials were obtained and held by Snowden is questioned as there are those who strongly refute that Snowden did not steal the documents, rather as they were on his computer and software, they belonged to Snowden and Greenwald. Those who subscribe to this argument claim the worst thing Snowden did with these documents by passing them onto *The Guardian* was to simply misuse them (Greenwald 2014). As these documents must have been on the NSA and GCHQ's IT systems, they were copied by Snowden onto his own software without the authority of the NSA and GCHQ. This is a form of appropriation that is the same as if Snowden physically got hold of the hard copies, copied them, and passed them on. As theft in the United Kingdom involves a person taking property belonging to another with the intention of permanently depriving the other of it,[†] Snowden showed his intent to permanently deprive the NSA and the GCHQ of them by passing them onto *The Guardian*. These actions show no intent of returning them to the NSA or GCHQ. As what Snowden had in his possession were copies of the documents, it can be argued that both the NSA and GCHQ had not been deprived of them. However, the theft lays in its contents, which are state secrets and it is the information that Snowden appropriated.

Crucial to proving theft is the action has to be dishonest. Although the Theft Act is silent in defining what factors amount to being dishonest, the act is clear on actions that would be or would not deemed to be dishonest. Those actions are where the person took the property:

1. In the belief that they had a right in law to deprive the owner of it.[‡]
2. They believed they would have had consent of the owner.[§]

As seen from the reaction of the US and UK governments, Snowden would not have had that consent and it is highly doubtful he would believe he had the consent of the NSA and GCHQ to copy the documents. If Snowden claimed that he did not do this for personal gain, but to show how the NSA and GCHQ conduct surveillance on a wide scale on citizens around the world, this would not negate an act of theft as the Theft Act is clear it is immaterial if the appropriation is made with a view to gain or is made for the thief's own benefit.[¶] Therefore, the proponents subscribing to the view Snowden simply

---

[*] *David Miranda v The Secretary of State for the Home Department and The Commissioner of the Police of the Metropolis* [2014] EWHC 255, paragraph 53.
[†] Theft Act 1968 section 1(1).
[‡] Theft Act 1968 section 2(1)(a).
[§] Theft Act 1968 section 2(1)(b).
[¶] Theft Act 1968 section 1(2).

misused the documentation on his software appear to have overlooked what actions amount to theft and it is submitted in the High Court in Miranda is correct in stating these documents were stolen.

In addition to this, the police believed the information Miranda possessed if released, even via the media where the intrinsic significance of the material was not understood, was deemed by the Court to be a "gift to the terrorist."* Although Greenwald claimed that journalists share with the government the responsibility of what is required by way of withholding publication for the protection of national security, this was dismissed as the Court made it clear that journalists have no constitutional responsibility.† This is an important point as the media cannot be held to account in law in this area the same way public bodies can be. These key points were influential in the Court finding that Miranda's Schedule 7 stop and detention was not only legitimate, it was also "very pressing" and in striking a balance between public interest or press freedom and national security, the Court found in favor of national security.

Detention Periods and Review of Detention

The maximum period a person can be detained under Schedule 7 is 6 h.‡ Originally, the maximum period of detention was 9 h, but the amendments contained in Schedule 9 paragraph 2 Anti-Social, Crime, and Policing Act of 2014 reduced the maximum period to 6 h. As his detention under Schedule 7 was prior to the amendments, Miranda was detained for the full 9 h. Even prior to the amendments coming into force, this period of detention was an exception rather than the norm. In his report on the UK terrorism legislation, Anderson found that of those stopped between 2009 and 2012 (carried out prior to the 2014 amendments), 97.2% of examinations lasted less than an hour, 2.02% lasted between 1 and 3 h with only 0.6% of examinations lasting the full 9 h. Following *Miranda*, the UK government found it necessary to reduce the maximum period for detention persons can be examined under Schedule 7 to 6 h. Regarding detention for examination under Schedule 7, another amendment under Schedule 9 of the Anti-Social, Crime, and Policing Act of 2014 was an addition to Schedule 8 of the Terrorism Act 2000. The amendment introduced the requirement that a person's detention under Schedule 7 is reviewed episodically. The first review must be carried out at the end of the period of 1 h by a review officer who is a senior officer of a higher

---

* Theft Act 1968 section 1(2), paragraph 58.
† Theft Act 1968 section 1(2), paragraph 71.
‡ Terrorism Act 2000 Schedule 7 paragraph 6A(3).

rank than the examining officer*and who has not been directly involved in the questioning of the detained person under paragraphs 2 and 3, Schedule 7.[†]

Proportionality and the Interests of National Security or Individual Liberty

In *Beghal*, the High Court saw no violation of ECHR articles through the use of Schedule 7 as the Court found Schedule 7 powers not to be arbitrary[‡] as in the court's opinion these powers are proportionate and permissible. The Court said that while rights protecting a defendant from prejudice are important, applying the legal principle of proportionality what outweighs individual rights is the protection of the public in combating terrorism.[§] On this point, Lord Justice Gross LJ said:

> Inhibiting or deterring the travel of someone otherwise engaged in the commission of acts for terrorism serves, in our view, manifestly rational purpose related to port and border control. ... realistically the ability to question widely is necessary to build up a picture of the travel in question and its connection (if such there be) to acts of terrorism.[¶]

This theme was also made in *Miranda* regarding the seriousness of the nature of the stop and examination being the prevention of terrorism. In *Miranda*, Ouseley J said that officers using this power must act in good faith for the purposes of the Terrorism Act 2000 and be able to explain the way they act as they do, adding:

> [An officer] cannot act on a merely arbitrary basis, but he can act on, for example, no more than a hunch or intuition, especially given the speed with which they may have to act. This is not a power of last resort.[**]

Regarding the *Miranda* case, Anderson raises concerns that the court's decision highlights the remarkable breadth of the UK's legal definition of

---

* Code of Practice for examining officers under Schedule 7 to the Terrorism Act 2000, paragraph 20K(7)(a).
† Code of Practice for examining officers under Schedule 7 to the Terrorism Act 2000, paragraph 20K(2).
‡ *Sylvie Beghal v Director of Public Prosecutions* [2013] EWHC 2573 (Admin), paragraph 112.
§ *Sylvie Beghal v Director of Public Prosecutions* [2013] EWHC 2573 (Admin), paragraph 143.
¶ *Sylvie Beghal v Director of Public Prosecutions* [2013] EWHC 2573 (Admin), paragraph 106.
** *David Miranda v The Secretary of State for the Home Department and The Commissioner of the Police of the Metropolis* [2014] EWHC 255, paragraph 91.

terrorism (Anderson 2014, p. 29). Among his concerns is that the publication or threatened publication of words may constitute terrorist action where the writing is for the purpose of advancing a political, religious, racial, or ideological cause designed to influence a government (Anderson 2014, p. 30). For Anderson, this had a "chilling effect" as

1. Possession of articles connected with publication or articles likely to be useful to publishing material of that kind would be punishable under sections 57 and 58 of the Terrorism Act 2000 leading to imprisonment.
2. Where a newspaper is printing such material that is politically motivated to influence a government, it could become a proscribed organization.
3. In such a case, the newspaper and its journalists could be designated under terrorist asset-freezing legislation.
4. Anderson thinks that potentially TPIMs could be imposed on journalists (Anderson 2014, p. 31).

While respecting Anderson's expertise on terrorism legislation, he appears to have exaggerated the potential implications of the *Miranda* decision. This is not just from a legal perspective as Laws LJ made it clear that this would not be the case, saying:

> There is *no suggestion* that media reporting on terrorism ought *per se* to be considered equivalent to assisting terrorists [my emphasis].*

If Anderson's assertions are correct that where a state condoned journalistic reporting containing a political motive to be an act of terrorism, such a move would be political suicide for any democratic state. The fallout for any party in government would not only be in the international condemnation of such action, but also in that state's citizens' condemnation of such an application of terrorism laws. That citizens' condemnation would inevitably be reflected in the voting behavior in the ballot box where undoubtedly the number of votes for the party in government that allowed this would greatly decrease and potentially result in that party remaining in the political wilderness for many years. As a result, it is highly unlikely that this would be the situation. To reiterate the point made by the High Court in *Miranda*, it was not examining a situation solely related to journalistic material that was politically motivated to influence a government because the case would be concerned with a blanket fettering of the freedom of the media. In *Miranda*,

---

* *David Miranda v The Secretary of State for the Home Department and The Commissioner of the Police of the Metropolis* [2014] EWHC 255 [35].

the application of Schedule 7 powers and whether the material Miranda had in his possession related to terrorism was what the court had to consider. The High Court's decision centered on the theft of 58,000 secret files, the content of which if were inadvertently released or lost and might have had fallen into the wrong hands would have a devastating consequence for national security, especially the national security of the United States and the United Kingdom. The role of a free media plays an important role in a democracy. Through their freedom of expression, the free media is a watchdog by acting as a check on political and other holders of power that could influence a government, hence its nickname of the Fourth Estate.* What was at issue in Miranda was balancing the genuine needs of national security with protecting the rights and freedoms of an individual. As Laws LJ said, the objective of the Schedule 7 objective in Miranda's case was

> ... not only legitimate, but very pressing ... In a press freedom case the ... requirement of proportionality involves as I have said the striking of a balance between two aspects of the public interest: press freedom itself on the one hand, and on the other whatever is sought to justify the interference; here national security.[†]

Even to the most fervent advocate of individual liberty, there are occasions when they must accept national security has to take precedent over individual rights, and *Miranda* was one of those occasions.

Summary of the High Court's Decision in *Miranda*

The result counterterrorism agency officers want in their investigations is to prevent acts of terrorism from occurring. This is an outcome governments also desire, not merely to demonstrate the potential to, but to actually keep its state's citizens safe and of course it is what citizens also desire. Schedule 7 of the UK's Terrorism Act 2000 has been subject of much criticism by those who have a deep concern for individual rights and freedoms. However, as seen in the judicial decisions, another imperative is in meeting the needs of national security as acts of terrorism can affect everyone. The terror effect results not only in deaths and serious disabilities of those injured in attacks, but impacts on the wider population who may change their daily behavior. This can range from changing methods of travel to restricting their own movements to particular locations where a terrorist attack is likely to occur. To prevent terrorist

---

* Sir Brian Leveson, *An Inquiry into the Culture, Practice and Ethics of the Press Volume 1* (The Stationary Office 2012), 65.
† *David Miranda v The Secretary of State for the Home Department and The Commissioner of the Police of the Metropolis* [2014] EWHC 255 [73].

attacks investigators need wide powers. This is a point conceded by Anderson who, in his criticism of how wide terrorism-related powers are being used, recognizes the need for "tough laws." He says, they are required to allow for terrorists to be arrested more easily and prosecuted for behavior falling short of traditional attempt, conspiracy, or incitement law, a position he recognizes the public accept, "... so long as they are used only when necessary."[*] It is submitted counterterrorism officers do only use these powers when it is necessary and *Miranda* should not be used to portray the norm in how the state and the judiciary deviate in the application of terrorism-related powers. As stated, the *Miranda* case was exceptional as Miranda was carrying government documents stolen from the US and UK's security agencies. As a result, this case was more about national security than the freedom of the press and as stated, the judgment given in Miranda is clear that its findings are not about restricting that freedom or extending the circumstances where terrorism-related legislation is applied to journalistic activity.

Conclusion

As stressed in this chapter, from government polices to the rationale behind introducing statutory preventative measure, the primary aim of a counterterrorism investigation is to prevent terrorist acts from occurring. This is evident in the offenses related to possessing and providing materials that support acts of terrorism. In using the examples of the legislation from the United Kingdom and the United States, we can see how wide the definition related to the offense of possession is, especially in relation to what actual articles or materials amounts to possessing to support terrorism. In turn, this widens the scope for investigating officers to arrest individuals and to apply for search warrants to seize such items. This has not given counterterrorism agencies carte blanche powers to bring individuals who would not normally be associated with acts of terrorism into their system and label them as terrorists. As seen in the UK court decisions, they have fettered to a degree any over-enthusiastic application of these offenses by laying conditions down when a person can be convicted for these offenses.

The statutory measures related to membership of proscribed or banned groups are also introduced to assist in preventing acts of terrorism both in the home state and abroad. As seen in the examples given from Canada, UK, and the US states have similar lists regarding groups they have proscribed and they are not fixed lists as states can add or delete groups each year when

---

[*] David Anderson QC, Independent Reviewer of Terrorism Legislation, Press release to The Terrorism Acts in 2013, July 22, 2014, retrieved from https://terrorismlegislationreviewer.independent.gov.uk/ [accessed July 22, 2014].

appropriate to do so. By having offenses related to terrorist groups is it makes it more difficult for them to operate openly and in their ability to raise funds to their cause. Of course, this can bring in those individuals who have sympathy for certain groups. If these individuals take action to support the groups, then they can be arrested, or by having such offenses it has the potential to prevent individuals from taking action beyond simply having sympathy as no criminal offense can be committed by simply having mens rea; actus reus is also required.

Having what is termed as quasi-criminal measures and wide powers granted to officers at a state's port and border controls have also been criticized. In using the example of the UK's TPIM orders, one could argue they are ineffectual in preventing terrorism and are simply a political statement that emphasizes the state is taking measures to ensure the safety of its population. What the examination of TPIMs has shown is how the courts, in balancing the interests of national security with a person's rights and liberty, have come down heavily in favor of individual liberty. This is seen in the cases related to orders controlling the movement of persons who have not been convicted of terrorist offenses. This may be due to the fact that in such cases individuals subject of the orders are simply suspected of being involved in acts related to terrorist activity. As seen, this was not simply a concern for the UK courts, but also within the EU and Australia with Kirby J's judgment in *Thomas v Mowbray*.[*]

As seen in the UK's *Miranda* case related to the application of a stop and search procedure contained in Schedule 7 of the UK's Terrorism Act of 2000 the courts will also decide there are circumstances where the interests of national security can over-ride the interests of an individual's liberty. As discussed, Schedule 7 is a power that appears so draconian that when the legal test of proportionality is applied it would be expected to be found to contravene human rights legislation. Yet, when the UK courts examined Schedule 7 in four cases since August 2013, they held the provisions contained within the Schedule did not violate any of the ECHR articles. Where concerns were made by the courts that Schedule 7 could contravene human rights legislation, the UK government introduced amendments in the Anti-Social Behavior, Crime, and Policing Act 2014 that ensured Schedule 7 powers are more proportionate. *Miranda* involved more than what would be expected in the circumstances surrounding terrorism-related activity a Schedule 7 stop and search entails. Another legal issue examined in *Miranda* was what amounts to journalistic material. As seen with Miranda and all terrorism statutory related offenses and powers the courts will balance the needs of national security with an individual's rights and liberty, where

[*] *Thomas V Mowbray* [2007] HCA 33.

in *Miranda* the Court found the needs of national security, overrode the Miranda's rights. Courts do not make these decisions lightly. The proponents of individual rights should accept the courts' decisions and the fact in the fight against terrorist activity there are occasions when the needs of national security are more important.

Surveillance and International Terrorism Intelligence Exchange

3

Balancing the Interests of National Security and Individual Liberty

Introduction

Former US NSA employee Edward Snowden's passing onto media sources classified documents relating to the practices of the NSA and the UK's GCHQ, in particular the PRISM project, resulted in condemnation of wide surveillance practices carried out by counterterrorism agencies. Underpinning this concern was how respective states' anti-terror legislation widened those agencies' powers to an extent it is effectively suffocating individuals' liberty and widens the scope of criminalization. This chapter examines the legislation governing surveillance related to terrorism in the United States and the United Kingdom along with an analysis of the judicial scrutiny of state agencies' practices in cases related to the legislation both pre and post the Snowden revelations. This leads to an explanation of why agencies like the NSA and GCHQ require wide surveillance powers and the impact the revelation of stolen classified documents such as those passed on by Snowden to UK's *The Guardian* newspaper can have on national security.

In the examination of these issues, this chapter looks at the surveillance powers used in terrorism investigations and how the intelligence obtained is exchanged between the United Kingdom and the United States. The coverage of the intelligence exchange includes an analysis of the role of the EU's policing agency Europol, which facilitates this exchange. This leads to an examination in how the legal principle of proportionality is applied by the respective states' judiciary when balancing the interests of national security and individual rights. This examination includes a study of legal challenges to made against US surveillance laws and clashes in the findings of the UK judiciary and the European Court of Human Rights on matters related to human rights provisions.

The argument presented here is that in balancing the interests of national security and individual liberty the two are inclusive as the state has a responsibility to protect an individual's personal liberty, but equally important the state must also protect its population from terrorist attacks. Therefore such powers are needed to keep people safe from indiscriminate terrorist attacks even if on occasions it infringes slightly on personal liberty.

Surveillance Powers Used in Terrorism Investigations

In gathering intelligence on terrorist-related activity, statutory powers allowing covert surveillance is a vital investigatory tool. In doing so it is important state agencies work within the rule of law. It not only ensures their practices are legally proportionate, but by working within the rule of law it allows for transparency of those agencies' operations revealing operational methods along with a transparency of accountability regarding decision making on granting authorities and misuse of powers by state officials (International Commission of Jurists 2009, p. 68).

US Powers

There are two significant statutes authorizing electronic surveillance in the United States. Section 2516(1) Title 18 United States Code allows for covert surveillance to obtain intelligence on terrorist related activity when the Attorney General authorizes a Federal judge to grant a Federal agency an order to intercept wire or oral or electronic communications. The second statute granting authority for electronic surveillance is the Foreign Intelligence Surveillance Act 1978 (FISA) where with Attorney General approval a Federal agency applies to a Foreign Intelligence Surveillance Court[*] for an authority to conduct electronic surveillance on "agents of foreign powers" including persons suspected to be engaged in international terrorism.[†]

The 2008 Foreign Intelligence Surveillance Amendment Act (FISAA) introduced important changes on the NSA's electronic surveillance powers including that the focus of the order is purely on the communications endpoint with no requirement of targets being specified. If the covert surveillance involves the likes of hidden microphones then there is a reasonable expectation of privacy by a citizen and the warrant must specify the target (Liu 2013, p. 7). One impact of the FISAA amendments is by authorizing surveillance on non-US citizens outside US territory, those citizens' personal data now comes under the range of US jurisdiction (Bigo et al. 2013, p. 3). While surveillance orders on US citizens located in the US has to have cognizance of the rights to privacy under the fourth amendment, no such right is applicable to foreign citizens.

---

[*] 50 USC section 1804.
[†] 50 USC section 1807(b)(1)(C).

UK Powers

Section 28(3) Regulation of Investigatory Powers Act 2000 (RIPA) allows a court to grant when necessary in the interests of national security, or in preventing or detecting crime or disorder, an authorization to specified agencies including the police[*] and UK intelligence services[†] to conduct covert surveillance. Although RIPA provides an extensive range of circumstances how the surveillance can be conducted, the surveillance is limited to the United Kingdom. A RIPA authorization must be compatible with the provisions of the European Convention on Human Rights (ECHR).

Intelligence Exchange between the United States and the United Kingdom: The Role of Europol

Since 9/11 the international sharing of intelligence between counterterrorism policing and national security agencies has increased. Between the United States and the United Kingdom this has invariably been carried out through the European Union's (EU) policing agency, Europol. With a mandate to collect, store, process, analyze and exchange intelligence (Berenskoetter 2012, p. 41) the 2009 Treaty of Lisbon (ToL) states Europol's mission:

> … is to support and strengthen action by member states police authorities and other law enforcement agencies through mutual co-operation in preventing serious crime affecting two or more member states, terrorism and forms of crime which affect interest by EU Policy.[‡]

Following 9/11 the EU prioritized the fight against terrorism and within ten days of the attack the EU's Justice and Home Affairs Commission (JHA) adopted an action plan in the fight against terrorism resulting in acceleration in the development and implementation of measures to counter the threat international terrorism posed (Joffe 2008, p. 158; Kaunert 2010, p. 653). Having the authority to sign international agreements, the agreement between Europol and the United States signed in 2001 is the most advanced. Intelligence is shared between the EU's member states' policing agencies and specified US agencies (Kaunert 2010, p. 664) that includes the FBI, US Secret Service, the Drug Enforcement Administration and the US postal Inspection (Den Boer et al. 2008, p. 10).

---

[*] RIPA Schedule 1(1).
[†] RIPA Schedule 1(5).
[‡] Article 88 ToL.

The Impact of the European Union's
Treaty of Lisbon on Cooperation

The EU tightened up its member states' cooperation with Europol through articles 84–88 of the ToL. As all EU Treaties are primary sources of EU law, the legal principle of supremacy of EU law over member states' national law* applies. The impact of this legal principle is that EU member states are legally obligated to the ToL's articles. Article 84 ToL allows for the more potent EU legal instrument of directives being issued requiring member states to cooperate with Europol.[†] As EU directives come under the jurisdiction of the EU's court, the European Court of Justice (ECJ), under the principle of the supremacy of EU law it allows the ECJ to ensure compliance among the member states.[‡] This is supported by article 87 of the ToL that states member states will adhere to police cooperation and this cooperation will include *all* national agencies involved in counterterrorism and investigating organized crime with the agencies including customs agencies and other "specialized law enforcement agencies." Perhaps the most significant development is article 88 that changed Europol's role from simply supporting, facilitating and requesting action by national police agencies to now being in a clear and implicit partnership with the member states' agencies. To ensure genuine partnership exists between the member states and the EU, article 88 ToL states another EU legal instrument, regulations, will be introduced to ensure compliance among the member states.[§]

These changes bolstering Europol's role are important for two reasons that center on accountability. Firstly, through the hierarchy of agencies associated with the JHA, Europol has a vertical legal legitimacy that is identifiable when compared the horizontal role of agencies made under the multi-lateral agreements (Den Boer et al. 2008, p. 106). This is important regarding the second reason concerning accountability as by bringing Europol under the jurisdiction and scrutiny of the ECJ and the EU Parliament, under the ToL provisions, Europol's actions come under the of rule of law where

> The constitutive role of the rule of law relates to the means by which the community is governed: through law. The law regulates social relationships and therefore effective enforcement of the law is constitutive for the rule of law (Murphy 2012, p. 35).

In its desire to ensure it can be an effective international actor, the EU's counterterrorism measures have led to an increased divergence of member

---

* Case 26/62 *Van Gend en Loos* [1963] ECR 1.
† Once passed through the EU Parliament, directives must be implemented and brought into national law by member states within the period specified in the directive.
‡ Article 87 ToL.
§ Once passed through the EU Parliament, EU Regulations will be implemented and brought into national law by member states straight away.

states' law that can be achieved by replacing the framework decisions with the more effective regulations and directives (Murphy 2012, p. 225). As well as enhancing the reputation and reliability of Europol's role as an international actor with member states and third countries, the rationale behind the ToL changes is because the volume of EU criminal law and counterterrorism measures are set to increase in the coming years (Murphy 2012, p. 241) requiring a stricter adherence to mutual cooperation between the Members States and Europol. In turn this will impact on the UK's legal position in exchanging intelligence with third countries, including the United States. An issue that may act as a brake to this improvement is what Argomaniz terms as the "Brusselsization" of terrorism that has produced a plethora of committees, expert groups agencies and bodies. He sees this as having led to inefficiencies in EU counterterrorism measures because of overlapping between structures within and outside the EU Framework (Argomaniz 2012, p. 69), which has resulted in a degree of inter-institutional friction (Argomaniz 2012, p. 70). That said, the ToL is the best opportunity the EU currently has to address these problems and weaknesses (Argomaniz 2012, p. 76).

The Snowden Affair, National Security Interests, and Protecting Individual Rights

In June 2013 the UK newspaper *The Guardian* and the US newspaper *The Washington Post* broke with the news story regarding the NSA and the PRISM program that gave US federal agencies direct access to servers in the biggest web firms including Google, Microsoft, Facebook, Yahoo, Skype, and Apple.* Snowdon released top secret documents to a *Guardian* journalist, Glenn Greenwald, who, in the first of a number of reports, revealed the NSA was collecting telephone records of millions of US customers under a top secret order issued in April 2013 adding that "... the communication records of millions of US citizens are being collected indiscriminately and in bulk regardless of whether they are suspected of any wrongdoing" (Greenwald 2013). Adding the NSA's mission had transformed from being exclusively devoted to foreign intelligence gathering Greenwald said it now focused on domestic communications.

As the revelations from the documents Snowdon passed on regarding the NSA's activities increased, *The Guardian* reported that GCHQ also gained access to the network of cables carrying the world's phone calls and Internet traffic and processed vast streams of sensitive personal information, sharing this with the NSA (MacAskell et al. 2013). This followed on

---

* BBC News June 7, 2013 "Web Privacy—outsourced to the US and China?" retrieved from http://www.bbc.co.uk/news/technology-22811002 [accessed September 1, 2013].

from earlier reports that GCHQ accessed the NSA's PRISM program to secretly gather intelligence, where between May 2012 and April 2013, 197 PRISM intelligence reports were passed onto the UK's security agencies, MI5, MI6 and Special Branch's Counterterrorism Unit (Hopkins 2013). GCHQ's actions led to the German Justice Minister writing to British ministers regarding an allegation of mass surveillance by British intelligence asking for reassurance the actions were legal and if they were targeting German citizens.[*] With reports from *The Guardian* that NSA actions were posing a threat to the privacy of EU citizens, this was a cause of concern for the EU's Justice and Home Affairs (JHA) resulting in EU's Justice Commissioner Viviane Reding stating:

> The European Commission is concerned about the possible consequences on EU citizens' privacy. The Commission has raised this systematically in its dialogue with the US authorities, especially in the context of the negotiations of the EU-US data protection agreement in the field of police and judicial co-operation ... (Watt 2013).

During this dialogue the difference in legal culture between the EU and the United States raised its head regarding individual's rights in the respective jurisdictions with the EU's focus being the dignity of citizens. In protecting fundamental human rights under the aegis of the rule of law the EU requires a system of protection of an individual citizen's data privacy (Murphy 2012, p. 149). There is no such explicit protection to a general right to privacy under the US Bill of Rights rather it is inferred in the First, Fourth, Fifth, and Ninth Amendments (Whitman 2004, p. 1155). This is important as Snowdon's revelations had the potential to damage not only diplomatic relations between the US and EU member states, but also affect the terrorism intelligence sharing between European counterterrorism agencies via Europol and US federal agencies. To prevent US/UK diplomatic relations with the rest of the EU member states deteriorating further, senior US and UK politicians were forced to speak openly and defend the actions of the NSA and GCHQ. The UK's Foreign minister, William Hague, said that both nations "... operated under the rule of law," with GCHQ being "... scrupulous in complying with the law" and used the intelligence to protect citizens' freedoms.[†]

As a result of handing the secret documents to journalists the US Justice Department filing criminal charges against Snowden for espionage and theft of government documents and a provisional arrest warrant was issued by

---

[*] BBC News June 25, 2013 "Germany seeks UK surveillance assurance" retrieved from http://www.bbc.co.uk/news/uk-23048259 [accessed September 1, 2013].
[†] BBC News June 26 "US-UK intelligence-sharing indispensable says Hague" retrieved form http://www.bbc.co.uk/news/uk-politics-23053691 [accessed September 2, 2013].

a federal court in the Eastern District of Virginia.[*] To evade prosecution Snowden left the United States where he was granted temporary asylum by the Russian Government, causing further friction in the political relations between the United States and Russia.[†] Referring to "top secret" documents Snowden passed on to them, *The Guardian* reported that from 2010 to 2013 the US government paid GCHQ£100 million to secure access and influence over the UK's intelligence gathering programs (Hopkins and Borger 2013). As these revelations were claiming to come from the secret documents Snowden passed on to Greenwald, it triggered the security services to act to retrieve the documentation at the earliest opportunity.

The Importance of the Snowden Documents to UK Authorities

Hopkins and Ackermann reported the United Kingdom was useful to the United States regarding gathering and storing intelligence as the legal framework in the United Kingdom is more flexible than the legal framework the NSA works under (Hopkins and Ackermenn 2013). To understand Hopkins and Ackerman's point the two main pieces of UK legislation governing GCHQ surveillance are the Intelligence Services Act of 1994 (ISA) and RIPA. The function of the secret intelligence service (commonly referred to as MI6)[‡] is to obtain and provide information relating to the actions or intentions of persons outside the British islands and to perform tasks relating to the actions or intentions of such persons[§] adding this function is only exercisable when

1. It is in the interests of national security, in particular regarding the defence and UK foreign policy.
2. It is in the interests of the economic well-being of the UK.
3. It is in support of the prevention or detection of serious crime.[¶]

We can see the influence of the article 8 (right to privacy and family life) ECHR qualifications in the wording of section 1 ISA as these qualifications to allow interference with citizens' rights are virtually verbatim. In the UK

[*] BBC News June 22, 2013 "NSA leaks: US charges Edward Snowden with spying" retrieved from http://www.bbc.co.uk/news/world-us-canada-23012317 [accessed September 1, 2013].
[†] BBC News August 1, 2013 "NSA spy leaks: Snowden thanks Russia for asylum" retrieved from http://www.bbc.co.uk/news/world-europe-23541425 [accessed September 2, 2013].
[‡] MI6 are concerned with external threats to the UK whereas the national security service, MI5, is concerned with internal threats to the UK's security.
[§] Section 1(1) ISA.
[¶] Section 1(2) ISA.

section 1(2) of the Security Services Act 1989 provides a legal definition of what amounts to national security, which is

> The function of the [security service] shall be the protection of national security and, in particular, its protection against threats from espionage, terrorism and sabotage, from the activities of agents of foreign powers and from actions intended to overthrow or undermine parliamentary democracy by political, industrial or violent means.

It is the latter part of the definition that includes action not conforming to submissive behavior that is sufficiently wide for the state to monitor UK citizens as well as foreign nationals, thereby allowing security agencies a wide leverage to interfere with citizens' liberties.

When in the interests of national security or the economic well-being of the UK or to support the prevention of crime or disorder, GCHQ's function is to monitor or interfere with electronic or acoustic communications and provide assistance to UK government agencies and its armed forces.[*] To carry out these functions GCHQ require a warrant issued by the Home Secretary.[†] GCHQ also can utilize the powers of communication interception under RIPA.[‡] Only when GCHQ can show the interception is proportionate to what is sought to be achieved will a RIPA surveillance warrant to intercept is issued under the provisions of international mutual assistance agreements.[§] This would apply to agreements between the NSA and GCHQ. From this agreement *The Guardian* reported that 36% of all the raw information GCHQ obtained was passed onto the NSA giving the NSA access to *all* the sifted and refined intelligence GCHQ obtained (Hopkins et al. 2013). When breaking down these sections of the relevant UK statutes, one can see why the media came to the conclusion that by having wide and flexible powers the UK has a place at the top table of intelligence agencies (Hopkins and Ackermenn 2013).

With Hopkins and Ackerman revealing they saw documentation on how and why GCHQ searched for material, including intelligence on the political intentions of foreign governments, political postures of foreign governments, terrorism, international trafficking, and fraud, it caused a high degree of disquiet among UK government officials, the UK national security agencies (in particular GCHQ) and the UK's Special Branch Counterterrorism Units. One of the main concerns for the security agencies appeared to be what the documents Snowden passed on revealed regarding the methods of surveillance, technical capability the agencies' surveillance equipment and, the identity of Her Majesty's Government personnel working in the area of

---

[*] Section 3 ISA.
[†] Section 5 ISA.
[‡] Section 4 RIPA.
[§] Section 5(3) RIPA.

national security. The main concern of the agencies was if the documentation fell into the hands of those preparing or in the commission of acts of terrorism, the intelligence contained within the documentation would be useful to them (Sparrow et al. 2013 citing Lowe from BBC News 24). It is estimated that at least 58,000 UK documents classified as top secret and secret information were stolen by Snowden from GCHQ* that contained information on personnel and details of surveillance methods that could put the general public's lives at risk.[†]

Balancing the Interests of National Security with Individual Rights: Democracies, Neo-Democracies, and the Legal Principle of Proportionality

Since 9/11 a significant amount, if not the majority of, criminological and legal writing on the impact terrorism has had on democratic states and individual rights has focused on how recent terrorist acts have legitimized states' illiberal legislative and policy responses to the terrorist threat they face resulting in a rights-based democracy being replaced by a "siege mode of democracy" (Palmer 2012, pp. 521–522). Referring to this transformation as "dressing the window" Gearty's concern is that the fear of terrorism is a facilitator to neo-democracies (including the United Kingdom and the United States) where on its surface liberty, security, and fundamental freedoms present themselves but in reality are only available to the few (Gearty 2012, pp. 55–56). If left uncontrolled, Gearty argues that by using the remit of terrorism, states can extend the core element of terrorism from being an indiscriminate assault on civilians to cover all sorts of conduct that when looked at closely is removed from what most people's perception of terrorism is (Gearty 2012, p. 33). This can result in the introduction of what he labels quasi-criminal law provisions that may have the appearance of freedom but in reality has no substance (Gearty 2012, p. 46). Fenwick's examination of post 9/11 UK anti-terror legislation found a significant rise in the adoption of authoritarian powers to policing agencies to curtail the liberty of persons who may be a terrorist threat in order to prevent terrorist activity before it occurs that places a strain on individuals' rights (Fenwick 2008, pp. 259–260). In the post 9/11 era these powers include widening electronic surveillance on targets that includes subgroups as well as individuals, even communities who are perceived to be a threat and consequently the "enemy within" (Palmer 2012, p. 522).

---

* From Laws LJ's judgment in *Miranda v The Secretary of State for the Home Department and the Commissioner of the Police and Metropolis* [2014] EWHC 255, paragraph 64.
† From Laws LJ's judgment in *Miranda v The Secretary of State for the Home Department and the Commissioner of the Police and Metropolis* [2014] EWHC 255, paragraph 53.

This is not a new response by states to threats to their national security. Bunyan chronicles how since its inception in 1880s the UK's Special Branch has conducted surveillance on individuals and communities ranging from a variety of political activists who have been seen as a threat that included telephone tapping and mail interception (Bunyan 1976, pp. 131–150). Gill provides a similar chronology of state agencies conducting surveillance from the early 20th century in the United Kingdom and the United States (Gill 1994, pp. 151–170). Donohue's work shows how not only in the United Kingdom where prior to 1985 both the national security services and the police conducted widespread surveillance using telephone taps and mail interception (Donohue 2008, pp. 188–190) but also how the United States has been imbued with a surveillance culture, especially since the 1920s during the Hoover/FBI period (Donohue 2008, pp. 218–229). What today is termed electronic surveillance carried out by state agencies on individuals and groups considered as subversive or a threat to security through program like PRISM should not come as a surprise as in democratic states this activity has taken place for many years. The issue to be concerned with is in relation to ownership of the electronic data, the authority the surveillance is conducted under and the legal provisions to protect citizens' privacy (Bigo et al. 2013, p. 5).

Legal Challenges to US Surveillance Laws

Court Decisions Pre-Snowden

Balancing the provisions of state surveillance and individuals' liberty under the Fourth Amendment was established by the US Supreme Court in *Katz v United States** who held the test for privacy is only dependent where one would have a reasonable expectation of privacy. Justice Harlan stated that society is prepared to expect an intrusion into their privacy by state agencies only when it is reasonable for those agencies to do so. Justice Harlan did emphasize the point that the situation changes when a citizen exposes their activities with others then privacy is not protected by the Fourth Amendment.[†] In *Katz* the Court emphasized the Fourth Amendment was introduced to protect people not places (Donohue 2008, p. 221).

In balancing the rights of citizens to protecting national security Pious comments there should be the best combination of guarantees within the due process of law that protects citizens' privacy that can run alongside:

> … strong government action that protects national security and our personal security as we travel on buses, trains, and airplanes (Pious 2006, p. 13).

---

* 389 US 347 (1967).
† 389 US 347 (1967), paragraph 361.

The rationale for adhering to due process of law is that it not only protects the accused, but it also helps guard against the prosecutorial zeal that sends false signals about who is a terrorist and what terrorists might be doing (Pious 2006, p. 16). An example of the United States protecting individuals' safety by focusing on liberty rather than the dignity of the individual is seen in the surveillance powers granted to US federal agencies where the Patriot Act 2001 amended the FISA provisions by changing the wording regarding the aim of intelligence gathering under the original FISA from a "primary" purpose to a "significant" purpose (Pious 2006, p. 34). This allowed intelligence to be obtained from a wider range of potential sources (Gearty 2012, p. 78), as these amendments bypass the US Constitution's Fourth Amendment regarding citizens' right to be secure in their persons, houses, paper and effects against unreasonable actions by government and police actions.

The United States Foreign Intelligence Surveillance Court of Review considered the implications of this subtle change *In Re Sealed Case* N.02-0001.* The Court held the shift from "primary" to "significant" purpose is a relaxation of the requirement of government to show its primary purpose was other than criminal prosecution saying:

> … In many cases, surveillance will have two key goals—the gathering of foreign intelligence, and the gathering of evidence for a criminal prosecution. Determining which purpose is the "primary" purpose of the investigation can be difficult, and will only become more so as we coordinate our intelligence and law enforcement efforts in the war against terror. Rather than forcing law enforcement to decide which purpose is primary—law enforcement or foreign intelligence gathering, this bill strikes a new balance. It will now require that a "significant" purpose of the investigation must be foreign intelligence gathering to proceed with surveillance under FISA. The effect of this provision will be to make it easier for law enforcement to obtain FISA search or surveillance warrant for these cases where the subject of the surveillance is both a potential source of valuable intelligence and the potential target of a criminal prosecution.†

As a result of the Court's decision, the FBI can now help local law enforcement agencies bypass the Fourth Amendment requirements in gathering evidence in matters related to foreign intelligence even where it might not be for wholly related ordinary crimes (Pious 2006, p. 48; Donohue 2008, p. 234; Gearty 2012, p. 78).

Another example of how national security can override individual's liberty provisions in US anti-terrorism law is seen in *Clapper (Director of*

---

* 310 F.3d 717 (2002).
† 310 F.3d 717 (2002) at 723.

Notional Intelligence et al.) v Amnesty International.[*] The US Supreme Court was asked to examine the FISAA amendments to section 702 FISA and the warrantless wire-tapping power. The respondents (who were lawyers, and, human rights and media organizations) claimed that in by-passing their Fourth Amendment rights, the surveillance powers contained in the amendment was unconstitutional. The foundation of their claim was they were regularly engaging in sensitive international communications with individuals likely to be targets of surveillance and being US citizens they stated their Fourth Amendment rights were breached by the surveillance orders. By a 5-4 majority, the US Supreme Court dismissed the respondents' claim as purely speculative. In delivering the judgment, Justice Alito said:

> … respondents have no actual knowledge of the Government's targeting practices. Instead, respondent's *merely speculate and make assumptions* about whether their communications with their foreign contacts will be acquired under s.702[†] [my emphasis].

This decision was subject to much criticism from US human rights and lawyer groups. The American Bar Association argued that the US President does have a constitutional obligation to authorize all surveillance (International Commission of Jurists 2009, p. 70). Opinions are summed up by legal advocates claiming the *Clapper* decision handed the US government a "get out of jail free" card for national security statutes (Sledge 2013). With no judicial supervision on the wire-tapping powers and, even if it was a speculative assumption, the fact there was the opportunity for the state to interfere. If this had gone before a European Court there is the likelihood that Court would have found for the respondents. This is supported by the four dissenting judges where Justice Breyer said the US Constitution does not require concrete proof only something where there is a "reasonable probability" or a "high probability."[‡]

Court Decisions Post-Snowden

In December 2013 two significant cases were heard where following the Snowden revelations the applicants claimed their Fourth Amendment rights had been violated by the NSA and the Federal Government. In *Klayman et al. v Obama et al.*[§] the US District Court for the District of Columbia heard a judicial review challenging the authorization of intelligence gathering

---

[*] (2013) 568 US No. 11-1025.
[†] (2013) 568 US No. 11-1025, paragraph IIIA.
[‡] (2013) 568 US No. 11-1025 at 20, paragraph 4.
[§] (2013) Civil Action Number 13-0881 (RJL).

relating to the wholesale collection of phone record metadata of all US citizens. An authority was granted by the Foreign Intelligence Surveillance Court in April 2013 concerning the applicants where in his judgment Justice Leon held the applicants have sufficient legal standing to challenge the constitutionality of the Federal Government's bulk collection of phone record metadata under their Fourth Amendment claim. In his deliberations Justice Leon said that while Congress has great latitude to create statutory schemes like FISA, "… it may not hang a cloak of secrecy over the [US] Constitution."[*] Distinguishing the applicants' claim in *Klayman* from the US Supreme Court's finding in *Clapper* Justice Leon said in *Clapper* the applicants could only speculate as to whether they were "surveilled" whereas in *Klayman* there was strong evidence their telephony metadata had been collected.[†] Underlying Justice Leon's judgment was his scepticism relating to the impact such wide surveillance practices has on identifying terrorists and thereby preventing terrorist attacks. He said:

> I am not convinced at this point in the litigation that the NSA's database has ever truly served the purpose of rapidly identifying terrorists in time-sensitive investigations, and so I am *certainly* not convinced that the removal of two individuals from the database will "degrade" the program in any meaningful sense[‡] [original emphasis].

Again concerning the NSA's collection of phone record metadata, eleven days after the *Klayman* decision Justice Pauley III from the US District Court of Southern District of New York took an opposite view in his judgment in *American Civil Liberties Union et al. v James R. Clapper et al.*[§] After commencing his judgment with pre-9/11 example of the hijacker Khalid al-Mihdhar who had seven telephone calls intercepted by the NSA but who could not capture the telephone number identifier and if they could they would have been able to pass onto the FBI that he was calling a Yemeni safe house from inside the United States,[¶] Justice Pauley III cites a number of NSA investigations where he justifies the effectiveness of NSA's surveillance through bulk telephony metadata.[**] Acknowledging that if left unchecked this investigative tool can imperil citizens' liberty along with the fact that Snowden's "unauthorized disclosure" of Foreign Intelligence Surveillance Court orders has provoked a public debate, he held these orders were lawful.[††] In his summation Justice Pauley III found there to be no evidence that the US government

---

[*] (2013) Civil Action Number 13-0881 (RJL) at 34.
[†] (2013) Civil Action Number 13-0881 (RJL) at 36.
[‡] (2013) Civil Action Number 13-0881 (RJL) at 66.
[§] (2013) 13 Civ 3994 (WHP).
[¶] (2013) 13 Civ 3994 (WHP) at 1-2.
[**] (2013) 13 Civ 3994 (WHP) at 48-49.
[††] (2013) 13 Civ 3994 (WHP) at 2.

had used any of the bulk telephony data for any other purpose than investigating and "disrupting" terrorist attacks* saying:

> The choice between liberty and security is a false one, as nothing is more apt to imperil civil liberties than the success of a terrorist attack ...[†]

This is important as the interests of national security and protecting individual liberties are not exclusive, they are inclusive. This is where the legal principle of proportionality plays an important part in judicial decision making. Utilitarian in nature, proportionality balances the interests of wider society with the interests of the individual.

UK Courts and the ECHR

UK Judiciary's Clashes with the European Court of Human Rights

Regarding the minimum rights citizens are entitled to expect, the UK has to take cognizance of the provisions contained in the ECHR. ECHR rights are broken in to three main categories, absolute rights which the state cannot interfere with, limited rights where the state has limited power to interfere and qualified rights. Regarding qualified rights the state can interfere with them provided certain provisions contained in the qualified rights are met and the interference is necessary in a democratic society. The ECHR article appertaining to surveillance and intelligence sharing is the qualified article 8 (right to privacy and family life). In *Klass v Germany* the European Court of Human Rights (ECtHR) examined article 8 and while acknowledging that surveillance is a necessary evil in a democracy, held that when the state carries out covert surveillance its actions must be proportionate.[‡]

One potential problem with intelligence sharing between the EU member states and the United States is the different focus on human rights legal culture. While the US focuses on liberty, the EU's focus is on the dignity of the citizen (Donohue 2008, p. 208; Murphy 2012, p. 149). Regarding cases brought to court related to terrorism statutory provisions and statutory provisions relating to evidence useful in counterterrorism investigations the UK's judicial decisions have been at odds to those made in the ECtHR. An example of this was in relation to the retention of DNA and fingerprint samples retained on a national database in England and Wales that went to

---

* (2013) 13 Civ 3994 (WHP) at 52.
† (2013) 13 Civ 3994 (WHP) at 52.
‡ (1978) (Application number 5029/71), paragraph 68.

the ECtHR in *S and Marper v UK.*[*] S and Marper provided samples during a police investigation and even though they were not convicted of a criminal offense, the samples were retained on national database. As result they both claimed their article 8 ECHR right to privacy had been violated. Both the High Court[†] and the House of Lords[‡] appellate courts held that there was no such violation. In dismissing S and Marper's appeal Lord Steyn stated that while accepting the Court must interpret the ECHR in a way that is in line with the ECtHR's jurisprudence he held that

> The whole community, as well as the individuals whose sample was collected, benefits from there being as large a database as it is possible ... The benefit to the aims of accurate and efficient law enforcement is thereby enhanced.[§]

While Lord Steyn was adopting the approach that interests of the wider community overrides the interests of the individual, when the case went before the ECtHR they saw the dignity of the individual as overriding the interests of the wider community saying:

> ... have due regard to the specific context in which information at issue is recorded and retained, the nature of the records, the way in which these records are used and processed and the results that may be obtained.[¶]

In this judgment the ECtHR emphasized that for powers to be compatible with the rule of law there must be adequate legal protection against arbitrariness and accordingly indicate with sufficient clarity the scope of discretion on the competent authorities and the manner of its exercise.[**] This decision was instrumental in forcing the UK government to introduce legislation that took account the ECtHR's decision that where a person is not convicted of a criminal offense their DNA and fingerprint samples are destroyed.[††]

Another example where the UK appellate court decision making was in conflict with the ECtHR is seen in *Gillan and Quinton v UK*[‡‡] that resulted in

---

[*] (2008) (Application numbers 30562/04 and 30566/04).
[†] *R(S) v Chief Constable of South Yorkshire Police and the Secretary of State for the Home Department* and *R(MARPER) v Chief Constable of South Yorkshire Police and the Secretary of State for the Home Department* [2002] 1 WLR 3223.
[‡] *R(S) v Chief Constable of South Yorkshire Police and the Secretary of State for the Home Department* and *R(MARPER) v Chief Constable of South Yorkshire Police and the Secretary of State for the Home Department* [2004] UKHL 39.
[§] *R(S) v Chief Constable of South Yorkshire Police and the Secretary of State for the Home Department* and *R(MARPER) v Chief Constable of South Yorkshire Police and the Secretary of State for the Home Department* [2004] UKHL 39, paragraph 78.
[¶] (2008) (Application numbers 30562/04 and 30566/04), paragraph 67.
[**] (2008) (Application numbers 30562/04 and 30566/04), paragraph 95.
[††] Section 1 Protection of Freedoms Act 2012.
[‡‡] (2010) (Application no. 4158/05).

section 44 of the UK's Terrorism Act 2000 being repealed. A stop and search power, section 44 allowed police officers to stop and search persons and vehicles* for articles that could be used in connection with terrorism.[†] Authorized by a senior police officer of at least assistant chief constable rank,[‡] when carrying out this search, a police officer did not require any grounds for suspecting the presence of articles that could be used in terrorism.[§] Especially following the London bombing in 2005, an unpopular side-effect in the use of this power was the majority of citizens stopped by the police were disproportionately of Black or Asian ethnicity (Parmar 2011, p. 370). The ECtHR held that section 44 violated article 5 (right to liberty) ECHR as account must be taken of a whole range of criteria such as type of search, duration, effects on the person and the implementation of the measure[¶] and article 8 ECHR where the ECtHR held:

> ... the public nature of the search may, in certain cases, compound the seriousness of the interference because of an element of humiliation and embarrassment. Items such as bags, wallets, notebooks and diaries may, moreover, contain personal information which the owner may feel uncomfortable about having exposed to the view of his companions or the wider public.[**]

Applying the legal principle of proportionality we see the ECtHR seeing the dignity of the individual prevailing over the interests of the wider community that is related to the needs of national security.

UK Appellate Courts Decisions That Changed Anti-Terror Laws

It is not just individual sections of UK anti-terror laws that have been required to change following human rights case decisions. Large parts of statutes, even whole statutes themselves have been repealed because the protection of individual liberties took precedence over national security. These changes were brought about as result of decisions made by UK appellate courts where they took cognizance of the ECHR. An example of this is the UK's Terrorism Prevention and Investigation Act 2011 (TPIMs). The evolution of the act can be traced back the decision in *A and others v Secretary of State for the Home Department*[††] where in 2001 the House of Lords' decision resulted in Part IV of the Anti-Terrorism, Crime and Security Act 2001 (ATCSA) being repealed. Under Part IV the Home Secretary could authorize the imprisonment of

---

* Section 44 (1) Terrorism Act 2000.
† Section 45(1)(a) Terrorism Act 2000.
‡ Section 44(4) Terrorism Act.
§ Section 45(1)(b) Terrorism Act 2000.
¶ *Gillan and Quinton v UK* (2010) (Application no. 4158/05), paragraph 56.
** *Gillan and Quinton v UK* (2010) (Application no. 4158/05), paragraph 63.
†† [2004] UKHL 56.

foreign nationals who were suspected terrorists without any judicial process. The House's concern was the lack of judicial supervision in imprisoning individuals and consequently found that Part IV of the act violated articles 5 and article 6 (right to fair trial) ECHR (Gearty 2012, p. 90). Introducing control orders for *both* foreign and national citizens who had to wear an electronic tagging device and abide by very strict bail conditions that severely impinged on the movement of those subject to an order, the Prevention of Terrorism Act 2005 replaced the repealed Part IV. Control orders were also challenged in *Secretary of State for the Home Department v AP.*￼ In the UK Supreme Court's decision in *AP* the dignity of the person was evident as the interests of individual liberty prevailed over national security as the Court held the 2005 Act violated articles 5 and 8 ECHR because the control order forced AP to live in a town 150 miles away from his family. A relevant point Gearty makes regarding the harshness in the conditions imposed on persons subject to control orders is that none of those persons have been charged with criminal offenses, adding that as a result control orders "… stood outside the normal law" (Gearty 2012, p. 92). As a result the Prevention of Terrorism Act 2005 was repealed and replaced with TPIMs that introduced surveillance orders issued on specific persons with less stringent controls on their personal life.

Issues Surrounding Control Orders and Blacklists

In their various conditions these UK counterterrorist orders have been subject to much controversy as they restrict the liberty of individuals suspected to be involved in terrorist activity where there is insufficient evidence to charge and convict them of terrorist offenses. Fenwick sees such orders as counterproductive as they were targeted mainly against members of the UK's Muslim community therefore making that community a "suspect community" resulting in making it more likely that some Muslims may be drawn into terrorist activity (Fenwick 2008, p. 268). In relation to the *A and others* decision Gearty is critical of the House of Lords decision to only declare Part IV of the 2001 Act as incompatible with the ECHR and not let the applicants "go free" (Gearty 2013, p. 90). Gearty fails to mention that UK courts cannot do this in relation to statutory provisions as unlike many other states' constitutions under the principle of parliamentary supremacy the UK judiciary do not have the power to declare a statute as unconstitutional as constitutionally the UK judiciary are subordinate to Parliament. In relation to statues, the judiciary's role is to interpret statutes giving effect to the will of Parliament

˙ [2010] UKSC 24.

(Barnett 2013, p. 78). Allowing UK appellate courts under section 3 of the Human Rights Act 1998 to declare statutory provisions as incompatible with the ECHR has been a significant move towards the judiciary in overturning Parliamentary statues. The UK courts have utilized this measure that has to some extent kept the UK's executive in check regarding anti-terrorist related statutory measures that are disproportionate, none more so than control orders. For example UK courts have held that 18-hour curfews in control orders were seen as excessive and disproportionate therefore violating article 5 (right to the liberty of the person) ECHR[*] and where following a review of evidence there was no possibility of a criminal prosecution in relation to terrorist offenses a control order was flawed.[†] As a result of these and other cases such as *AP* the UK courts did in effect force the UK Parliament to change the law.

Focusing on terrorist-related "blacklists," Gearty cites the examples of Nada (2013, pp. 38–41) and Kadi (2013, pp. 41–44) whose respective liberty and freedom of movement was at risk. This led him to say that "our security" must trump their freedom as blacklists (and one could add control orders) only apply to people like them (where one presumes Gearty is referring to Muslims) and therefore it does not affect "one jot" how we experience freedom (2013, p. 40) is disparaging. Two issues should be considered here. First, evidence of a true separation of powers is seen in the courts' decisions where the judiciary have demonstrated their independence from their respective states' executives. As discussed above both the UK and the US jurisdictions have in effect put the brakes on excesses into an individual's liberty incurred through terrorism related legislation. A further example of this was seen in the New York State Court of Appeal's judgment in *The People v Edgar Morales*[‡] where the Court held:

> The concept of terrorism has a unique meaning and its implications risk being trivialized if the terminology is applied loosely in situations that do not match our collective understanding of what constitutes a terrorist act.[§]

Secondly, for every Nada there is a Lee Rigby who dies at the hands of terrorists[¶] and for every Kadi there is an Erika Brannock who is permanently disabled after losing a limb in an indiscriminate terrorist attack.[**] Detention

[*] *Secretary of State for the Home department v JJ and others* [2006] EWHC 1623 (admin).
[†] *Secretary of State for the Home Department v E and another* [2007] UKHL 47.
[‡] (2012) No 186 NYLJ 1202581035138.
[§] (2012) No 186 NYLJ 1202581035138, paragraph 10.
[¶] BBC News (2013) Woolwich attack: Drummer Lee Rigby named as victim retrieved from http://www.bbc.co.uk/news/uk-22635206 [accessed March 1, 2014].
[**] The Baltimore Sun (2013) Seven months after Boston Marathon bombing, local victim walking retrieved from http://www.baltimoresun.com/news/maryland/bal-bs-md-erika-brannock-profile-20131110,0,5575246.htmlstory [accessed March 1, 2014].

can be temporary but death or disability is permanent. Naming individuals to personalize victims of excessive state terror provisions can also be applied to victims of terrorist attacks as this shows how imperative it is to ensure proportionality is applied by the courts in balancing the interests of wider society in the name of national security with the interests of the individual and their liberty. It is the court's duty to protect both.

Conclusion: The Balance between the Interests of National Security and Individuals' Liberty

The rationale behind preemptive counterterrorism powers is they are exercised on identifying individuals who might commit crimes related to terrorism with the aim of the investigators to remove the individual's ability to carry out terrorist-related activity (Murphy 2012, p. 234). Preemptive legislation invariably widens the powers of counterterrorism agency officers to intrude deeper into the everyday lives of citizens. As a result it gives those officers greater ability to bring an ever widening group of citizens into their gaze and consequently into their intelligence systems. As this discussion has emphasized, the interests of national security and individual liberty are not exclusive, they are inclusive. They are not opposing poles but a seamless web of protection incumbent upon the state (ICJ 2009, p. 21). While individual liberty is precious and must be protected from unnecessary state incursion by the judiciary, keeping citizens safe from terrorist attacks is equally important. As Yoo's study found this is what the majority of citizens want even if it is bordering on infringing individual liberty (Yoo 2010, pp. 347–350). In a poll held following revelations of NSA practices, in June 2013 nearly half of US citizens polled approved of everyone's emails being monitored if in doing so it might avert a terrorist attack.*

The former MI5 Director revealed in the UK between 2001 and 2012 43 serious terrorist plots or potential attacks were prevented, adding that the terrorist threat is real and remains with us today (Evans 2012, paragraph 11). As seen with the example of control orders, the danger is what Gearty refers to as quasi-criminal law provisions such as control orders being introduced as preventative measure. As seen above, when applying the legal principle of proportionality, judicial scrutiny ensured that legal measures are kept in check. It is not the media's role to do this. The role of a free media in a democracy is through their freedom of expression to act as a watchdog by acting as a check on political and other holders of power, hence its nickname of

---

* *Washington Post* (2013) Public reaction to NSA monitoring retrieved from http://www. washingtonpost.com/politics/public-reaction-to-nsa-monitoring/2013/06/10/90dd1e60-d207-11e2-a73e-826d299ff459_graphic.html [accessed March 2, 2014].

the Fourth Estate (Leveson 2012, p. 65). It is accepted that with Snowden passing on the NSA/GCHQ documents to *The Guardian*, the newspaper was attempting to do this. However it is not the media's role to handle stolen classified document and decide what to reveal from that documentation that they perceive is in the public interest and safe to publish without jeopardizing national security. The danger is in journalists inadvertently releasing information that would be useful to a terrorist. Following the Snowden revelations the current MI5 Director, Andrew Parker said, that making public the reach and limits of national security agencies' techniques is damaging adding:

> Such information hands the advantage to the terrorists. It is the gift they need to evade us and strike at will. Unfashionable as it might seem, that is why we must keep secrets secret, and why not doing so causes such harm (Parker 2013, paragraph 59).

In adopting preventative measures both governments and their counter-terrorism agencies must assess the risk such measures present to individual's liberties balanced with a proportionate application of those measures to prevent terrorist activity (Palmer 2012, p. 527). As discussed above, this is what the UK and US judiciary are assessing in their judgments. Palmer notes in his work that most writing in this area has been hijacked by a legal and academic elite rather than an enlightened political, legal and social order where he adds, "Ideology cannot address immanent [terrorist] threats" (Palmer 2012, p. 535). Adopting such a position does not denigrate the view that security and liberty interests are inclusive and the importance of ensuring individuals' liberty is not railroaded by terrorism related legislation. As Palmer opines, little has been written about the reality of countering terrorism, which includes the practical issues in confronting agencies tasked to protect the public from terrorist attacks (Palmer 2012, p. 536). It is hoped that by examining the judicial responses to terrorism-related legislation this work goes some way to doing that.

Funding Terrorism

4

Introduction

Terrorism is an expensive operation, especially if the group plans a prolonged period of conflict. While the financial cost of carrying out attacks can be relatively inexpensive, the main drain on terrorist groups' resources is in the running and maintenance costs such as purchasing materials, property, and travel arrangements (Donohue 2008, pp. 153–154; Danziger 2012, p. 213). While links to terrorist groups being involved in organized criminal activity have been proved to exist (Hesterman 2013), terrorist groups also use legitimate means to fund their activities. With the threat international terrorist groups pose to many states, the UN introduced the 1999 International Convention for the Suppression of the Financing of Terrorism, supported by the UN Security Council issuing Security Council Resolutions (SCR). This chapter will examine the statutory provisions, mainly the UK and US provisions, relating to the funding of terrorism. As the main controversy in the case reports and academic commentary has been concerned with asset freezing, the main focus of this chapter will center on the SCR's issued relating to orders regarding asset freezing of persons' finances and how this has been implemented.

Provisions Related to Funding Terrorism under the UK's Terrorism Legislation

Terrorism Act of 2000

Part III of the 2000 Act created offenses relating to funding terrorist groups. This ranges from

1. Fund raising.[*]
2. Use and possession of property for the purposes of terrorism.[†]

---

[*] Section 15 Terrorism Act 2000.
[†] Section 16 Terrorism Act 2000.

3. Becoming concerned in the arrangement of property, money for the purposes of terrorism.[*]
4. Money laundering in relation to terrorist property.[†]

The act also applies a duty on a person in the course of their employment, for example, those working in the financial sector, to disclose information where they suspect a person has committed an offense under section 15–18.[‡] Where a person is convicted of an offense under sections 15–18 Terrorism Act 2000 the court can make a forfeiture order of any money or property the person had in their possession at the time of the offense that had been used for the purposes of terrorism or was intended for such a purpose,[§] with the process of how this is carried out being outlined in Schedule 4 terrorism Act 2000.

Anti-Terrorism, Crime, and Security Act 2001 (ATCSA)

Part 2 of the act is concerned with freezing orders that can be made by Her Majesty's Treasury (HM Treasury) (2007) provided the Treasury reasonably believe the person's actions will be a detriment to the UK economy or that action constitutes a threat to the life or property of UK citizens (section 4 ATCSA). The order prohibits persons from making funds available to or for the benefit of persons named in the order.[¶] Freezing orders are only exercisable by statutory instrument and must be laid before Parliament to have an effect.[**] ATCSA also contains two schedules concerned with funding terrorism. Schedule 1 is concerned with terrorist cash where paragraph 2 allows an authorized officer to seize any cash they have reasonable grounds for suspecting is terrorist cash. As well as any coins or notes of any currency, cash includes postal orders, checks, bankers' drafts, and bearer bonds and shares.[††] Forfeiture of the cash can be authorized by a court.[‡‡]

Counter-Terrorism Act of 2008

Part 5 and Schedule 7 of the act are concerned with terrorist financing and money laundering. Schedule 7 defines terrorism financing as using funds or making funds available for the purposes of terrorism or the acquisition,

---

[*] Section 17 Terrorism Act 2000.
[†] Section 18 terrorism Act 2000.
[‡] Section 19 Terrorism Act 2000.
[§] Sections 23 and 23A Terrorism Act 2000.
[¶] Section 5 ATCSA.
[**] Section 10 ATCSA.
[††] Paragraph 1 Schedule 1 ATCSA.
[‡‡] Paragraph 6 Schedule 1 ATCSA.

possession, concealment, conversion, or transfer of funds that are directly or indirectly to be used for the purposes of terrorism.[*] Schedule 7 ATCSA allows the Treasury to make a direction that imposes requirements in relation to transactions or business relationships with a person carrying out business in the country, the government of the country, or a person resident in or incorporated in the country.[†] The direction may require the person named in it to undertake enhanced customer due diligence measure before entering into a transaction or business relationship with a designated person actually doing business with that person.[‡] Due diligence measures are measures to establish the identity of a designated person and obtain information about that designated person's business, the source of their funds and to assess the risk of the designated person being involved in relevant terrorist activities.[§] H.M. Treasury can give such a direction provided the Financial Action Task Force has advised the Treasury that such measures should be taken because of the risk of terrorist financing or money laundering. The Treasury must reasonably believe that there is a risk that terrorist financing or money laundering activities are being carried out and pose a significant risk to the UK's national interest. The Treasury also reasonably believes the development of nuclear, radiological, biological, or chemical weapons or any action is carried out that facilitates the development of such weapons poses a significant risk to the UK's national interests.[¶] Where financial restrictions proceedings emanating from UN terrorism orders in the UK Part 2 ATCSA or Schedule 7 of the Counter-Terrorism Act 2008 asset-freezing orders are issued on persons or groups named within the UN orders believed to be resident in the United Kingdom. Part 6 of the act covers the procedures that person can take in applying to a court to have those decisions set aside via judicial review.[**] The UN orders that section 62 apply to are the Terrorism (United Nations Measures) Order and the Al Qaeda and Taliban (United Nations Measures) Orders or any other related orders that apply under section 1 United Nations Act 1946.

Terrorism (United Nations Measures) Orders and Al Qaeda and Taliban (United Nations Measures) Orders

These have been the most controversial legal provisions related to the funding of terrorism. The important difference between the provisions in the funding of terrorism in the acts compared to the orders is the acts require

---

[*] Paragraph 2 Schedule 7 ATCSA.
[†] Paragraph 9 Schedule 7 ATCSA.
[‡] Paragraph 10 Schedule 7 ATCSA.
[§] Paragraph 10(3) Schedule 7 ATCSA.
[¶] Paragraph 1 Schedule 7 ATCSA.
[**] Section 63 Counter-Terrorism Act 2008.

a degree of mens rea. As mentioned above, the provisions in the respective Acts relating to the forfeiture or freezing of assets apply where a person is committing or has committed or has been convicted of terrorist-related offenses. However, this is not the case with Orders as the persons or groups (entities) are listed by the UN's Security Council in the SCR. Although the ability to freeze assets is often regarded as one of the most effective ways to combat terrorism (Ryder 2007, p. 832), as Lord Hope observed, the effect of the orders freezing a person's assets is to deprive that designated person of any resource whatsoever thereby effectively making them prisoners of the state. He added they do not just affect the persons designated, but also their spouses and family members.*

How the Orders Were Derived

Emanating from article 2 of the 1945 Charter of the United Nations that states to ensure to all its members the rights and benefits of UN member-ship they, "… shall fulfil in good faith all members the obligations assumed by them in accordance with the present Charter." In the Charter, article 41 states:

> The Security Council may decide what measures not involving the use of armed force are to be implemented to give effect to its decisions, and it may call upon the members of the United Nations to apply such measures.

As a result the UK government passed the United Nations Act 1946, where section 1(1) states that under article 41 of the Charter of the United Nations:

> … the Security Council of the United Nations call upon His Majesty's Government of the United Kingdom to apply any measure to give effect to any decision of that Council, His Majesty may by Order in Council make such provision as appears to Him to be necessary or expedient for enabling those measures to be effectively applied, including … provision for the apprehen-sion, trial and punishment of persons offending against the Order.

Following the 9/11 attacks by Al Qaeda in the United States, the UN Security Council issued Resolution 1373 outlining measures UN member states should take to deal with international terrorist activity where para-graph 1(c) of the SCR states that all States shall:

> Freeze without delay funds and other financial assets or economic resources of persons who commit, or attempt to commit, terrorist acts or participate in

---

* *H.M. Treasury v Mohammed Jabar Ahmed and others* [2010] UKSC, 2 paragraph 4.

or facilitate the commission of terrorist acts: of entities owned or controlled directly or indirectly by such persons; and of persons or entities acting on behalf of, or at the direction of such persons and entities, including funds derived or generated from property owned or controlled directly or indirectly by such persons and associated persons and entities.

As a result, the UK government introduced as a statutory instrument the Terrorism (United Nations Measures) Order 2001, regarding the granting of directions that froze assets of those listed by the UN Security Council. The 2001 Order was replaced by the Terrorism (United Nations Measure) Order 2006,[*] where paragraph 4 granted H.M. Treasury the powers to give directions on persons identified where it considered the direction was necessary for the purpose of protecting the public from a risk of terrorism provided "... the Treasury have reasonable ground for suspecting that the person is or may be ..." a person who commits, attempts to commit, participates in, or facilitates the commission of acts of terrorism, or is a person identified in the UN Council Decision, or a person owned or controlled directly or indirectly by a designate person or is a person acting on behalf or at the direction of a designated person.[†]

The Disproportionate and Oppressive Nature of the Terrorism Order Rendering It *Ultra Vires*

In *H.M. Treasury v Mohammad Jabar Ahmed and others*,[‡] the claimants stated the Terrorism Order went further that the relevant Security Council Resolution (SCR) required, saying the freezing orders were disproportionate and oppressive and the terms of the freezing orders were uncertain.[§] The focus of their claim was due to the wording of article 4 of the 2006 Terrorism Order where the Treasury could grant a direction where they had reasonable suspicion that a person is *or may be* involved in acts of terrorism made the order's provisions go further than the SCR intended resulting in the provisions being disproportionate and uncertain.[¶] This was an issue raised in *A, K, M, Q, & G v H.M. Treasury*[**] and was considered by the High Court where Mr. Justice Collins having said the phrase "or may

---

[*] SI 2006/1747.
[†] Paragraph 4(2) The Terrorism (United Nations Measures) Order 2006.
[‡] [2010] UKSC 2.
[§] *H.M. Treasury v Mohammad Jabar Ahmed and others* [2010] UKSC 2, paragraph 128.
[¶] *H.M. Treasury v Mohammad Jabar Ahmed and others* [2010] UKSC 2, paragraphs 130–132.
[**] [2008] EWHC 869 Admin.

be" lowered the threshold required when a direction can be ordered by the Treasury, adding:

> While I can see the force of an argument that reasonable suspicion may suffice
> … to implement the requirement of [the SCR] it is impossible to see how the
> test could properly be as low as reasonable suspicion that a person may be a
> person who commits etc. I do not accept … that it is limited to those who are
> proved by conviction to be committing or attempting to commit acts of ter-
> rorism. But it is impossible to see how the test applied in the [Terrorism Order]
> can constitute a necessary means of applying the resolution.[*]

This was the key legal issue that resulted in Mr. Justice Collins finding the power given to H.M. Treasury was ultra vires and stating that the order should be quashed.[†] In *H.M. Treasury v Mohammad Jabar Ahmed and others*, the Supreme Court had a similar concern. In relation to the Terrorism Order Lord Hope said by introducing reasonable suspicion as a means of giving effect to the SCR:

> … the Treasury exceed their powers under section 1(1) of the 1946 Act. This is
> a clear example of an attempt to adversely affect the basic rights of the citizen
> without the clear authority of Parliament.[‡]

Lord Mance compared the asset-freezing power of the Treasury in the order to that under Part 2 ATCSA 2001 saying in the ATCSA two pre-condi-tions limit the ability of the Treasury to give a direction on a person saying:

> … the first that the Treasury reasonably believe that action to the detriment of
> the United Kingdom economy or constituting a threat to the life or property
> of one of more United Kingdom nationals has been or is likely, but the second,
> critically, that the person taking or likely to take such action is a foreign gov-
> ernment or overseas resident.[§]

Two points come out of Lord Mance's judgment. One is that for a freez-ing order to be applied by the Treasury under ATCSA the freezing order must go before Parliament and be reviewed, provisions which were not in the order as it was introduced into English law via a statutory instrument that does not have full Parliamentary scrutiny (Danziger 2012, p. 220). The second is that in essence, as with all of the forfeiture and asset freezing provisions in the ter-rorism Acts, a greater degree of mens rea is required under the ATCSA provi-sions for a direction to be given on a person thus making it more difficult for a direction to be ordered. In stark contrast with the acts' provisions, with the

---

[*] *A, K, M, Q, & G v H.M. Treasury* [2008] EWHC 869 Admin, paragraph 40.
[†] *A, K, M, Q, & G v H.M. Treasury* [2008] EWHC 869 Admin, paragraph 49.
[‡] *H.M. Treasury v Mohammad Jabar Ahmed and others* [2010] UKSC 2, paragraph 61.
[§] *H.M. Treasury v Mohammad Jabar Ahmed and others* [2010] UKSC 2, paragraph 223.

Terrorism Orders having the phrase "or may be" added to the reasonable suspicion required by the Treasury significantly lowers the threshold of suspicion required to grant a direction thus making it easier for the state to freeze a person's assets. This is an important point as the disproportionate and oppressive nature of directions given under the orders can be seen in *M, A, MM v H.M. Treasury and Secretary of State for Works and Pensions,* where the judicial review applicants were housewives responsible for raising several children and received in their own right a number of social security benefits, but they all lived with persons listed in the designation granted under a Terrorism Order.[†] The applicants contended that the Treasury was mistaken in concluding the payment of their social security benefits fell within the scope of the direction issued against their respective spouses[‡] as these funds are made available only to the claimants, not through them for the benefit of any listed person.[§] The High Court held that such funds did fall within the requirements of the Terrorism Order. As Kenneth Parker QC (sitting as Deputy Judge of the High Court) stated that even though the Department of Works and Pensions paid the claimants on a regular basis, it can be reasonably expected they would use the funds for the benefit of their spouses who were listed persons in the Treasury's direction.[¶] On that basis, the court dismissed the applicants' grounds for judicial review.[**] Returning to the Supreme Court's decision in *H.M. Treasury v Mohammad Jabar Ahmed and others* [2010] UKSC 2, in a majority decision it held as the wording of paragraph 4 of the Terrorism Order 2006 provided a lack of legal certainty the 2006 Order was therefore ultra vires and the order be quashed.[††]

European Court of Justice's (ECJ) Decision Being Influential to the Supreme Court's Decision in *H.M. Treasury v Mohammad Jabar Ahmed and Others*

The EU's Council Regulation (EC) No 881/2002 was issued following the 9/11 Al Qaeda attacks on the United States. The regulation was introduced

---

[*] [2006] EWCH 2328.

[†] *M, A, MM v H.M. Treasury and Secretary of State for Works and Pensions* [2006] EWCH 2328, paragraph 1.

[‡] *M, A, MM v H.M. Treasury and Secretary of State for Works and Pensions* [2006] EWCH 2328, paragraph 3.

[§] *M, A, MM v H.M. Treasury and Secretary of State for Works and Pensions* [2006] EWCH 2328, paragraph 52.

[¶] *M, A, MM v H.M. Treasury and Secretary of State for Works and Pensions* [2006] EWCH 2328 paragraph 63.

[**] *M, A, MM v H.M. Treasury and Secretary of State for Works and Pensions* [2006] EWCH 2328 paragraph 83.

[††] *H.M. Treasury v Mohammad Jabar Ahmed and others* [2010] UKSC 2 Lord Hope at paragraph 83, Lord Phillips at paragraph 156, Lord Rodgers with Lady Hale agreeing at paragraph 187.

to ensure all EU member states imposed certain specific restrictive measures against persons and entities associated with Osama Bin Laden, the Al Qaeda network, and the Taliban. The regulation strengthened the member states' ability to impose flight bans and the freezing of funds and other financial resources in respect to the Taliban in Afghanistan. Article 2 of the regulation states that all funds and economic resources belonging to, or owned, or held by a person, group, or entity be frozen. Article 2 is specific in stating that no funds or economic resources should be made available to the person, group, or entity either directly or indirectly.

In *Ahmed Ali Yusuf and Al Barakaat International Foundation v Council of the European Union and Commission of the European Communities,*[*] the EU's Court of First Instance (CFI) examined the provisions of regulation No 881/2002 and on three grounds found that freezing of funds under this regulation did not infringe the fundamental rights of a person:

1. The SCR against Bin Laden, Al Qaeda, and Taliban was important in the fight against international terrorism and enhanced the legitimacy of the protection of the UN against actions of terrorist organizations.
2. Freezing of funds is a precautionary measure that unlike confiscation did not affect the substance of the rights to their property, only the use of the assets.
3. The SCR did provide a means of review as persons affected could present their case to the Sanctions Committee through the member state of their nationality or where they resided.[†]

The CFI added that it was not for them to review if the SCR was compatible with fundamental rights protected by the EU's legal order and key in that decision was the fact the CFI thought a person's interest in having a court hear their case is not enough to outweigh the public interest in the maintenance of international peace and security.[‡] However, the position of the EU's judiciary changed significantly in *Kadi v Council of the European Union,*[§] where the ECJ examined once more the asset freezing under SCR on Osama Bin Laden, Al Qaeda, and the Taliban and EU Regulation No 881/2002. Advocate General Maduro noted that Kadi had not had the opportunity to make a submission whether the sanctions against him were justified and if they should be kept in force, all of which centered on the

[*] (2005) Case T-306/01.
[†] *Ahmed Ali Yusuf and Al Barakaat International Foundation v Council of the European Union and Commission of the European Communities* (2005) Case T-306/01, paragraph 8.
[‡] *Ahmed Ali Yusuf and Al Barakaat International Foundation v Council of the European Union and Commission of the European Communities* (2005), paragraph 9.
[§] Joined cases C-402/05P and C-415/05P) [2009] AC 1255.

de-listing procedure a designated person can apply through. The problem Advocate General Maduro saw with this process was even though the
request can be submitted through the Sanctions Committee, it was only
governmental departments that considered the applications and there was
no judicial scrutiny or protection within the process.* Challenging the finding of the CFI in *Yusuf*, an important principle of EU law is that it is based
on the rule of law and that an international agreement could not affect the
autonomy of the Community's legal system and according to settled case
law fundamental rights formed an integral part of the general principles
the ECJ followed.[†] He said

> It follows … that the obligations by an international agreement cannot have
> the effect of prejudicing the constitutional principles of the EC Treaty, which
> includes the principles that all Community acts must respect fundamental
> rights, that respect constituting a condition of their lawfulness which it is for
> the Court to review in the framework of the complete system of legal remedies
> established by the Treaty.[‡]

Adding that judicial review of United Nations' legal orders was not
excluded,[§] Gearty sees this decision as "heroic" (Gearty 2012, p. 41). Gearty
states the CFI was wrong to genuflect to the UN as by not including a procedure for communicating the evidence it adversely affected the persons named
in the measures by restricting their right to an effective judicial review. For
Gearty Regulation No 881/2002 was fatally flawed and says that Advocate
General Maduro was right to insist on the protection of fundamental rights
(Gearty 2012, pp. 44–45).

UK's Terror Asset-Freezing Act of 2010 (TAFA)

As a result of the Supreme Court's decision in *H.M. Treasury v Mohammed
Jabar Ahmed and others*, the UK Parliament introduced TAFA that repealed
the previous Terrorism Orders. In outlining H.M. Treasury's powers to
make a final designation of a person to freeze their assets, in section 2 TAFA
the Treasury can still reasonably believe a person is or has been involved
in terrorist activity. However, the words "or may be" have been removed.

---

[*] *Kadi v Council of the European Union* Joined cases C-402/05P and C-415/05P) [2009] AC
1255, paragraphs 51–55.
[†] *Kadi v Council of the European Union* Joined cases C-402/05P and C-415/05P) [2009] AC
1255, paragraphs 281—283.
[‡] *Kadi v Council of the European Union* Joined cases C-402/05P and C-415/05P) [2009] AC
1255, paragraph 285.
[§] *Kadi v Council of the European Union* Joined cases C-402/05P and C-415/05P) [2009] AC
1255, paragraph 287.

section 26 TAFA clearly specifies that a person who has had a designation placed on them can appeal to the High Court against any decision made by the Treasury. Also, other than regarding a decision to which section 26 applies, section 27 allows a person affected by a Treasury decision to apply to the High Court to have that decision set aside with the court being allowed to grant any relief that can be given in the judicial review proceedings.

While there were similar provisions to be found in the UK's terrorism legislation, TAFA has placed all the relevant provisions in one statute. The effect of TAFA is it increases the threshold of reasonable suspicion the Treasury must have before placing a designation on a person to freeze their assets. While there is no judicial supervision in the granting of a designation, it places on a statutory footing the procedure for a person to access the court for a judicial review of the Treasury's decisions. The act also ensures compliance with section 1 United Nations Act 1946 by ensuring that SCRs are introduced through UK legislative provisions. With the introduction of TAFA, we are seeing the state balancing the needs of not just the national, but also international security, against the needs of an individual's rights. As seen above, it is important to consider that asset freezing can have a dramatic effect on the domestic finances of a family where a member of the family is listed. As the state's preference is to apply the provisions contained in the TAFA rather that the terrorism funding offenses in the terrorism Act of 2000, getting the balance right is important, especially when issuing asset freezing measures. This is seen in Anderson's study who found that between April 2008 and March 2012 only one person was charged in the United Kingdom with offenses under sections 15–19 Terrorism Act 2000 (Anderson 2013, p. 71). Under section 23A Terrorism Act 2000, when a person is convicted of a terrorism offense a court can order the forfeiture of any money or property that was in their possession at time. The question whether the family home of a convicted terrorist can be seized as property in their possession was examined by the High Court in May 2014. The Court held the family home of a convicted terrorist cannot be seized, with Sir Richard Henriques QC saying it would have an adverse effect on the innocent members of the family (BBC News 2014).

The US Statutory Provision in Relation to the Funding of Terrorism

Following the 9/11 Al Qaeda attack on the United States, two significant parts of the US strategy against terrorist finance were introduced. The Presidential Executive Order 13224 on blocking property and prohibiting transactions with persons who commit, threaten to commit, or support terrorism, and Part III Patriot Act 2001 that is also cited as the International Money Laundering Abatement and Financial Anti-Terrorism Act 2001.

Presidential Executive Order 13224

This order is concerned with blocking (freezing assets) of suspected or known terrorists and is administered by the US Treasury.* Under the order the term terrorism is defined as activity that involves a violent act or an act dangerous to human life, property, or infrastructure and appears to be intended to intimidate or coerce a civilian population or influence the policy of a government by intimidation or coercion or affects the conduct of a government by mass destruction, assassination, kidnapping, or hostage-taking.† As covered in the chapter regarding the legal definition of terrorism in this book, we see the difficulty in not having the one statutory definition in the United States as this is another derivation of the term "terrorism" applied by US Federal agencies. In the first 5 years, the order was operating:

1. Approximately 250 groups and individuals were designated as terrorist organizations.
2. US$36 million was frozen in 92 suspected terrorists' accounts.
3. 150 terrorist-related accounts were blocked.
4. More than 400 individuals and entities were designated terrorists or terrorist supporters.
5. Approximately 40 charities were found to be transferring money to Al Qaeda, Hamas, and other designated terrorist groups and denied access to the US financial system.
6. About 1439 suspected terrorist accounts were frozen that contained US$135 million (Ryder 2007, p. 832).

The financing of the actual 9/11 attack involved the terrorist hijackers wiring cash transfers that were not sufficiently exceptional to make them stand out or bring attention to them. For example, the terrorist hijackers opened accounts in US banks in their own names and they made a number of small withdrawals from ATM or credit cards that were normal (Danziger 2012, p. 215). Another practice by terrorist groups like Al Qaeda that came onto counterterrorism investigators' radar in relation to terrorism funding is through global fund raising built on a foundation of charities, nongovernmental organizations, websites, intermediaries' facilitators, banks, and other financial institutions. Greenberg et al. (2002) reported how many of the people who make donations under such practices know full well their money will further enable the illicit purposes of groups like Al Qaeda. Taking this

---

* Presidential Executive Order 13224 section 1(d).
† Presidential Executive Order 13224 section 1(d), paragraph 3(d).

into account it is easy to understand why the US government felt it necessary that drastic measures should be introduced in the order.

Part III Patriot Act: International Money Laundering Abatement and Financial Anti-Terrorism Act 2001

As with the presidential order, Part III Patriot Act was introduced shortly after the 9/11 attacks and in its findings it says:

> … money laundering, and defects in financial transparency on which money launderers rely, are critical to the financing of global terrorism and the provisions of funds for terrorist attacks.[*]

The act makes the US Treasury principally responsible for implementing the act's provisions (Van Cleef 2003, p. 73). Included in those provisions is an increase in the reporting obligations that permits the US Treasury to impose additional money-laundering requirements on financial and credit institutions (Ryder 2007, p. 835). As stated in relation to the introduction of the presidential order, as the financing of terrorist activities are not often derived from illegal activities prior to the introduction of the act it was difficult for US authorities to prosecute the funding of terrorist activities under the former money laundering laws (Weiss 2005, p. 7).

Key provisions in the act empower the US Treasury to require US domestic financial institutions to undertake special measures, which include obtaining information on beneficial ownership of accounts and information relating to certain payable-through and correspondent accounts.[†] This involves the financial institutions taking due diligence procedures and establish where necessary enhanced procedures and controls that are reasonably designed to detect and report instances of money laundering through those accounts.[‡] This due diligence measure includes in relation to foreign banks:

1. Ascertaining foreign banks shares are not publically traded, the identity of each of the owners of the foreign bank and the nature and extent of the ownership interest of each such owner.
2. Conducting enhanced scrutiny of such accounts to guard against money laundering and report any suspicious transactions.
3. Ascertain whether such foreign banks provide correspondent accounts to other foreign banks and, if so, the identity of those foreign banks and related due diligence information.[§]

---

[*] Part III Patriot Act section 302(a)(2).
[†] Part III Patriot Act 2001 section 311.
[‡] Part III Patriot Act 2001 section 312.
[§] Part III Patriot Act 2001 section 312 (2)(B).

In relation to private banking accounts, the due diligence procedure requires:

1. Ascertaining the identity of the nominal and beneficial owners of and the source of funds deposited into such account as needed to guard against money laundering and report any suspicious transactions
2. Conduct enhanced scrutiny of any such account that is requested or maintained by or on behalf of a foreign political figure or any immediate family member or close associate of a senior political figure that is reasonably designed to detect and report transactions that may involve the proceeds of foreign corruption (section 312 (3)).

The act allows for a judicial review of the assets seized due to the suspicion of terrorist activities and the "innocent owner" defense,* which is where a person did not know of the illegal activity or on learning of the illegal activity did all that was reasonable to terminate use of the property in question (Weiss 2005, p. 6). One caveat in using this defense is that a court may admit evidence that is otherwise inadmissible under the Federal Rules of Evidence but only if the court determines that the evidence is reliable and the compliance with the Federal Rules of evidence may jeopardize the national security interests of the United States.†

Sections 357–359 of the act covers the procedures related to Suspicious Activity Reports (SAR) which extends the procedure of filing SAR's to broker-dealers and allows the US Treasury Secretary the authority to pass on SAR's to US intelligence agencies to combat terrorism. Anyone who is engaged in a trade or business who receives US$10,000 cash in one transaction must file an SAR with the US Treasury identifying the customer in the SAR along with the amount and date of the transaction as the act makes it an offense to knowingly conceal more than US$10,000 in cash or other monetary instrument and attempt to transport it into or out of the United States (Weiss 2005, p. 8).

Judicial Response to Lack of Judicial Scrutiny of Asset-Freezing SCRs

Both the presidential order and Part III Patriot Act have increased powers that are extensive and intrusive into an individual or company's finances. As Lee pointed out, one of the most controversial aspects of the US government's ability to freeze assets can be seen in the US-based Islamic charities (Lee

---

* Part III Patriot Act 2001 section 316.
† Part III Patriot Act 2001 section 316(b).

2002, p. 5) and this came to light in *Kindhearts for Charitable Humanitarian Development Inc v Timothy Geithner et al.*[*] In *Kindhearts*, the District Court of the Northern District of Ohio Western Division found that Islamic charity, Kindhearts' assets being frozen by the US Treasury violated their fourth amendment rights (right of people to be secure in their persons, houses, papers, and effects against unreasonable searches and seizures). Although a blocked person can obtain a post-blocking judicial review, the Court found the power of the US Treasury to block (asset freeze) had no built-in limitation thereby curtailing executive discretion and putting individuals on notice their assets were being frozen.

The lack of judicial supervision in relation to SCRs is a legal issue that is not unique to the United Kingdom, European Union, or United States. In *Abdelrazik v The Minister of Foreign Affairs*,[†] the Federal Court of Canada found that Abdelrazik, who had been listed on the SCR, had his rights under the Canadian Charter of Rights and Freedoms breached. Mr Justice Zinn was scathing about the SCR saying there was nothing in the listing or de-listing procedure that recognized the principles of natural justice or that the SCR made provisions for basic procedural fairness. He said the SCR could not meet the requirement of independence or impartially, adding "The accuser is also the judge."[‡] What is a cause of concern in all of these cases is the lack of judicial involvement or supervision in the issuing of directions on persons freezing their funds and assets. As seen, this is a global concern.

Conclusion

Particularly from the case reports, what we see in the statutory response to the terrorist threat, in particular the threat international terror groups pose to national security related to funding terrorism, is how far the state is prepared to go in applying draconian measures related to terrorist activity that can be oppressive and disproportionate. These measures are potentially oppressive as the measures when deployed by the relative treasury agency not only curtail the financial transactions a listed person can make, but also on their family members' financial transactions. The effect of this is the potential to place that person's family into serious financial difficulty as they balance day-to-day financial activities related to normal living. To counter this, we also see the judiciary performing its important role within the separation of powers by applying the legal principles of the rule of law related in assessing if the state's powers are ultra vires and natural justice to ensure the law

---

[*] 3:08CV2400 August 18, 2009.
[†] [2009] FC 580.
[‡] *Abdelrazik v The Minister of Foreign Affairs* [2009] FC 580, paragraph 51.

is applied equitably. By doing so, as seen in the United Kingdom with the Supreme Court's ruling in *H.M. Treasury v Mohammad Jabar Ahmed and others* [2010] UKSC 2, the court's decisions resulted in the UK Parliament amending the law. What we see with the issuing of orders is how difficult it is for states to strike an equitable balance between meeting the needs of national security in freezing assets that can be used to fund indiscriminate attacks on its citizens and meeting the needs of an individual's liberty. Applying asset freezing measures that are oppressive puts not only the listed person at a serious pecuniary disadvantage but also members of the family they live with, which in the United States can affect their Fourth Amendment rights and in the United Kingdom their European Convention on Human Rights, article 8, right to a family life.

Investigating Terrorism

II

Lack of Discretion in High Policing

5

Introduction

Focusing mainly on counterterrorist investigations, this chapter examines the lack of operational police officers' discretion in applying the law in high policing (defined below) compared with officers carrying out low policing duties. Founded on data gathered from counterterrorist investigations conducted by the UK forces' Special Branch Counterterrorism Units (CTU) departments in the UK between 2006 and 2007, this chapter looks into an area of policing that has so far been out of the reach and eluded the rigor of academic study (Gill 1994, Chapter 1; Innes and Thiel 2008, pp. 554–555). The chapter places in context what police activities amount to high policing and explains the research method of covert participant observation from which the data were collected.

The primary concern of this chapter is high policing operational officers' subculture and their application of the law. While some similarities can be found within the generic operational culture reported in previous police studies in relation to high policing officers' attitude toward legislative changes, the key and important difference in the cultural approach is seen in how officers in high policing apply the law governing their actions (Waddington 1999; Reiner 2010, pp. 213–214). From the data obtained, the main difference this study found compared with previous policing ethnographical studies is there is little scope for the junior ranking operational officer to use discretion when applying the law (McLaughlin 2007, pp. 51–52; Walker 2007, pp. 325–326). This is down to the management and conduct of CTU investigations where lower ranking operational officers have greater stake in the outcome of the investigation compared with officers of a similar rank in low policing activity.

Research Methods Used

The primary data used in this chapter come from my own research, where I used covert participant observation. The data were collected through a variety of techniques. One technique was making hand-written notes at the time. This was achieved from volunteering to be a minute taker at meetings, to writing up observation logs where I could make my own notes without raising suspicion. One was through covert recordings using the department's equipment to record officers' conversations where possible. The final tactic was on hearing relevant information, I would have to leave the company of colleagues for a short period and make up retrospective notes on what was said. At the time of data collection, I was a Detective Sergeant (DS) in the CTU leading a team of Detective Constables (DC). If I had requested to conduct my research openly, it would have been unlikely that permission would have been granted. A result of this is, I would not have had access to the police staff and reports that were available to me being a covert observer. The lack of transparency of high policing agencies brought about by a veil of secrecy has resulted in a limited development of a critical perspective on contemporary high policing (Sheptycki 2007, p. 3). Therefore, it is important that opportunities are taken to conduct research into high policing departments like the CTU, not just low policing departments, to provide a more complete picture in relation to terrorism investigations.

Conducting covert participant research raises an ethical issue regarding the subjects of the study. Holdaway, who conducted a landmark piece of covert participant research into the uniform arm of the police in the United Kingdom, refers to this issue as the "calculated deception of trust" by the researcher (Holdaway 1983, p. 13). The 2003 Social Research Association's (SRA) Ethical Guidelines on avoiding undue intrusion states that social researchers must strive to be aware of the intrusive potential of their work, adding that

> The advancement of knowledge and the pursuit of information are not themselves sufficient justifications for overriding other social and cultural values (Social Research Association's Ethical Guidelines, 2003, Para 4.1, pp. 25–26).

As Holdaway's and my research was on the police, we were not dealing with vulnerable victims of crime where the betrayal of trust could have a detrimental effect on the subjects of the research. Holdaway says he conducted a covert strategy on the police, as they are a powerful institution of our society who deals with the less powerful (Holdaway 1983, p. 4). That maxim is still true today. Justifying the use of covert participant observation on the police Holdaway says it

> ... [Is] strengthened by the central and powerful situation of the police within our social structure. The police are said to be accountable to the rule of law, a constitutional constraint which restricts their right to privacy but which they can neutralize by maintaining a protective occupational culture. When such an institution is over-protective, its members restrict the right to privacy they possess. It is important that they be researched (Holdaway 1983, p. 5).

The difference between Holdaway's research and mine is that Holdaway researched a visible arm of policing, uniform police officers, which is low policing, while I examined an invisible and secretive arm of policing. In my research, I anonymized the police force and the individuals to prevent them from being identified. Perhaps the key issue regarding the ethical implications is the betrayal of trust.

Betraying the trust of your subjects is an important implication when utilizing covert participant observation, and one that was seriously considered in my research. The SRA's ethical guidelines state in relation to the use of covert observation that can only be justified

> ... where there is no other ethically sound way of collecting accurate and appropriate data. If research requires any kind of deception, then only by the clear demonstration of the benefits of the research can it be justified (Social Research Association's Ethical Guidelines 2003, Para 4.3(d), p. 34).

At that time, there was no other research method open to me to study a policing agency that in effect polices politics.

That breach of trust is not only in reporting my findings, but also in the fact my former colleagues saw me as one of them, having no idea that I was observing them for the purposes of academic research. As Liebling and Stanko point out, "Ethical research is typically defined as that which safeguards the rights and feelings of those who are being researched" (Liebling and Stanko 2001, p. 424). Liebling and Stanko discuss dealing with victims of violent crime as subjects of research; to abuse any trust between the researcher and the subject for such vulnerable victims is clearly unethical. The issue for this research is whether the police officers are as vulnerable.

I took care not to infringe any of the individual subject's "private space" (Social Research Association's Ethical Guidelines 2003, para 4.3(a), p. 31). All the qualitative data used in my research are related to national security work while being careful not to breach my obligations under the Official Secrets Act. During the years I conducted the research, I was privy to conversations that included topics related to officers' private lives and their private thoughts on issues not related to their work. Although some of these thoughts were inadvertently recorded, I disposed of them and they are not used in this study.

High Policing

Brodeur introduced the concept of separating policing into two distinct categories, high policing and low policing. He identified high policing as policing based on the collection and processing of valid information that reaches beyond criminal intelligence and goes into the realms of economics and

politics, while low policing refers to the traditional activities of police departments such as patrol, order maintenance, and the control of street crime
(Brodeur 2005, p. 810). Basing his thesis on Napoleon's Minister of Police,
Joseph Fouche, Brodeur states the explicit distinction between the two is that
high policing establishes the political order whereas low policing is "piece-
meal policing" (Brodeur 2007, p. 2). Key to identifying a high policing agency
is its involvement in the protection of national security. He says the protection of the security of the nation is the raison detre of high policing where
the intelligence collated is analyzed, threat assessments are made in relation
to the data and disseminated on a need-to-know basis (Brodeur 2007, p. 3).

In comparison, Innes and Thiel identify low policing as that which

> ... tends to be concerned with classical notions of protecting the public from
> everyday volume of crime and maintaining public order by preventing and
> solving crimes directed at individuals or small groups (Innes and Thiel 2008,
> p. 560).

Low policing is primarily a reactive response, although over the past
few years even the uniform police departments deploy resources based on
intelligence-led policing (Ratcliffe 2008, p. 36). In essence, low policing is the
public face of policing, such as the uniform departments that carry out the
everyday policing tasks from taking crime reports for burglaries and thefts,
to arrests for minor disorder to overt patrol work, what Innes and Thiel refer
to as micro-crime (Innes and Thiel 2008, p. 560).

High policing deals with macro-crime where the victims can be the
whole of society. Regarding counterterrorism, as Gill points out, the specific
role of the security intelligence agencies "... is the surveillance of the population for evidence of particular forms of resistance and deviance" (Gill 1994,
p. 61). To carry out this surveillance effectively, it requires a different form
of policing from that seen in low-policing activity. As Innes and Thiel state:

> As terrorism is a "macro-crime," counter-terrorism is thus predominantly
> carried out by secretive high policing agencies that place significant emphasis
> upon their capacity to access covert organisations in order to develop pre-
> emptive intelligence with which to direct their operations (Innes and Thiel
> 2008, p. 260).

Low-policing targets range from individuals to small groups, whereas
in counterterrorism the targets are populations (Gill 1994, pp. 145–151).
During my first posting to the Branch's counterterrorist unit in the late 1980s
and early 1990s, the targets were members of the Irish nationalist community residing in mainland Britain. During my second posting, the primary
focus of counterterrorist investigations had changed from watching the
Irish community to predominantly watching the Asian Muslim community.

In counterterrorism investigations, surveillance of targets by CTU officers is not solely in keeping certain, identified persons under surveillance, they are also watching for any signs of deviance or a threat from the whole of the targeted population that could pose a potential threat to the stability and peace of the nation. This includes members of extremist political parties or groups. It is not just members of extremist groups that come under the CTU's radar; if intelligence is received in relation to associations with various individuals perceived as a threat to national security, it can include those seen as pillars of the community. In other words, the CTU target *anyone* they see as a threat, not just the stereotyped hoody or small-time drug using criminal targeted by low-policing departments.

The Dichotomy between Previous Police Research and This Study

Compliance with the law is paramount in CTU counterterrorist investigations. The main reason for this is that arrests and searches carried out by the CTU receive high profile media attention. Evidence obtained by not following the law is likely to result in suspects being freed without charge or found not guilty in a subsequent trial. When this occurs, the finger of blame will not only be pointed at the DC or DS who failed to follow legal procedure, but also to the head of the CTU, if they were the senior investigating officer (SIO) and possibly chief officers. This raises the issue of whether the law is synonymous in controlling police activity.

Holdaway maintains that informal rules of police subculture determine police behavior with the law being primarily presentational (Holdaway 1983, p. 163). To apply Holdaway's hypothesis in relation to current low policing could still be relevant regarding the operational culture of uniform policing with the caveat that Holdaway's hypothesis is dated as it does not take into account the legislative changes in police governance. In the UK, this can be traced through various police acts from the Police and Magistrates Court Act 1994[*] to the police reform in the early 21st century with the Police Reform Act 2002[†] and the Police and Justice Act 2006.[‡] The second point

---

[*] This Act changed the formation of police authorities and increased the control of the Home Secretary over provincial police forces. Key to this is the budgetary control of the Home Secretary over provincial forces.

[†] This Act introduced three key changes to the control of policing, the introduction of the National Policing Plan, where KPI's are set by the Home Secretary, the introduction of the Independent Police Complaints Commission and the power of Home Secretaries to remove ineffective chief officers.

[‡] A key change to the control of policing in the act is the introduction of the National Policing Improvement Agency.

regarding Holdaway's thesis is that it focuses primarily on uniform police work. To apply a one-fits-all explanation to all forms of policing can skew any subsequent analysis, as it does not take into account other equally powerful policing subcultures. As I found in my research, there is no one homogeneous police culture, neither is there a single homogeneous CID culture. Identifiable subcultures exist in each policing department.

The folly of applying a one-dimensional approach to understanding police culture is seen in Waddington's examination of how the police use and enforce the law (Waddington 1999). His data emanate from uniform policing, covering incidents from drunk and disorderly behavior to other minor disorder. He discusses how uniform officers on the street face the issue of authority. To maintain their authority, uniform officers have to maintain control and not lose face while adopting a degree of pragmatism in deploying their authority. For example, Waddington refers to how a senior constable changed the literal account of events in the arrest evidence written by a recruit because it would save completing additional work. Waddington says that what was rewritten was true but entirely misleading (Waddington 1999). This demonstrates the contrast between low policing that deals with minor incidents and high policing that deals with serious criminal activity such as policing national security. To get the job done, uniform officers tend to find themselves in the invidious position of having to make the law fit the situation they are dealing with. In comparison, CTU officers have wide powers that meet virtually all the incidents they have to deal with. This is one factor that explains why operational officers in high policing do not have much use of their discretion when applying the law. Unlike their uniform colleagues, they do not have to make a square law peg fit a round operational hole.

Initial Action Taken in CTU Counterterrorist Investigations: It Is Ownership, Not Discretion

In the United Kingdom, the majority of CTU investigations commence with external triggers such as intelligence reports from MI5. If there is a global aspect to the investigation, the intelligence could have emanated from agencies outside Europe and passed on through Europol to MI5 and/or the intelligence unit in the national Crime Agency, formerly the Serious Organized Crime Agency (SOCA). Once the CTU section DS is handed, the investigation package, the Detective Inspector (DI) would brief the DS on a one-to-one basis or it could be by the DI to the whole section. This depended on the intricacy of the subject of the investigation. On most occasions, it was a one-to-one briefing between the DI and the DS after which the DS examines the investigation package to assess the best line of approach to conduct the investigation. This involves considering the types of surveillance to use and how section members would be deployed during the surveillance. It is not uncommon for the DI to later join a DS's briefing to the section. The role of the DI was mainly to give a pep talk. A typical example of the sort of input from the DI is from one investigation relating to a suspected Islamic-based terror group. The DI said:

> I just want to add to what XXXX has told you. This must be carried out with sensitivity and you must be careful not to be compromised. The intelligence from MI5 has been verified and we need to confirm the intelligence is reliable. You'll be working in other force areas so be mindful of your actions and don't raise suspicion with the local bobbies be they uniform or the local jacks as well as the locals themselves. Keep to speed limits. Don't park on double yellows, all the usual things. If you do get a ticket, you pay for it; we don't want to compromise the investigation (D1/DI1).

All the members of the investigation team go through the intelligence contained in the package and have a say in how it should be conducted, as many CTU investigations take months to complete. It is important team members become familiar with the targets. Apart from studying the intelligence stored on the CTU computer systems, they familiarize themselves with photographs and video recordings, addresses, and locations. In the familiarization process, the team would study maps of the area associated with the target. From these, not only would the team discuss possible observation spots to conduct static surveillance but they also study the area for potential hazards and escape routes. To help in the decision making, the team would also study satellite photographs of the location, especially in areas members of the team were unfamiliar with. This process was essential if the team was assisting another force area's CTU, as CTU counterterrorism work is run at a coordinated regional level. In setting up static observation points, members of the team would leave the office and reconnoiter the area looking mainly for empty property from which to set up a static observation post.

Once the team was familiar with the geography of the area, the DS planned with the team the most appropriate methods of surveillance, the equipment that would be needed and the roles and responsibilities that should be assigned to members of the team. The detectives on the teams had a lot of experience and a diversity of skills that was an important source for the DS's to tap into. The skills members of the team possessed were officers who were highly trained and skilled in mobile surveillance, intelligence analysis, informant handling, or suspect interviewing. Once the team was in agreement, the DS submits an operational plan to the senior management team via the DI for its approval. One important point to note here is that although the lower ranking officers have more of a say in how the investigation is conducted and in drawing up the operational plan, they have little or no say when action can be taken against a target. That was the prerogative and responsibility of the SIO.

This approach by DCs and DSs in major investigations is an important issue when understanding the operational culture and practice of high-policing investigations. Not only do the junior ranks have a major say in how the investigation will be run, but the detectives feel they have ownership of the investigation and their input is valued. From a cultural point of view, this demonstrates the difference between uniform and CID work. In policing major events, from demonstrations to football matches, uniform officers are generally ordered as to what they will do. Uniform constables have no say and uniform sergeants virtually no say in the planning or running of the operation. They are not given any ownership in the responsibility of the running of the operation, they are ordered to carry out specific tasks. Unlike uniform constables and sergeants who during the policing of major events display a degree of cynicism to the decision-making process in major incidents, being a major part of the decision-making process, CTU DCs tend to have a desire to ensure success. If events do not go as planned, unlike their uniform colleagues, part of the responsibility lies with them not just with senior managers.

Intelligence Gathering

Once the surveillance authorities are in place, the investigation begins in earnest. Surveillance has a wide connotation. It is not simply occupying premises and watching targets. Surveillance includes ascertaining bank account details, ascertaining landline and mobile telephone numbers and monitoring calls, monitoring Internet access and email accounts, observing debit and credit card transactions, vehicle tagging (either with a specialist device or through the use of the vehicle's satellite navigation system) and travel ranging from scheduled and chartered flights, and ferry passenger lists to monitoring vehicle movement on roads. The different categories of surveillance carried out by the ISB are varied and numerous and can include requests to see records from other agencies, for example the UK's Benefits Agency or the National Health Service. During the research, I started to measure the length of time it took to ascertain a workable profile of a person who came into the investigation through an association with the target. I selected 10 random counterterrorist investigations (this included investigations conducted by other sections in the unit in the 12 month period 2006–2007). In each investigation, I selected five persons who were peripheral associates of the main target in each investigation and the mean time it took the CTU to build a workable profile was just above 26 h. I know from working with my section, if it took 48 h plus it was viewed as a disappointing time period. This form of information exchange and target profiling is not unique to national security policing. It takes place in virtually all forms of contemporary policing (Ratcliffe 2008, pp. 127–130). Although Ratcliffe says information sharing and information management is "time-consuming" (Ratcliffe 2008, p. 130) and appears at variance to my findings, one possible explanation for this is that Ratcliffe researched a wider sample of policing departments than I. Also, when requests are made under the interests of national security, other policing departments and public agencies appeared to give the requests from departments like the CTU top priority.

The first stage of the surveillance was building up a personal data pattern on the targets and their associates. This would involve section DCs carrying out static surveillance from safe premises. Initially, this would involve video and photographic evidence gathering. On each static surveillance point, a surveillance log is maintained to record location, time, and a description of the targets and their associates' movements. To demonstrate the advance in technology, digital cameras speed up the process and the teams would have a number of chips for the camera. Once a series of photographs is obtained, the chip is taken out of the camera, placed into a computer, and the photographs would then be matched to a photograph database. Once frequently used premises and vehicles are identified, there is a discussion between the team and the SIO as to whether further intrusive surveillance methods should be deployed. This could be to record and/or film conversations in private dwellings, work places, or other frequently used premises, as well as electronically tagging vehicles. It is important to note it is the SIO that makes the final decision, not the DS and the DC's on the team.

CTU Operational Officers' Attitudes Toward the Law: Followed to the Letter or Just a Rough Guide?

It can be argued that all police officers need black-letter law as a framework within which they can make their decisions, but as previous ethnographical research has revealed, there are other factors governing police behavior. Holdaway sees subcultural rules and police policy under the powerful symbolic canopy that the police operate under as governing police behavior rather than strict interpretation of the law (Holdaway 1983, p. 163). He says, "Law and policy are not obliterated within the occupational culture but re-worked, refracted in one direction or another as they do or do not resonate with the themes of the occupational culture" (Holdaway 1983, p. 65). Although not taking the culturalist position on how law governs police action, McBarnet's empirical study also revealed that the police approach the law as raw material to be worked on, "… the law is something to be used, manipulated, crafted to suit their interests. She found the police approach focused less on the content of law and more on exploring its methods, structures, and ideologies, its facilitative form, and how it could be actively used" (McBarnet 1992, p. 248). This demonstrates how officers view the law as something not to be followed through strict interpretation. Dixon's research among police officers revealed that "… in their work they see legal controls as generally wide and flexible so as to interfere minimally with everyday police work based on common sense and cultural standards of reasonableness" (Dixon 1997, p. 38).

There is some data from my research supporting these findings. One example is from a "mop up" human rights training session I conducted with the CTU. It was referred to as a "mop up" session as most of the officers who attended these sessions were those who found training in law and policy as an unnecessary distraction to carrying out operational policing. This particular session was run 10 months after the act had commenced. An example of the attitude toward the law was seen in an email response from one of the officers asking if their attendance was necessary as he was "busy with an investigation." The training sessions were obligatory and this type of response endorses the view of some officers that training should not supersede what they see as "real" police work. Even during the session I was asked a number of times, "How do we get around this?" as opposed to what is the best method of applying the requirements of the ECHR to our role.

I found the attitude of wanting to know how to circumnavigate the law among some of the officers in a number of the training sessions that I ran. When I was running the training sessions on the Terrorism Act 2000, a positive attitude was displayed when I explained to the officers their powers had widened. There was one change in the act that caused some disquiet. The act allows terrorist suspects the right to consult a lawyer as soon as is reasonably practicable, privately, and at any time.* (Prior to the 2000 Act terrorist suspects only had the right to a lawyer after being in police detention for 48 h under the previous Prevention of Terrorism [Temporary Provisions] Act 1989.) There was a feeling of disquiet about this change, and in one session an officer asked me, "How are we going to get into them before the brief arrives? Human rights! It's a pain in the arse" (D3/HRATE2/DC3). This response was typical of many of the officers who were informed of this change and who saw it as another obstacle to overcome in their work. However, comments like these were borne out of frustration in the sense that CTU officers knew that this was the law they *would* have to follow.

Another question I was frequently asked during the training sessions was in relation to what the force policy was on the application of the law. Dixon's research also found that force policy was an important issue in the application of the law by the police, saying "From the perspective of police

* Paragraph 7(1), Schedule 8 Terrorism Act 2000.

management, the gap between the law and practice should be bridged by the formulation and implementation of policy" (Dixon 1997, p. 26). Force policy is an example of what Waddington refers to as the epitome of organizational bureaucracy where police forces attempt to orchestrate the behavior of their officers through a dense set of rules and procedures, which officers, just like they do with the law, try to subvert or circumvent (Waddington 1999). Waddington gives the example of a Metropolitan police sergeant who saw force orders and policy as a set of rules introduced to be used when something goes wrong (Waddington 1999). In relation to the law appertaining directly to CTU work, another common response was asking what the "Met's national policy" was. Where it had not been decided, my frequent response to these questions was that they will follow the will of Parliament adding that is what parliamentary sovereignty and the rule of law is about. In one session, an officer said in relation to this response, "That's all well and good but we follow force policy" (D3/HRATE5/DC6).

There are different levels of rules that officers follow in an ascending order. First, there is the statute itself that outlines what the offenses are and the police powers to deal with that offense. Consideration is given to the UK's Human Rights Act 1998 and the associated articles in the ECHR to ensure that the police as a public body act in a manner that is compatible with the ECHR.* This is followed by a combination of Home Office guidelines and Force policy, and in the case of the ISB, Branch national policy that emanates from the Metropolitan Police SO13 department. Within these three rules that influence police work, there is a hierarchy in that Home Office guidelines and Branch national policy is considered first and then Force policy. The aim of the policies and the guidelines are to ensure there uniformity as well as conformity in how the law is carried out by the police. The final set of rules to be considered is the departmental or area orders. The purpose of these orders is to inform officers of the practice of how to apply and from whom authorities are obtained.

In relation to police officers' approach to these levels of rules, once again we see a difference in how they are applied between officers involved in high and low policing. The uniform officers, as shown by the ethnographic research in this area, deal with low-level incidents of public order and criminal activity. One problem officers have in dealing with this type of criminal activity is that on many occasions they do not have specific powers to meet the situation they are dealing with. Explaining why uniform police officers feel the need to make the law fit the scenarios they face, Dixon states:

> The police do not have legal powers for everything that they do. Like other citizens, they may do anything that the law does not forbid. Indeed, most

* s 6 Human Rights Act 1998.

policework entails duties which do not involve the use of coercive powers: the police do not mainly operate as crime-fighters or law-enforcers, but rather as providers of a range of services which beggars description … crime-fighting has never been, is not, and could not be the prime activity of the police (Dixon 1997, p. 66).

In high-policing work, like counterterrorism, this is not the case as CTU officers have legal powers to cover virtually any situation they come across. They do not have to make the law fit a situation like their uniform colleagues have to do as found in Reiner's and Waddington's work. The "ways and means" Act that uniform officers have to apply to many situations they deal with (Waddington 1999) do not apply to CTU officers.

Terrorism Legislation: Extension of Power or Extension of Discretion?

Regarding terrorist offenses, it is interesting to note that for some of them the mens rea threshold is so low they are not far off from being ones of strict liability. For example, s 11 of the 2000 Act, being a member of a proscribed organization, simply states:

A person commits an offense if he belongs or professes to belong to a proscribed organization.

There is a very low threshold of mens rea regarding this offense. There is nothing in the definition of this offense that says a person commits an offense if they knowingly belong to an organization or are reckless as to whether it is a proscribed organization. This offense is useful for UK counterterrorist agencies in relation to arresting persons believed to belong to Islamic-based groups. A number of these groups are listed in Schedule 2 of the 2000 Act, including Al Qaeda. If a person using Internet sites (especially chat-rooms) professes membership to one of these groups, or even a link, regardless how tenuous, as occurred during investigations carried out during the research period, they could be arrested and interviewed. Although there is a defense under s 11(2) for the defendant to prove that the organization was not proscribed on the occasion they became a member and that they had not taken part in the activities of the organization at any time while it was proscribed, it could be argued that the section is totally silent on mens rea.

As found in my research, unlike investigating groups such as the Provisional IRA that was one cohesive unit with a hierarchical structure among its membership, during the investigations ascertaining actual membership of the proscribed Islamic-based terrorist organizations was not as easy. The problem during those investigations was in identifying who among a large number of disaffected Muslim youths logging onto extreme Islamic cites promoting hatred toward the West were genuinely professing membership of a proscribed organization. Posting messages on these sites encouraging hatred does not necessarily mean they are all members of a proscribed group. Schedule 2 of the UK's Terrorism Act 2000 lists proscribed groups and they include Al Qaeda, Armed Islamic Group, Harakat Mujahideen, and Ansar Al Islam, among others. During the investigations carried out during the research period, this gave the SIO-wide leverage to authorize arrests, especially on fringe players, to gain further information on the main targets.

As pressure on CTU officers is to prevent acts of terrorism, offenses silent on mens rea such as being a member of a proscribed organization are useful to them in their investigations, as the evidence required is minimal to suspect that the target has committed an offense. If there is insufficient evidence to charge the suspect, they will be released, but only after providing fingerprint and DNA samples. Such action also allows the potential for agencies like the CTU to recruit informants.* Another example of the low level of mens rea required is seen in s 58 Terrorism Act 2000, where a person commits an offense if they possess a document or record containing information that is likely to be useful to a person committing or preparing an act of terrorism. This section is virtually silent on mens rea making it easier for the police to take that important preventative step.

An example of this was seen in the UK case *R v M, Z, I, R, and B.*† The evidence that led to the defendants being charged was based on possession of computer data, a video recording and paper documents involving extreme Islamist and terrorist propaganda. There was no evidence they used it to assist a terrorist in planning an act of terrorism. One of the defendants was a 17-year-old boy who left home, leaving a note to his parents that he was going to fight abroad and they would meet up again in heaven. He actually went to Bradford University to meet up with the other defendants he encountered in a chat-room devoted to Islamic fundamentalism. He returned home 3 days later. In the meantime, his parents had contacted the police who found incriminating materials on R's computer. R was released on appeal, but R came into the security intelligence system due to the nature of the messages he posted on the extremist Islamic sites as well as the materials found in his possession. Due to the nature of the contents of the material that was found in relation to R, a decision was taken to arrest him. From the facts of the case, R was an impressionable young man and what this case demonstrates is how misguided but innocent behavior can result in a person being arrested and entering the criminal system labeled as a terrorist.

---

* Chapter 7 covers informant recruitment in counterterrorism investigations in more detail.
† [2008] Crim LR 80.

These are examples of Walker's point that the police are given a greater breadth of discretion against terrorists than when dealing with "ordinary decent criminals" (Walker 2007, p. 336). Perhaps Walker's use of the word "discretion" is inappropriate; legal power might be more applicable here. This is more than semantics in differentiating between the words "discretion" and "power." In both examples for sections 11 and 58 of the 2000 Act, the state has given the police the power to assist in taking preventative action in a counter-terrorist investigation rather than discretion. This involves making decisions as whether to arrest, whether to search someone, decisions that uniform officers routinely make when on patrol, away from the gaze of their managers or other operational colleagues. This is not the situation in CTU investigations, where officers are working under the gaze of their colleagues and it is the SIO who will make the decision as to whether an arrest or a search is to be made. Why offenses like sections 11 and 58(2) widen an operational CTU officer's powers is in the fact a person either is or is not a member of a proscribed organization, or a person either has or has not got a document or record in their possession that will assist a terrorist. Through their actions alone, they are either simply committing the offense or they are not. The investigating officers do not have to find much evidence of mens rea. The only issue regarding the burden of proof in s 58 is whether the article is of the type that would be likely to be useful to a person preparing or committing an act of terrorism. The word "likely" in and of itself widens the power available to CTU officers as they do not have to prove the article would *definitely* be of use to a terrorist. During the investigations in the research period, once such evidence against the target was relayed to the SIO (usually a DI or the Detective Chief Inspector operations), it is the SIO's decision whether an arrest should be made or to use that evidence to justify a further period of surveillance on the target. As stated above, while lower ranking operational CTU officers have a greater input in the decision making on operational issues regarding an investigation, for example selecting the best observation point, they have no real freedom to decide when to arrest and search targets and targets' premises. That decision is made by the SIO.

My findings differ from previous empirical police research that found uniform constables have greater discretion compared with their senior officers such as the uniform inspector. For example, when a uniform officer deals with a motorist caught speeding the officer may either issue a fixed penalty notice or summons or may just give a warning. There is no such opportunity for lower ranking CTU officers to issue a warning for terrorist-related offenses. Even where evidence is coming out from an investigation that a target has committed terrorist-related offenses, such as possession of a document or record that may be used in terrorist-related incidents,* it is not

---

* s 58 Terrorism Act 2000.

the DC or even the DS's decision to arrest, it is at the least the SIO's decision whether to arrest at that stage of the investigation.

Due to the technology used by investigating officers, there is little discretion for CTU DC's and DS's as to what they do and do not record during the course of an investigation. All audio and visual recordings are timed and dated and given an identification or exhibit number. All recording devices are sealed before use and have a reference number. These numbers are recorded at the CTU office before the devices are taken out into the field. Those that are used are sealed after use and given an exhibit number while a working copy is kept. Apart from the use of technology, CTU officers are also under the gaze of their colleagues affording little, if any opportunity for DC's and DS's to conceal evidence. Apart from their own team colleagues, they are working alongside colleagues from other force areas and other EU member states. This restricts a CTU officer's use of discretion as to what they record. In essence, lower ranking CTU officers active in the operational field are themselves under the surveillance of their fellow DC's, their immediate supervisor, and the intelligence or evidence gathering process. The latitude for selectivity as to what to record is extremely narrow. This is the opposite from most of the uniform police officers' work where the only record of what was said and done in an incident is written in their pocket notebook. The lack of an actual record or accountability as to what is recorded by uniform officers allows them a greater latitude to be selective as to what is said and done by a suspect (Reiner 2000, p. 104).

It could be argued there is a degree of naivety in this submission as the evidence from other ethnographic research on the police reveals the loyalty of police colleagues where they act defensively to shield police officer deviancy from the gaze of bureaucracy, be it a "code of silence" or a "blue shield" that can usurp the system (Waddington 1999; Reiner 2000, pp. 91–92; Holdaway 1983). Reiner sums up the police research regarding the powerful code of internal solidarity saying there is the need of officers to rely on colleagues in a tight spot, "… and a protective armor shielding the force as a whole from public knowledge of infractions" (Reiner 2000, p. 92). This factor was considered and examined when collecting and analyzing my research data. One powerful finding that came out of my data concerns the DCs' ownership in an investigation. As stated earlier, DCs have a say in the operational plan of how the investigation will be run, tasks to be performed, and the knowledge that the investigation is likely to take a considerable period of time before it is concluded. This investment of their valued opinion, skill, and time gives them shares in the desire of a successful outcome to the investigation. It came across during the research that success is important to the team members, and it was not just for self-pride but it demonstrated to the SIOs their effectiveness, which in turn they believe will assist in them staying in the CTU and not be posted out.

During the research, using discretion to shortcut the procedure only became a problem once during the intelligence gathering stage of the investigation. An experienced DC, but inexperienced in CTU work (this was his first major CID department posting) was causing consternation among members of the team by not following to the letter the law and policy regarding the recording of intelligence or evidence. The senior service DC on my team came to me and told me that he was "not playing by the rules" and that he and a couple of others on the section had spoken to him but he was not doing anything about it. I called this officer back to the CTU office and we went into a quiet room where I told him what had been said, informed him that it was unacceptable (and why) and that he would be out of the ISB, and out of the CID if he continued. He accepted what I said and apologized, however I had to see if he could be moved onto another section as he had upset my section's team spirit, as I got the feeling they no longer trusted him. After speaking to my DI, the move was completed within the week and he was transferred to the Port Unit with a Port Unit officer transferred to my section. This incident shows the power the ownership CTU DCs have in an investigation.

Conclusion

Stating that high-policing detectives have little or no discretion contradicts all the previous ethnographic police research. Previous ethnographic police research found wide levels of discretion, minor infringements by police officers when applying the powers and a high degree of solidarity among the officers in the operational field, including support for officers who commit minor transgressions. The only similarity between CTU officers in my research and the general police culture in previous research was the perception and sense of frustration during the CTU training events that legislators keep placing obstacles in their way to doing their job. That said, even though there may have been mumblings of disquiet, by the end of the training events, there was an acceptance that the law is what they will have to follow.

When it comes to going out in the field and conducting investigations, there is little opportunity for officers to use their discretion in applying the law. As shown, there are a number of reasons for this. There is the fact that the law governing counterterrorist investigations is wide enough to cover virtually every eventuality the officer comes across during an investigation, reducing the need of officers in having to make the law fit the situation they have to deal with. Second, the nature of a high-policing investigation is the constant supervision of the SIO, who is a senior ranking officer and it is the SIO that makes the decisions. The third reason why officers are fettered in their use of discretion is due to the attitude of the members of the investigation team.

As shown, all the team members have a say in how the investigation is run and subsequently have a stake in the outcome. Of course, it could be argued that the method of evidence gathering in high policing is in itself a form of surveillance on the officers as their actions are recorded. In addition to the technology, as shown above, CTU officers, like officers in other high-policing departments, tend to work alongside colleagues from departments based in other police forces as well as officers from agencies based in other states. This reduces the scope for an officer to apply their own values in using discretion as they are under the gaze of other officers. All these factors are instrumental in understanding why in high policing, operational officers have little scope to use their discretion when applying the law.

Radicalization of Terrorist Causes

6

A Study of the 32CSM/IRA Threat to UK Security

Introduction

Since 2009, the significant increase of violence from Irish dissident groups has broken the relative peace in Northern Ireland brought about by the 1998 Good Friday Agreement (GFA). Being the largest and most active of the Irish dissident groups, this chapter focuses on the IRA. The original focus of the research was on the then largest republican group, the Real IRA (RIRA) and its political wing, the 32 County Sovereignty Movement (32CSM). However, during the data collection period, RIRA amalgamated with another republican dissident group, Republican Action Against Drugs (RAAD) and disaffected former members of the Provisional IRA (PIRA). The increase in size of the group has consequently increased its capability to mount a period of violence in Northern Ireland and, potentially, mainland Britain.* As a result, the research focus changed slightly by examining this new IRA group. The danger the 32CSM/IRA pose, cannot be understated. The 2012 Northern Ireland Peace Monitoring Report states as a result of the threat Irish dissident groups in the Province pose to UK security, the Terrorism Risk Index placed the United Kingdom at a greater risk than any other Western nation. (Nolan 2012, p. 43).

This chapter focuses on the radicalization process the 32CSM/IRA use to gain support, mainly from Catholic republican or nationalist communities (including recruiting individuals to the IRA). Just as there is difficulty in deriving one agreed definition of what actions amount to an act to terrorism, when examining the empirical work carried out on radicalization, it too contains conflicting findings. This chapter applies radicalization theories to the methods the 32CSM/IRA use to gain support from their use of e-sources, symbols, and ceremonies. In the process, we can make links to the offenses examined in Part 1 of the book, being members of a proscribed organization, possession of articles that are likely to assist those preparing or committing acts of terrorism and offenses related to terrorist funding.

---

* NI's dissident groups to unite under IRA banner. http://www.bbc.co.uk/news/uk-northern-ireland-19009272 [accessed August 5, 2012].

Primary data for this research were obtained from nationalist, republican, and unionist politicians, police officers (mainly the Police Service of Northern Ireland [PSNI] and Ireland's An Garda Siochana), and members of the Catholic community in Northern Ireland (many who had connections with PIRA and Sinn Fein). The analysis of the primary data draws comparisons with the findings of the 2012 Northern Ireland Peace Monitoring Report and the events that led to PIRA's breakaway from the IRA at the start of the 1969–1998 Irish Troubles (now on referred to as the Troubles) to assess if through a radicalization process the 32CSM/IRA can eventually emulate PIRA and Sinn Fein during the Troubles. This research found the IRA is building a capacity to mount a sustained campaign of violence in Northern Ireland, which, through their radicalization of English-based supporters could expand to carrying out attacks in England. If the IRA achieves this, it would result in the United Kingdom having a terror war on two fronts with Irish and jihadist terror groups.

Radicalization

The more one examines radicalization the more one finds that radicalization is a complex, multifaceted phenomenon (Carpenter et al. 2009, p. 327). There is no one-size-fits-all theory to radicalization, as some situations and issues that apply to certain groups will not to others. As a result, no one satisfactory theory exists (Hutson et al. 2009, p. 18). This may be due to the diverse types of terrorist activity around the world being affected or influenced by a variety of issues and events that triggers their cause. On the danger radicalization poses to security of its member states, the EU states radicalization should be

> ... viewed as a complex interaction of factors that does not necessarily lead to violence. Since the process can evolve in many different directions, including non-violent ones, radicals can engage in non-violent behaviour without terrorist intent yet still be considered radical. As such, although not every radical becomes a terrorist, every terrorist has gone through a radicalization process (OT Institute for Safety, Security and Crisis Management 2008, p. 5).

Recognizing the importance of the radicalization process, under a prevention of terrorism strategy, the EU listed among their key priorities the development of a common approach to spot and tackle problem behavior (including misuses of the Internet), the promotion of good governance, democracy, education, and economic prosperity in the EU, and, the development of a media and communication strategy to explain EU policies (OT Institute for Safety, Security and Crisis management 2008, p. 61). While the underlying tone of the document is to deal with jihadist extremism, these points also apply to political motivated terrorism. As the United Kingdom and Ireland are EU member states, this policy also applies to actions by the 32CSM/IRA in the radicalization process.

Coming out of the data in this research is the concern that the current economic recession could assist the 32CSM/IRA's cause. Social and economic status has raised differing views in the radicalization process. Examining the processes of jihadist radicalization, Silke states that research has not found a clear link between poverty and deprivation along with the membership of extreme organizations. In explaining this, he says as the impoverished are less likely to vote, they are also less likely to become engaged in terrorist organizations (Silke 2008, p. 109). Githens-Mazer challenged this and many of the empirical studies that state low income is not a cause of terrorism. He found that an attraction to jihadist violence exists where the individual suffers "difficult" social, political, and *economic* circumstances (Silke 2008, p. 7). Githens-Mazer's findings are supported by other studies, certainly in regard to jihadist-based extremism. For example, Hutson, Taylor, and Page's study found in poverty stricken areas that economic deprivation was a factor in the radicalization process (Hutson et al. 2009, p. 21). One agreed finding in most of the empirical studies into radicalization is that where a multi-situational position exists, it results in a more politically, socially, and economically deprived landscape making it more fertile to allow a process of radicalization into extremism (Vertigans 2011, pp. 77–87). Such a landscape Silke recognizes as existing during the Troubles. He says the multi-situational position of economic deprivation, educational underperformance, and insufficient representation were important radicalization factors that increased support for Sinn Fein or PIRA from the Catholic community (Silke 2008, p. 112). During the Troubles, the radicalized individuals who joined PIRA were not deranged or insane. Punch's study on the Troubles found that while individual members came from a degree deprivation, they were, "resilient, relaxed and stable" (Punch 2012, p. 49).

These themes will be examined in more detail as the actions of the 32CSM/IRA regarding recruitment and how they get the message of their cause across to a global population are analyzed.

Research Method Used

Sample Size

Apart from examining official data and reports of actions by Irish dissident groups, I visited Northern Ireland to interview republican, nationalist, and unionist politicians (14), police officers (6), and members of the Catholic community (24). The latter group included informers I handled as a detective during the Troubles, community leaders and members of republican organizations. In England, I also interviewed members of Liverpool's Catholic community that were members of republican flute bands (RFBs). All consented to be interviewed and have it tape recorded. The interviews took place from June 2012 to October 2012, with most interviews lasting 1 h.

Research Strategy

In assessing the IRA's capability to mount a sustained campaign that could escalate to Britain, the research was founded on four areas:

1. How active the IRA are
2. The link between the IRA and 32CSM
3. Support for the IRA and the 32CSM in Northern Ireland
4. Support for the IRA and the 32CSM in Britain

Semi-Structured Interview

The primary data used in this research emanate from semi-structured interviews. Prior to the interviews, I forwarded onto them a set of topic areas the interview would cover (Bayerns and Roberson 2011, p. 110). The aim of this was to focus the subjects' minds (Baker 1998, p. 136) on the subject matter so as to minimize disruption from the interviewer by having to keep the subject discussing solely the topic areas (Baker 1998, p. 137). The research findings were verified with data from other sources. This is important as Mythen and Walklate state that data from politicians and the police can be discursively shaped because of their involvement in risk definition (Mythen and Walklate 2006, p. 389). By passing on the terrorist scare, it can be used as a form of disciplinary control as politicians and police officers harden domestic security objectives (Mythen and Walklate 2006, p. 330). To minimize any discrediting of the responses, in particular those from the politicians and the police, it was important the validity and reliability of the data were maintained by comparing them with data found in other empirical studies in the topic area.

Ethical Issues

The 2003 Social Research Association's (SRA) Ethical Guidelines states that social researchers must strive to be aware of the intrusive potential of their work. As Liebling and Stanko point out, "Ethical research is typically defined as that which safeguards the rights and feelings of those who are being researched" (Liebling and Stanko 2001, p. 424). The Community Relations Council recently reported a deep-rooted sectarian divide still exists in the Province.* As a result of this divide, Irish dissident groups have a propensity toward violence against those who speak out or who are vehemently opposed to them. It was paramount that whatever was disclosed was dealt with sensitively. This is the reason why the subjects interviewed remained anonymous. A second reason the ethical guidelines were relevant was, in handling data it was important nothing was revealed that could hinder or obstruct any on-going or recent operations or investigations into the 32CSM/IRA.

Background to the Research

RIRA

RIRA broke away from PIRA at the time PIRA and Sinn Fein agreed to the GFA in 1998. RIRA announced their opposition to the GFA with the 1999 Omagh bombing killing 29, making it the worst single atrocity during the Troubles (Vaughan and Kilcommins 2008, p. 80). Feeling betrayed by PIRA and Sinn Fein for agreeing to the GFA, RIRA viewed the Agreement as a concession to an imperial state's (Britain) continuance to govern their country, supported by forces of occupation. Resigning from PIRA's executive, Mickey McKevitt formed a breakaway dissident group, Oglaigh na hEireann (Harden 2000, p. 311). Oglaigh na hEireann became known as the RIRA following the staging of illegal roadblocks in 1998 where its members told motorists, "We're from the IRA. The Real IRA" (Harden 2000, p. 312).

The Northern Ireland Peace Monitoring Report identifies three republican groups, the Real IRA, Oglaigh na hEireann and Continuity IRA (Nolan 2012, pp. 44–45). This builds on MacDonald's 2008 report on the threat to security in Northern Ireland identifying the same three groups who at that time had no unified command (MacDonald 2008). My research found the numbers of activists in these groups is higher than those reported by MacDonald. Following a relative lull since 2001, there has been an incremental rise in RIRA attacks in Northern Ireland commencing with the killing of two British Army soldiers at Massereene barracks in March 2009 in County Antrim,[†] up to bomb attacks in Derry 2012[‡] and the targeting PSNI officers

---

* BBC News Sectarian division still deeply rooted in NI. http://www.bbc.co.uk/news/uk-northern-ireland-18076231 [accessed May 15, 2012].

† BBC News Two Soldiers killed at Massereene Barracks March 2009. http://news.bbc.co.uk/1/hi/northern_ireland/7930837.stm [accessed May 15, 2012].

‡ BBC News Real IRA bomb attacks January 2012. http://www.bbc.co.uk/news/uk-northern-ireland-16645604 [accessed May 15, 2012].

in early 2013.* This has included killing PSNI officers† and bombing the UK's national security service MI5's Belfast headquarters.‡ As the frequency of attacks have increased, at the inception of the research it was important to assess if the RIRA supported by the 32CSM could achieve their main target, to carry out a bombing campaign in England (Nolan 2012, p. 45).

"New" IRA

At the end of July 2012, a statement was released by RIRA saying they had joined RAAD and other former prominent PIRA members to form a unified structure under a single leadership thereby increasing their capacity and capability to maintain a sustained campaign of violence.§ Based predominantly in Counties Derry and Tyrone, in essence RAAD was a vigilante group comprising of former PIRA members who carried out punishment beatings on individuals suspected to be involved in drug dealing or drug abuse and anti-social behavior in predominantly Catholic neighborhoods.¶ They operated in a similar fashion to PIRA during the Troubles, where to tighten their grip within their community they regularly gave punishment beatings to those they found stealing, involved in drugs or anti-social behavior, which often took the form of shooting the victim's kneecaps (Taylor 1997, p. 287). This was a natural alliance between both groups as both groups RIRA and RAAD's cause is similar.

Since this alliance, the IRA has carried out a number of attacks. In November 2012, a Maghaberry prison officer, David Black, was killed while on his way to work by the IRA.** In November and December 2012, the PSNI found a number of horizontal mortar bombs across various locations in Northern Ireland that are capable of piercing the armor of police vehicles. This resulted in an off-duty PSNI officer finding an explosive device under his car on New Year's Eve in 2012.†† In January 2013, an off-duty PSNI officer saw people at the back of his house causing the officer to draw his firearm and shoot at them. The following day, a pipe bomb was found at the officer's

* BBC News Omagh police bomb incident was attempted murder. http://www.bbc.co.uk/news/uk-northern-ireland-21247711 [accessed January 30, 2013].
† BBC News PSNI Officer, Ronan Kerr killed by Real IRA April 2011. http://www.bbc.co.uk/news/uk-northern-ireland-13001728 [accessed May 15, 2012].
‡ BBC News Bombing of MI5 HQ at Palace Barracks, Belfast April 2011. http://www.bbc.co.uk/news/uk-northern-ireland-13223966 [accessed May 15, 2012].
§ BBC News "What does dissident republican 'merger' statement mean?" http://www.bbc.co.uk/news/uk-northern-ireland-19014981 [accessed September 6, 2012].
¶ BBC News "Who are the dissident republicans?" http://www.bbc.co.uk/news/uk-northern-ireland-10732264 [accessed September 6, 2012].
** BBC News Prison officer murdered on NI motorway. http://www.bbc.co.uk/news/uk-20164563 [accessed January 7, 2013].
†† BBC News Dissident republicans "remain determined to kill." http://www.bbc.co.uk/news/uk-20164563 [accessed January 7, 2013].

house.* Such incidents have increased from occurring occasionally to what now appears to be a weekly basis. These actions in such a short period demonstrate the IRA's mission to kill military personnel, police and prison officers, and those who work for the British is no idle threat.

32CSM

Parallel to the rise of the IRA is the growth of its political wing, the 32CSM. Formed in December 1997 (Taylor 1997, p. 328) the 32CSM is not a political party per se and has not stood any candidates in Northern Ireland Assembly or local elections. Having a political wing associated to a terror group is not unique to Ireland. In Spain, Euskadi ta Askatasuma (Eta) had a political wing, Batasuna, a coalition of leftist national parties containing Eta members among its ranks (Whittaker 2012, pp. 120–122). The political wings take on the role of legal representatives of terror groups to be an avenue of dialogue (Tuman 2010, p. 20). During the Troubles Sinn Fein was PIRA's political wing. In 1983, it was led by Gerry Adams who would neither condone nor condemn PIRA's violent actions (O'Callaghan 1998, pp. 172–173). Addressing Sinn Fein's *ard fheis* (party conference) in 1989, Gerry Adams said:

> The history of Ireland and of British colonial involvement throughout the world is that the British government rarely listens to the force of argument. It understands only the argument of force. This is one of the reasons why armed struggle is a fact of life and death in the six counties (Adams 1989).

From 1983 to the GFA, Sinn Fein adopted a strategy referred to as the "armalite and the ballot box" where they pursued an electoral strategy alongside PIRA's armed struggle (Taylor 1997, pp. 281–282). This strategy was successful bringing about the GFA and Sinn Fein is currently the largest political party from the Catholic community in the Northern Ireland Assembly.

In building a political position from which to defend the nationalist community, rather than having just an armed struggle, Sinn Fein advocated putting more energy into a political solution (Adams 1996, p. 263). While some observers may spot anomalies in Sinn Fein's assertion, Sinn Fein always claimed they were separate from PIRA (Adams 2003, pp. 46–47). At the time of its inception, the 32CSM leadership attempted to adopt a similar position. Its leader, Bernadette Sands-McKevitt, claimed the 32CSM was a single issue group with no connection to any paramilitary wing. At the time this assertion was made, two members of the 32CSM Executive were charged with

---

* BBC News Omagh Bomb incidents: assembly member believes police officer was targeted. http://www.bbc.co.uk/news/uk-northern-ireland-21247711 [accessed January 30, 2013].

possession of materials for bomb making (Taylor 1997, p. 358). Three months later members of the 32CSM were linked to several bombings. The former Royal Ulster Constabulary (RUC) chief constable, Ronnie Flanagan, admitted intelligence reports on the 32CSM revealed its membership included a significant number of dissident elements of PIRA, concluding:

> Undoubtedly people close to the [32CSM] Committee have knowledge, expertise and experience in the terrorist field and probably have access to materials to allow that expertise and experience to be brought to bear in the carrying out of attacks. So I think people close to the [32CSM] Committee pose a very significant threat indeed (Taylor 1997, p. 358).

Whether the 32CSM pose a similar threat today, both the PSNI and An Garda Siochana officers interviewed agreed they do, with one officer saying:

> Just look at who the members are. There's Marian Price an ex-Provisional, who is in prison after holding a statement read out by a member of the Real IRA at the 32CSM's commemoration of the Easter Rising in Derry's Creggan cemetery in 2011. Then there's the Duffy's who were in the Provisionals with Colin only recently acquitted at the Massereene Barracks murder trial. I could go on with the names who are members of the 32CSM we suspect are also members of the Real IRA. There isn't even an attempt by the 32CSM to distance themselves from the IRA. The arrests of members of the Real IRA we've made over the last year are all connected to the 32CSM.

Six months after this officer was interviewed, Paul Duffy, Damien Duffy, and Shane Duffy, all members of the RIRA and 32CSM, were charged with the offenses of collection of information likely to be of use to terrorists,* conspiracy to murder and conspiring to cause an explosion.[†] This extremely close relationship between the 32CSM and the IRA shows how dangerous the 32CSM is, not only to peace in Northern Ireland, but to peace in Britain, especially England.

Radicalization Process in Ireland

Economic Deprivation

Regarding IRA activity within the nationalist communities, a community member who had connections with PIRA summed up a concern many of the politicians and community members had, saying:

---

* Section 58 Terrorism Act 2000.
† BBC News Duffy relatives on terror charges. http://www.bbc.co.uk/news/uk-northern-ireland-18128778 [accessed May 28, 2012].

[The IRA] are bigger and more influential in parts of the community than is reported in the papers or on television. I know old hands from my days in the Provisionals are in their ranks and kids who basically have no job, no future and who are bored. As these are hard line fanatics, if things get just a little worse, then God help us.

By "getting a little worse," this respondent referred to the economic recession. Republican and nationalist politicians were concerned that as the UK government's austerity measures bite deeper, this could turn disaffected young people to the dissident groups. A Social Democratic Labor Party (SDLP) politician interviewed said:

Poverty's affected many of my constituents. There's no jobs [sic], cuts in benefits and these are starting to hurt. Some of those I see in my surgery don't see this as a global problem or even an Irish problem. They're blaming the Government in Westminster for making the Irish pay the price. No matter how misinformed it is, this type of thinking only causes further disaffection and if it gets worse there's no doubt in my mind they'll turn to extreme republican groups like the 32CSM and the IRA ... in desperation as they get carried away with blaming England.

The Poverty Site's latest annual survey of hours and earning (updated in December 2010) shows Northern Ireland is not the most economically deprived area of the United Kingdom. It is on par with Scotland and the midlands area of England, with Wales, North East England, and Yorkshire being worse off (The Poverty Site 2011). There is a similar pattern regarding income inequalities and total weekly income (The Poverty Site 2011) showing a number of UK areas are economically worse off than Northern Ireland. One set of data does support the concern poverty is a potential recruitment tool for the 32CSM/IRA. After deducting housing costs, in Northern Ireland 26% of Catholic households are found to be below the median income compared with 16% of Protestant households (The Poverty Site 2011). The deprivation indicators show the percentage of Catholics suffering is far higher than Protestants. For example, 66% of Catholics are behind in one or more household bill compared with 33% Protestants, and 62% of Catholics are unable to heat the home compared with 31% Protestants (Nolan 2012, p. 89).

Suffering worse economic and social conditions compared with their protestant counterparts, in 1968 Catholics aired their grievances through the nonviolent Civil Rights Movement with marches and protests (Coogan 1995, pp. 60–64). From 1970 onwards, Catholics began moving their support from the Civil Rights Movement to PIRA with the watershed being Bloody Sunday in January 1972. With the state response to their grievances being violence meted out by RUC police officers on civil rights marchers, they felt they were not being listened to (O'Callaghan 1998, p. 167). Just prior to Bloody Sunday, Coogan said in the *Irish Times*:

> In the North the Catholics have said: we have had enough ... the IRA are the hard cutting edge of their grievances and, horrible though many of the deeds which have been done in the North are, the IRA continue to draw support (Coogan 1995, p. 133).

After Bloody Sunday, where the British Army's Parachute Regiment opened fire on civil rights marchers in Derry, killing 14 unarmed marchers, support for PIRA from the Catholic community increased to a point where PIRA had more potential recruits that it could cope with (Martin 2013, p. 87; English 2009, p. 70). English states this situation was not produced by violence alone, "But the cumulative experience of blood stained friction" (English 2009, p. 71). Underpinning this was Catholics suffering greater poverty compared with Protestants (Taylor 1997, pp. 38–40). This is not unique to Ireland. Kirby's study on jihadist radicalization found that after the 7/7 London Bombing, individuals who experience economic and social difficulties in their lives are ripe for radicalization (Kirby 2007, p. 416).

There are links to an individual's socioeconomic status and susceptibility to radicalization. Kirby, Hutson, Long, and Page found that socioeconomic status plays a role in determining the relationships an individual is able to build (Hutson et al. 2009, p. 21). Radicalization to violent groups is conceived in the context of local conditions and drivers that vary from case to case (Githens-Mazer 2008, p. 26). In essence, the empirical studies agree that where socioeconomic status applies to radicalization the poorer that status, the more likely the radicalization process to extremist groups occur, whereas the more prosperous democratic societies that respect the rights of their citizens are more resilient and less susceptible to political instability and radicalization. Carpenter, Levitt, and Jacobson explain this is so because "Its grievances can be peacefully expressed and mediated through democratic institutions, citizens are less apt to turn to more extreme opinions" (Carpenter et al. 2009, p. 303). Yet, regarding radicalization to 32CSM/IRA causes, an anomaly exists.

As mentioned earlier, during the Troubles, in addition to economic deprivation there were also two other factors present in the radicalization process, educational underperformance, and insufficient political representation (Silke 2008, p. 112). These last two categories do not currently exist in either the 6 northern or 26 southern counties of Ireland and can explain why the 32CSM remains on the fringes of Irish politics. Post-GFA, the traditional republican or nationalist community does have political representation where Sinn Fein is currently the largest party from that community in the

Northern Ireland Assembly, with the deputy leader of the Assembly being a Sinn Fein MLA. Education opportunities are equal among both Catholic and Protestant communities. While economic deprivation in the current economic climate applies to both communities, it is the disparity between the Catholic and Protestant communities that is a cause for concern, but should be tempered with the absence of the political representation and educational underperformance.

Radicalization through Fundraising

When the subjects were asked if the IRA has the financial capability to sustain terror attacks over a prolonged period, the police responses in particular acknowledged there had been an incremental increase in fund raising capacity by the 32CSM/IRA in the last 12 months. The politicians agreed with this. One unionist politician said:

> We worked hard for peace in Northern Ireland with both sides ceding some of their ideals to achieve peace. The problem is we never really got rid of the fringe fanatics on both sides. The IRA have the resources to raise enough to finance a terror campaign and lead us back down the slippery slope of sustained violence.

Maintaining a continuous terror campaign is expensive. In 1983, Gerry Adams estimated that for Sinn Fein and PIRA to function at the level of operations at that time cost around £2,000,000 a year (O'Callaghan 1998, p. 167). The cost to the United Kingdom of the security measures taken during the Troubles was an estimated £9.826 billion (Valino et al. 2010, p. 18). The attack on the World Trade Center and the Pentagon on the 11th September 2001 cost Al Qaeda an estimated US$300,000 (Martin 2013, p. 520). Martin identifies four main categories where funds are raised to finance terror campaigns:

1. Criminal activity
2. Personal Fortunes
3. Extortion
4. Charities and foundations (Martin 2013, p. 521)

While there is little evidence that PIRA had personal fortunes to tap into, there is evidence PIRA were involved in the other three methods to raise money to fund their activities. During the Troubles PIRA carried out bank and post office robberies in both the northern 6 and the southern 26 counties of Ireland (O'Callaghan 1998, pp. 205–207).

PIRA also used extortion to raise funds. One of their main methods of extortion was targeting wealthy Irish and non-Irish residents in all 32 Irish

counties demanding protection money to prevent them from being kidnapped (O'Callaghan 1998, pp. 166–167). This tactic has been used by other
terror groups in different conflicts. Groups like the Revolutionary Armed
Forces of Columbia (FARC) and the Filipino Abu Sayyaf have used the
threat of kidnap to raise essential funds. An important element of this tactic is to restrict the number of kidnappings, not only to heighten the fear of
being kidnapped, but when a kidnap occurs it raises the publicity of a terror group's profile (Vertigans 2011, p. 113). PIRA also raised a levy on the
Falls Taxi Association (each driver contributing £15 a week), was involved in
tax swindles and social security fraud (O'Callaghan 1998, p. 167). The most
well-known PIRA international fund-raising campaign was NORAID (Irish
Northern Aid). Founded by Martin Flannery, an IRA veteran in the United
States, NORAID raised millions of pounds sterling for PIRA to buy muni-
tions (Taylor 1997, p. 84). Other forms of PIRA fund raising were in its drink-
ing clubs, most of which were in Belfast, some raising more than £150,000 a
year (Taylor 1997, p. 67).

Europol's 2012 T-Sat Report states that current IRA criminal activity
used to raise funds include robberies, fraud, extortion, and tobacco and fuel
smuggling (Europol 2012, p. 24). In September 2012, Alan Ryan, a RIRA
member (later the IRA) was killed by criminal gangs in Dublin as Ryan was
involved in extortion practices to raise funds for the 32CSM/IRA as well as
the IRA being involved in drug dealing themselves to also raise funds (BBC
2012). Prior to Ryan's murder the 32CSM/IRA were found to be involved in
drug dealing to raise funds to their cause in 2010 following the killing of a
former RIRA member, Kieran Doherty. Doherty was cultivating a cannabis
farm in a house in County Donegal on behalf of RIRA, and after a police
raid on the house and it coming to light RIRA were running a cannabis farm
they murdered Doherty on the border of Counties Donegal and Derry (BBC
2010).

All respondents said the IRA was involved in criminal activity to raise
funds. A typical response from one of the republican politicians interviewed was:

> You can't discount that robberies are still one way of raising funds but more
> subtle criminal activity is also being used. I know from the area I represent
> that social security fraud and Internet fraud is common. Added to that are
> extortion and protection rackets they run be it through pseudo security com-
> panies or plain threats to individuals or criminals involved in drug dealing
> where the IRA take a cut of their takings.

An example of this type of IRA extortion activity came out during the
trial of the murder of two drug dealers in Cornwall where two men from
Liverpool (England) were tried for the murder. During their trial, under

oath, one of the defendants admitted they were working for an Irish republican group based in Liverpool and their activities were financed by the IRA
for fund-raising purposes (Rossington 2012).[*]

If possible, future IRA action to raise funds would involve kidnapping,
the respondents in my research suggest that this would be unlikely. Several
reasons were given. From the community members interviewed one reason
was because currently 32CSM/IRA are not in a position of strength to carry
out successful kidnappings. As one of the community members said:

> The IRA mightn't have as much muscle the Provos [PIRA] had yet, but they're
> pretty powerful and that threat's increasing and kidnap's one possibility they
> could use in the future [sic].

The police officers interviewed were agreed that a main reason why
extortion through kidnapping was not a viable option for 32CSM/IRA at
the moment is because of the risk involved in kidnapping. These views were
summed up by one of the officer's responses, saying:

> To raise funds through kidnapping carries a greater risk of detection. Apart
> from the likes of Internet fraud, a more lucrative form of fund raising is tak-
> ing on the drug dealers as well as being hypocritical and dealing in drugs
> themselves.

Irish history shows the IRA in whatever form it takes to prepare for a
long war. This is seen from the Irish Republican Brotherhood from the 1860s
with their bombing campaign in London in the 1880s (Staniforth 2010, p. 79;
Vaughan and Kilcommins 2008, p. 54; Bunyan 1976, pp. 104–111) to the
Troubles themselves. In addition to finances, the ability to maintain a sustained campaign ranges from the strength of republican history and suffering to more mundane but significant momentum provided by organizational
dynamics such as training, fund raising, commemorations, and organizing
structure (English 2009, p. 74). The IRA has incorporated these dynamics
alongside their fund raising over the last couple of years. An IRA training
camp was found in Omagh, where four members were arrested for training
IRA members in small arms use.[†] To assist the maintenance of their campaign, the IRA frequently attend marches and assemblies to commemorate
Irish republican events to reinforce the history of the Irish struggle against
British imperialism, which is a powerful symbol to legitimize their fund raising from their traditional communities.

---

[*] BBC News "Cornwall shooting death men 'worked for IRA drug gang.'" http://www.bbc.
co.uk/news/uk-england-16543286 [accessed January 20, 2013].
[†] BBC News Four remanded over "terror training camp" near Omagh. http://www.bbc.
co.uk/news/uk-northern-ireland-18130609 [accessed May 28, 2012].

Radicalization: The Power of Language and Symbolism to Demonstrate Mutual Empathy

How groups like the 32CSM/IRA use language to raise the profile of their message is important (Taylor 1997, p. 291). During the Troubles, Sinn Fein referred to prisons such as Long Kesh as concentration camps (Adams 1990, p. 11) and republican prisoners as prisoners of war (Adams 1990, p. 13). The 32CSM's 2012 New Year statement refers to all republican prisoners detained at Maghaberry and Portlaoise as prisoners of war. An important 32CSM cause is the imprisonment of Marian Price. Price joined PIRA in 1970 (Dillon 1994, p. 164) and was imprisoned for the bombing of the Old Bailey courts in London in 1973 along with her sister Dolours Price* (Taylor 1997, pp. 154–155). She is currently on remand for holding a written statement at the 32CSM/IRA's Eater Rising commemoration at Creggan Cemetery for a masked RIRA member to read out in April 2011 and is facing possible charges related to the killing of the two soldiers at Massereene Barracks in 2009.[†] The 32CSM portray Price as a victim of British imperial law, referring to her imprisonment as internment. The potency of the 32CSM's message infiltrating mainstream politics is seen in the nationalist SDLP's Alban McGuiness' response to Price's imprisonment, referring to it as *internment*.[‡]

Significant in 32CSM's 2012 New Year statement is the rhetoric regarding their position over British sovereignty of Northern Ireland, referring to it as imperialism. Their main cause of supporting the IRA is in intensifying armed conflict because a political discourse for a solution continues to be out of reach, saying:

> The Real IRA are not the cause of conflict in Ireland they are a response to the conditions created by Imperialism in Ireland. The 32CSM believes that there is no room for ambiguity on the issue of resistance.[§]

Similarities to the potency of the language used by 32CSM/IRA to that used by republicans during the Troubles is seen in the language used by Sinn Fein, who also referred to the British as imperialists (Adams 1996, p. 123), and any initiative taken by the British Government in Northern Ireland was perceived as a pogrom against the Catholic community (Adams 1996, p. 119). Demonstrating mutual empathy during the annual commemoration

---

* Dolours Price died peacefully in her Dublin home in December 2012 and has become another "martyr" to the 32CSM/IRA cause. http://www.32csm.net/#!/2013/01/32csm-condolences-to-family-of-late.html [accessed January 30, 2013].

† BBC News Derry terrorist Easter rally charges dismissed. http://www.bbc.co.uk/news/uk-northern-ireland-18022527 [accessed May 24, 2012].

‡ BBC News Marian Price being interned says SDLP's Alban McGuiness. http://www.bbc.co.uk/news/uk-northern-ireland-18049635 [accessed May 16, 2012].

§ 32CSM 2012 website.

of the 1916 Easter Rising at Creggan Cemetery in Derry, the 32CSM/IRA demonstrate the lack of ambiguity on the issue of armed resistance to British sovereignty. Although referring to groups in the United States, Vertigans recognizes how items of clothing, badges, and flags used at demonstrations develop mutual empathy among terror organizations and their supporters (Vertigans 2011, p. 101). Over the last few years, the numbers of supporters or attendees at Creggan Cemetery has risen for the Easter Rising commemoration. In 2012, a 32CSM/IRA color party dressed in a black military style uniform with black berries, on which is the white Easter lily badge, carried the Irish tricolor and the flags of the four districts of Ireland to present them before the republican memorial stone. This was followed by speeches from leading members of the 32CSM. At the 2011 commemoration, the color party consisted of balaclava wearing IRA members dressed in khaki uniform. In the last few years, a member of the IRA wearing a balaclava appears from the crowd, stands next to the memorial stone and reads out a statement reiterating what the IRA stands for. In essence, it is that more attacks will be carried out on the police and army as well as those who oppose them.[*]

The Easter Rising commemorations provide a powerful theater for those with republican leanings as not only does it project mutual empathy, it is also one of the steps in a radicalization process used for recruitment (Stuttmoeller et al. 2011, p. 84). With the 32CSM/IRA using these traditional republican symbols, we see two processes at work. First what Vertigans refers to as "we-ness." Founded on networks based on friendship, camaraderie, similar backgrounds and beliefs (Vertigans 2011, p. 98), we-ness is a collective effervescence based on shared beliefs, practices, and heightened emotions providing definitions and meaning (Vertigans 2011, p. 94). The 1916 Easter Rising commemoration is an important commemoration for Irish citizens and in the Irish Republic the official commemoration outside the GPO Building in Dublin is attended by the Irish President and Taoiseach (Prime Minister).[†] Therefore, the 32CSM/IRA commemoration not only shows Irish solidarity, they can show their commemoration is not in itself subversive and neither is the color party nor are the flags displayed symbols of a proscribed organization. The gold, white, and green tricolor is the internationally recognized flag of the Irish Republic. These symbols together demonstrate the mutual empathy, not just to the 32SCSM and its supporters, but to republicans in all the 32 counties. This mutual empathy can be linked to an early stage of radicalization the 32CSM/IRA will want to achieve. Demonstrations and symbolic

[*] Ulster TV–32CSM's Easter Rising commemoration. http://www.u.tv/News/Six-held-after-RIRA-threatens-police/4dda6662-5c13-4949-b287-102c977cb25c [accessed May 30, 2012].

[†] 1916 Easter rising Commemoration Ceremony 2012. Dublin http://www.youtube.com/watch?v=c76-K_ZsNuo [accessed May 26, 2012].

resistance is one of the first steps of radicalization (Horgan 2009, p. 42) and this activity does not have to be violent (Stuttmoeller et al. 2011, p. 83). It is worth noting that demonstrations and protests account for 17.2% of the recruitment strategies deployed by violent groups like the IRA (Stuttmoeller et al. 2011, p. 92).

The final symbolic gesture demonstrating mutual empathy is the balaclava-wearing member of the IRA making a statement to the assembly. It is symbolic as the balaclava echoes PIRA's dress code, illustrating little difference between the two factions. Using the term *Oglaigh na hEireann* is also symbolic. Meaning "soldiers of Ireland," it was used by the original IRA that fought the British in 1918–1921 and is the title of the Irish Republic's Defense Forces.* Trying to show there is little difference between them and other Irish republican movements, the main difference is in their threats. Using this difference, the 32CSM/IRA is reinforcing the point whereas PIRA may have stopped fighting and decommissioned its weapons in 2005 (Whittaker 2012, p. 303), in their eyes the IRA are continuing the war against the British imperialism and traitors who work for them, including Sinn Fein. This is the self-identification stage part of the radicalization process bringing about personal awareness resulting in that person exploring the ideology of the group (Stuttmoeller 2011, p. 84).

On representativeness among the wider nationalist community and if there is mutual empathy toward the 32CSM/IRA, one of the SDLP councilors interviewed said:

> While they hold demonstrations that resonate with members of the nationalist community, they're not representative at all, but I've noticed a shift in attitude in republican voters towards Sinn Fein. While canvassing in the last elections [May 2011] on the doorstep I came across a lot of disillusioned Sinn Fein supporters. By becoming part of the British establishment in Stormont they see the Shinners [Sinn Fein] as having sold out. That's the danger with the 32CSM, should they ever stand they could take disillusioned Sinn Fein votes.

Being seen as selling out by republican voters is starting to cause alarm in Sinn Fein. One Sinn Fein MLA said:

> They think we've sold them out yet nothing can be further from the truth … Republicans now have a voice in Northern Irish politics. The 32CSM's causes are outdated. I've offered to speak to Marian Price but she refuses to see me even though I've criticised her imprisonment in the Assembly and the press, saying it's internment. I know some of the 32CSM members when they were Sinn Fein. Some are good people but they're caught in a time warp.

---

* Oglaigh na hEireann: Defence forces Ireland website. http://www.military.ie/ [accessed May 28, 2012].

This particular MLA was asked if he could understand that with Sinn Fein power sharing with the Democratic Unionist Party, coming out in support of the PSNI and working with a British Northern Ireland Minister why some republicans are disillusioned. His response was:

> I've said this before … these people are living in the past. Their efforts to turn the clock back are futile. They want to return to the days of armed struggle and the misery this will cause.

During the interview with this MLA, it was pointed out in 1986 he said that Sinn Fein was:

> … a socialist republican movement, a movement that supports the use of armed struggle in the six counties and the establishment of a socialist republic in the thirty-two counties of Ireland (English 2009, p. 88).

When asked what the difference was between this message and the message given by the 32CSM/IRA, his response was:

> At that time Sinn Fein was fighting for rights for the nationalist community … we were in a struggle with the British having to fight their violent and vicious pogrom. Republican voters should look at what we've done not at what we haven't … What I said in 1986 was in a different Ireland to what we have now.

The demonstration of mutual empathy is a powerful strand of radicalization as the Easter Rising commemoration is a powerful piece of theater, one that for the 32CSM/IRA cannot be criticized for holding in Ireland as similar commemorations are run all over the 32 Irish counties. The rhetoric used in the speeches and proclamations of the 32CSM/IRA is also powerful in demonstrating mutual empathy that is close to Sinn Fein policies. It can be difficult for some members of the traditional republican or nationalist community to differentiate between the two; the 32CSM/IRA is stealing the symbols of legitimate events, commemorating those that sacrificed their lives to establish an Irish state that promotes the values of democracy and peace. The 32CSM/IRA are replacing those values with the promotion of murder, extortion, and other forms of criminality. This view was mentioned by some of the other subjects, especially from the Republican politicians and community members. A response from one of the community members encapsulates the sentiment given by the subjects on this topic:

> Being a republican party Sinn Fein still have the desire that all thirty-two counties are unified under the rule of the Dail, Dublin. The difference is how they go about it. Sinn Fein want to use the political process like a referendum. I can't say the 32CSM want to continue with the armalite and ballot box approach. As they won't stand at elections that tells me they supporting IRA violence is the only way to achieve this goal.

Radicalization via the Internet

Terror groups and their political wings need to gain support not just from the community they claim to represent but also from the global community. The use of the Internet and social media is an important source for garnering sympathy or at least a measure of understanding of their cause to a wider audience. If terrorist groups use the Internet they can successfully achieve in spreading their message (Martin 2013, p. 45). Focused on jihadist terrorism, Sageman's work in this area demonstrates how the Internet is a useful, inexpensive tool to send a group's message quickly to potentially billions of people (Sageman 2008, Chapter 7). This returns us to Vertigans' "we-ness," as the Internet provides terror groups with new opportunities to gain potential recruits (Vertigans 2011, p. 80). With the Internet producing 27.9% and 38.7% of its membership for both violent and nonviolent groups, respectively, the Internet is an important recruitment tool (Stuttmoeller 2011, p. 92).

The 32CSM/IRA has used e-sources as a platform to create a dialogue with a global audience that has triggered Irish mainstream political responses. Now a Dail Techta Dala (TD),* Gerry Adams is looking to help Irish dissident groups by offering to hold talks in an attempt to bring about a cessation of their violence. In response to widening their message via e-sources in May 2012, the Northern Irish Assembly Deputy Leader, Martin McGuiness, told the Sinn Fein *ard fheis* the war with the British is over and groups like the IRA's actions are pathetic and attempts to turn back the clock are futile.[†] Concerned the 32CSM/IRA message was getting through to the nationalist community, he did not dismiss the possibility of a united Ireland believing it could be brought about by peaceful means, not through an armed struggle. Extolling the peace process for allowing a national reconciliation with unionists that he saw as necessary for constitutional change, he said, "A peaceful and democratic path to a united Ireland is there" (DeBreadun 2012). Sinn Fein TD Martin Lewis called on Sinn Fein to renew its commitment to the unification of the 32 counties by campaigning to the Irish Government to commission a Green Paper on unity (Moriarty 2012). It appears the concern that disaffected republican voters turning away from Sinn Fein with the corresponding increase in support for the 32CSM regarding its main aims of a united Ireland has forced Sinn Fein to respond.

To date, the 32CSM/IRA are some way off emulating PIRA and Sinn Feinduring the Troubles in achieving widespread mutual empathy with nationalist communities and a global audience. One example is seen where social media were used to oppose the IRA and the impact the 32CSM hoped

---

* Irish Member of Parliament.
† BBC News "Gerry Adams says dissident republican talks offer is genuine." http://www.bbc.co.uk/news/uk-northern-ireland-18225884 [accessed May 28, 2012].

to achieve following the IRA's killing of a Catholic PSNI officer in 2011. With a Facebook protest group "not in my name" set up, it showed the IRA they did not achieve their aim of intimidating Catholics from joining the PSNI or even getting the message across they are fighting in their cause. A week after being set up, this Facebook group organized a protest resulting in thousands of people assembling on the streets of Omagh to demonstrate against the IRA's killing of the police officer, Ronan Kerr.[*]

While the IRA does not use any social media or Internet websites as these would reveal the details of its members, the 32CSM overtly spread the IRA's message through their websites and social media pages. Regionalized, but all carrying the same message, the 32CSM websites have been effective in raising international awareness of their cause. This included organizing a protest in Canada on 22nd May 2012 for the release of Marian Price[†] and seven arrested IRA suspects.[‡] A report written by USA 32CSM/IRA sympathizers refers to the imprisonment IRA suspects as internment, with the suspects being called prisoners of war.[§]

While this use of the Internet appears to have some impact, it is not replicated among the grass roots feelings of the politicians and community members who were interviewed. One of the republican politicians said:

> Apart from wanting a united Ireland free of British rule it's hard to associate with their cause. I know that's what many of my constituents think. Political movements like 32CSM or Irish Socialist Republican Party or Republican Sinn Fein are a minor voice in Ireland. They don't stand at elections as they wouldn't get many votes because the majority's not interested in their message.

Recruitment to Causes via Social Media

Another advantage in using social media such as Facebook, Twitter, and YouTube is it offers terror groups opportunities to demystify their opponents to bring in new supporters and prevent current supporters from drifting away by focusing them into more constructive pursuits (Seib 2012, p. 69). Through the 32CSM's use of social media we see Sageman's radicalization

---

[*] BBC News "Omagh remembers murdered policeman at rally." http://www.bbc.co.uk/news/uk-13029286 [accessed April 4, 2012].

[†] BBC News Derry terrorist Easter rally charges dismissed. http://www.bbc.co.uk/news/uk-northern-ireland-18022527 [accessed May 24, 2012].

[‡] John Bonnar "Toronto group demands immediate release of Irish republican political prisoner" *Online newsletter for activists.* http://rabble.ca/blogs/bloggers/johnbon/2012/05/toronto-group-demands-immediate-release-irish-republican-political-pr [accessed May 28, 2012].

[§] 32CSM Derry website–The Irish Republican Immersion Experience—Perspective from America. http://www.derry32csm.com/#!/2012/05/irish-republican-immersion-experience.html [accessed May 24, 2012].

model operating. Radicalization is not a specified linear process for him. He states there are four prongs to radicalization:

1. Moral outrage.
2. Interpretation.
3. Resonance with personal experience.
4. Mobilization through networks that interact with each other (Sageman 2008, pp. 57–62).

The 32CSM's Free Marion Price Facebook page,* set up to create a moral outrage, has 3519 supporters.† Although not a large support compared with other Facebook protest pages, it was successful in mobilizing more than 1000 protesters gathering in Belfast on the May 27, 2012, to raise wider public support for the Free Marian Price campaign. Regardless of the high numbers this rally attracted, it was not reported in the UK mainstream news media, including Ulster TV and BBC news Northern Ireland. This includes the print media where the UK newspapers, including the Northern Ireland-based *Belfast Telegraph* failed to report on the event. Coverage of the rally can only be found on Internet sites linked to the 32CSM.‡ On the same weekend of the 32CSM's rally, the Marian Price cause did result in increasing more pressure on Sinn Fein with one of their MLA's, Raymond McCartney, calling for the release of Price at their *ard fheis* (Moriarty 2012).

Marian Price's imprisonment has not totally evaded the UK media. In January 2012, Eamonn McCann reported in *The Guardian* on Price's imprisonment, referring to it as a "scandal." McCann commented that Price is not being held for any crime other than the belief the United Kingdom would be better off without her, interpreting her imprisonment as internment (McCann 2012). A reason why this has evaded mainstream UK media could be linked to what Tuman found. Examining media reporting on terrorist-related activity, he states that key to what was reported lay with the media's public relations experts and media consultants who help decide what is and what is not covered (Tuman 2010, p. 166).

The 32CSM-related Facebook page with the most supporters is the Long Kesh Facebook group§ having more than 4910 supporters. It has already

* 32CSM Tyrone website. http://www.facebook.com/search/results.php?q=32+County+Sovere ignty+movement+Tyrone&init=quick&tas=0.5166589089280618#!/FreeMarianPriceNOW [accessed May 28, 2012].
† http://www.facebook.com/author.davidlowe#!/FreeMarianPriceNOW?fref=ts [accessed January 30, 2013].
‡ 32CSM Tyrone website. http://www.facebook.com/search/results.php?q=32+County+Sovere ignty+movement+Tyrone&init=quick&tas=0.5166589089280618#!/FreeMarianPriceNOW [accessed May 28, 2012].
§ 32CSM Tyrone website. http://www.facebook.com/search/results.php?q=32+County+ Sovereignty+movement+Tyrone&init=quick&tas=0.5166589089280618#!/profile. php?id=100002091740429 [accessed January 30, 2013].

posted on its wall pictures and support for the Duffy brothers (referred to above), who they refer to as the "Duffy 3." Once more, we see a moral outrage mobilizing support. Very soon after their arrest, details of a meeting in the Cock Inn, Euston Station in London were posted on the Long Kesh page, accompanied by an arrangement for fly posting in London to raise awareness of the Duffy brothers' imprisonment.

Another social media source used to good effect by both the 32CSM/IRA in the radicalization process is YouTube. A 32CSM recruitment video, posted on the June 1, 2011, attracted 2119 views,[*] with an earlier video, posted on the June 14, 2008, *The 32CSM—who we are* attracting 11,452 views. A video posted on YouTube raising awareness and support for Marian Price posted in December 2011 has attracted 2457 views.[†] The Real IRA has also been active in posting video clips on YouTube. One posted in November 2007 showing Real IRA operatives on maneuvers accompanied by a soundtrack of Irish rebel songs has been successful in attracting more than 167,329 views.[‡]

While using social media to promote their causes, the 32CSM/IRA are quick to denounce those who also use social media with a critical voice to their actions. In June 2011, a Scottish journalist, David Leggat, reported that the 32CSM was linked to RIRA. In a strongly worded response, the 32CSM repudiated Leggat's claim saying they only support Republican Prisoners of War (the likes of Marian Price, a convicted PIRA bomber, and Campbell, a convicted RIRA terrorist).[§] In January 2013, I too have been a victim of the 32CSM's vitriol containing veiled threats to those like me who deign to associate them with the IRA. Based on the research covered in this chapter, a lecture I delivered to my students was filmed and placed on YouTube. Following a prolonged email exchange with the 32CSM that questioned my findings, as there was no initial backing down from me to retract my findings, the 32CSM threatened to protest outside my university and accost students attending the degree program I run. As a result, the lecture was removed from YouTube accompanied by a polite email from me to the 32CSM. I can understand my university's fears of having 32SCSM/IRA members protesting as they are a violent and threatening group who can easily intimidate those they confront.[¶]

---

[*] YouTube "Join the 32 County Sovereignty Movement." http://www.youtube.com/watch?v=ss3j0wTyMs4 [accessed January 30, 2013].

[†] YouTube "Free Marian Price." http://www.youtube.com/watch?v=MUqivvLi6Ws [accessed January 30, 2013].

[‡] YouTube "Oglaigh na hEireann Real Irish Republican Army News Report." http://www.youtube.com/watch?v=7zx-bafKRtA&feature=related [accessed January 30, 2013].

[§] 32CSM website. http://32csmscot.blogspot.co.uk/2011/06/leggat-claims-repudiated.html#comment-form [accessed January 30, 2013].

[¶] http://www.youtube.com/watch?v=ur96ylrWphI [accessed January 30, 2013] this clip shows how violent this group can get when protesting.

E-media demonstrate the potential for increasing support and recruits to their cause. Having Facebook "likes" or "friends" or the views on YouTube in thousands demonstrates how successful the fringe political voice of the 32CSM has been in attracting to their causes via social media. No doubt a situation will develop that Seib points out above that through the use of this relatively cheap and accessible media new followers will be recruited to their cause as the 32CSM/IRA attempt to demystify their message. The potential danger is it can attract British supporters who may want to go further than declaring their support for the 32CSM/IRA by clicking the Facebook "like" button to physically helping IRA operatives on the British mainland to carry out bombing attacks.

Loyalist Paramilitary Violence: Fueling and Legitimizing the Fire of 32CSM/IRA's Cause?

An issue that came out of the research was how 32CSM/IRA activity could provoke a violent response from loyalist paramilitary groups like the Ulster Volunteer Force (UVF). The impact the rise of UVF activity can have on peace in Northern Ireland should not be underestimated. Many accounts claim the Troubles was ignited by loyalist politicking that encouraged UVF activity (Bamford 2005, p. 582). Coogan records the activities of the Reverend Ian Paisley (former leader of the Democratic Unionist Party and the Northern Ireland Assembly) in stirring up the loyalist community at the start of the Troubles. Coogan states this led to loyalist demonstrations and attacks on Catholics resulting in the killing of prominent republicans (1999, pp. 47–50; Taylor 1997, p. 30). As one of the police officers interviewed said:

> One knock on effect of the rise in republican dissident activity is an escala-tion of loyalist dissident group activity. As well as an increase in UVF activity, there's been the emergence of a small group, the Real Ulster Volunteer Force, which we believe to be a response by loyalists to the emergence of the Real IRA. Our intelligence states they came about following discontent with the lack of reaction by the UVF to the killing of the officers in Lurgan and Omagh along with the bombings carried out by the Real IRA over the last few years.

Should loyalist dissident groups carry out attacks against republicans it would play into the hands of the 32CSM/IRA. Nolan states, in 2007 the UVF pursued a nonmilitarized role, but by 2010 the UVF returned to vio-lence including murders of Catholics (Nolan 2012, p. 46). The UVF's politi-cal wing, the Progressive Unionist Party, failed in gaining electoral success in the 2011 elections, leading to a resurgence of UVF street activity and a significant increase in gable end street murals depicting UVF men (Nolan 2012, p. 47). Any increase in UVF violence will result in Real IRA's equally violent responses under the cause of protecting the nationalist community. During the Troubles, PIRA saw themselves as the main protectors of the Catholic community, which included violence against loyalist groups (Bamford 2005, p. 583). The 32CSM/IRA is likely to adopt a similar strategy.

The community members interviewed were concerned about UVF violence. A former PIRA operative who now works for Sinn Fein said:

> It's unlikely in XXXX the UVF will do anything, but in districts in Belfast like Short Strand and areas where there's a small nationalist community like Antrim is where the damage can be done. All it'll take is a few shootings of Catholics and the IRA will claim the PSNI can't or won't protect the Catholic community because the PSNI is the RUC* in disguise. Some will fall for this bullshit, some possibly joining the IRA.

This danger has become a reality. Since December 2012, and up to the time of writing in January 2013, Loyalists organized by the UVF have held regular violent protests against Belfast City Council's decision to only fly the Union flag on certain days rather than 365 days a year, which have done up to that date.[†] In addition to injuring a number of PSNI officers in the riots that followed the demonstrations, Loyalists have attacked republican, nationalist, and Alliance Party premises, a police car with a police officer inside was petrol bombed and violence escalated in other cities and towns in Northern Ireland including the Catholic populated Short Strand area of Belfast that led to a conflict between the Loyalists and the Catholic residents of Short Strand.[‡]

In addition to an increase in Loyalist violence that has echoes of the mid-1960s, Loyalist violence against republican and nationalist targets, for the 32CSM/IRA to have greater success in getting their message across in Ireland and globally, it only takes for the economic and social conditions in Ireland to worsen or for another event where republicans suffer violence to inflame a situation. One of the republican councilors summed the current situation in Northern Ireland saying:

> You don't take a naked flame into a room full of petrol. Even if it's a match that's running low it can be enough to ignite it. That's the north of Ireland at the moment.

---

[*] The Royal Ulster Constabulary.
[†] BBC News Timeline of attacks in Northern Ireland political parties. http://www.bbc.co.uk/news/uk-northern-ireland-20720406 [accessed January 29, 2013].
[‡] BBC News Police car petrol bombed near MP Naomi Long's office. http://www.bbc.co.uk/news/uk-northern-ireland-20676315 [accessed January 29, 2013].

Conclusion: Radicalizing Individuals in Britain Support to the 32CSM/IRA Cause

Background to British Support for Irish Republican Groups

Throughout the various Irish wars, Irish dissident groups have received support from Irish communities living in Britain. During the Irish war of Independence, when the founder of the IRA, Michael Collins, arrived in England in 1919, he received support from the Liverpool Irish Republican volunteer unit (Mackay 1996, p. 136). In early 1939, the IRA sent an ultimatum to the British Prime Minister demanding the British leave Northern Ireland. Not receiving a reply, the IRA bombed English cities with assistance from Liverpool Irish republican supporters (Hewitt 2008, pp. 14–15). During the Troubles, O'Callaghan, an active PIRA operative, describes the help he received from Liverpool Irish republican sympathizers when he was sent over to England on a bombing mission (O'Callaghan 1998, pp. 149–151). During the Troubles Liverpool was never attacked by PIRA's English Department. The main reason for this is the large ethnic Irish Catholic community in the city, a number of whom had sympathies for Sinn Fein and PIRA. In fact, it went beyond sympathy to actual physical support for PIRA's English Department and PIRA cells' attacks in England. In Liverpool and the wider Merseyside area, PIRA had a number of safe-houses, quartermasters, and activists who were Liverpool born Catholics descended from Irish immigrants as far back as the 1840s (Dillon 1994, pp. 283–286). O'Callaghan is adamant that one reason for PIRA's English Department success was the support they got from British-based sympathizers, those based in Liverpool in particular (O'Callaghan 1998, pp. 112–115).

The 32CSM/IRA and British RFBs

The influence of the 32CSM/IRA's use of social media and websites present in Britain can be seen in the *32CSM England, Alba & Cymru* website.[*] Its 2013 New Year message reinforces the opposition to British rule in Northern Ireland.[†] This is seen in the website's links regarding support for Marian Price[‡] and the IRA. This includes a web page dedicated to the recently killed IRA member Alan Ryan, where the video link has been removed.[§]

---

[*] http://gaughanstaggcumann.blogspot.co.uk/?view=magazine#!/ [accessed January 30, 2013].

[†] http://gaughanstaggcumann.blogspot.co.uk/?view=magazine#!/2012/12/32-county-sovereignty-movement-new-year.html [accessed January 30, 2013].

[‡] http://gaughanstaggcumann.blogspot.co.uk/?view=magazine#!/2012/12/wherever-there-is-conflict-women-must.html [accessed January 30, 2013].

[§] http://gaughanstaggcumann.blogspot.co.uk/?view=magazine#!/2012/11/ballad-of-alan-ryan.html [accessed January 30, 2013] and "The Ballad of Alan Ryan" http://www.youtube.com/watch?v=Bs-YkfXdtCo [accessed January 30, 2013].

Nowhere near on the scale of Northern Ireland, sectarianism is present in Liverpool and can be traced from the 1840s when Liverpool's Catholic Irish émigrés built a community in the north of the city around Scotland Road and Everton with the subsequent support for the Orange order from the Protestant community. There is strong support for the RFBs, the largest being the Liverpool Irish Patriots RFB). A spokesperson for the band was interviewed who said:

> We don't support the 32CSM or the Real IRA. We support Sinn Fein and never had any connection with the Provo's ... While celebrating Irishness and Irish music, we're a socialist movement supporting the working class here in Liverpool and in Ireland ... In Liverpool it's the likes of the James Larkin Republican Flue Band that supports the 32CSM. We have no connections with them.

Founded in 1996, the James Larkin RFB openly support the 32CSM and the Real IRA. No one from the James Larkin RFB agreed to be interviewed for this research. Taking their name from a Liverpool-born socialist of Irish Catholic parents, Larkin was active in organizing the trade union movement in Liverpool and Ireland. By introducing industrial dispute into mainstream Irish history, Larkin created a positive view of enabling strike tactics into a moral struggle linked to the armed struggle for Irish independence (O'Connor 2002, p. 102). Showing no alignment to the trade union movement, in the James Larkin RFB's Liverpool address is a reaffirmation of the 32CSM/IRA's politics and actions:

> The Anglo Irish conflict is not resolved. The British Parliament and Crown still maintains a sovereign claim over part of Ireland. Acts of insurgency against this claim continue. Irish POW's remain incarcerated. No amount of emotional rhetoric or flawed references to democracy can mask these blatant truths ... The starting point for democracy in Ireland is an immediate British withdrawal. The terms for a just peace must begin with self-determination for the Irish people. Every generation has asserted these rights. Acts of the British Parliament can have no place in the sovereign affairs of the Irish people ... The claims of British neutrality toward the Six Counties are a sham.

The James Larkin RFB has joined the West of Scotland Band Alliance, which is also aligned to the 32CSM. One of the largest members of the alliance is the Glasgow based Parkhead RFB, also aligned to the 32CSM, who march in commemoration parades organized by the 32CSM. As one of the Liverpool community members interviewed said:

> It's groups like that [James Larkin and Parkhead RFB] that can turn young heads on the mainland to get caught up in the romance of fighting for a unified thirty-two county Ireland. They're surrounded by the tricolor, hear heroic

tales of the Troubles, learn the rebel songs and so on. It only needs a few of them to help the IRA in England. Just one successful attack will tell Britain and the world the IRA is back … There are times I look at some individuals and know they'd assist an IRA mission.

The James Larkin RFB's own website* and its Facebook page† make it very clear that the band supports the 32CSM. The James Larkin RFB Facebook page, which is kept more up to date than their website, supports the "Irish prisoners of war" like Marian Price. It also advocates the end of British rule over the six northern Irish counties and promotes the actions of IRA. This is all part of the radicalization via e-sources showing mutual empathy discussed above. The danger is that all it takes is for a few supporters based on the British Mainland to make arrangements for the IRA to bomb targets in England.

How Extortion and Murder Have Become a Romanticized 32CSM/IRA Cause

The propaganda the 32CSM/IRA produce on both sides of the Irish Sea to radicalize individuals, show how they have portrayed extortion and RIRA member Alan Ryan's murder to martyrdom to the 32CSM/IRA cause. Among the most potent case studies that demonstrate the threat the 32CSM/IRA poses is the portrayal of Ryan as a martyr. Ryan was based in Dublin and ran a security company that was involved in extortion, including violence and threats to drug gangs, to raise money for the 32CSM/IRA (shortly before his death he was admonished by the senior commanders of the IRA for pocketing some of the money for his personal use) (BBC 2012). In September 2012, after upsetting too many criminal gangs in Dublin, a hit man was hired to kill Ryan. The week after his death Ryan was given a full IRA paramilitary funeral in his hometown district of Donaghmede that included a volley of shots fired over his coffin by an IRA color party. The murder and particularly the funeral caused outrage among Irish citizens and politicians (Irish Independent 2012). The report of the murder and the funeral of Alan Ryan in the *Irish Independent* sums up the outrage encapsulating the points found and raised in my research. Describing Ryan as an "extortionist and a killer," the *Irish Independent* is critical of how the 32CSM/IRA choreographed Ryan's funeral as they turned him into a martyr for republicanism who was fighting drug barons on behalf of the downtrodden working class, with the report saying that 32CSM/IRA now have their equivalent of Bobby

---

* http://jimlarkinrfb.blogspot.co.uk/ [accessed January 30, 2013].
† http://www.facebook.com/people/James-Larkin-Rfb/100001306623263 [accessed January 30, 2013].

Sands. The report exposes how the 32CSM tutored its members as to what to say publically to media outlets and how certain members of the 32CSM/IRA were selected as spokespersons.* The article sums up the events and the dangerous consequences of such 32CSM/IRA actions and portrayal of events such as those surrounding Ryan, saying:

> The Special Branch has already established an intricate network or informants in the RIRA camp and the gang responsible ... Meanwhile the RIRA will not seek vengeance for a while. The godfathers will manage it as carefully as they did the funeral. They see this as an opportunity to make inroads into hard-pressed communities and recruit a new generation of gullible kids (Irish Independent 2012).

This is why the 32CSM/IRA cannot be taken lightly. Europol's 2012 TE-SAT report states as well as building support, the IRA has had continued success in the deployment of Improvised Explosive Devices, which is a cause for concern as it shows that in the past 2 years the IRA has improved their engineering and technical capabilities (Europol 2012, p. 24). Not only does the 32CSM/IRA pose a security threat to Northern Ireland, they are increasing their capability to pose a security threat in England. Regardless of which terrorist group it is radicalizing individuals to their cause, one key issue this study shows is that terror groups' use of e-sources cannot be underestimated. Such use can reach millions of people that can influence thousands to have sympathy for their cause and in turn can result in hundreds becoming active. Even if those who become active are less than a hundred, it is still a cause for concern for the state and counterterrorism officers as they try to ascertain within a community individuals who pose a threat to security. IRA activity is a classic example of the communal terrorism model (Martin 2013, p. 11). Not often commanding international headlines, but being deeply rooted in cultural memories of conflict against the British and Irish Protestants, communal terrorism is vicious and intractable (Martin 2013, pp. 119–120). As 3284 people died during the Troubles (Martin 2013, p. 121), to avoid a repeat of this it is paramount that a political and policing effort against the 32CSM/IRA is a top priority. As PIRA's Brighton bomber, Brian Magee, who targeted the British Prime Minister in 1984 poignantly stated, the security services have to be lucky all the time, while the IRA only have to be lucky once (Taylor 1997, p. 253).

---

* To support this hear the interview by Ireland's Ocean Radio with Paul Stewart of the 32CSM on Ryan And his funeral. http://www.youtube.com/watch?v=FwZkvLuBk-g [accessed January 30, 2013].

Recruiting Informants in Counterterrorism Investigations
Is Loss of Integrity a Noble Cause?

7

Introduction

This chapter focuses solely on the recruitment of informants who are detained in police custody following their arrest. All the subjects of the research were informants I handled when I was a detective in counterterrorism and forms part of wider research covering the recruitment and handling of informants in counterterrorism investigations. Due to the research revealing various tactics used by police officers, this work focuses solely on the recruitment of informants who are suspects in police detention. Twenty-one subjects were interviewed in the research and they were informants who are no longer active. Using semi-structured interviews, they were asked questions regarding their methods of recruitment, why they decided to inform and how they felt during the recruitment process. These topic areas produced some illuminating data regarding the recruitment of informants.

In my data, inducements offered to potential informants by police officers questioned their integrity, a behavior that could amount to noble cause corruption. Noble cause corruption is a relatively new concept (Cooper 2012, p. 170) and this article examines what is meant by the term. Emanating from Cooper's work, the examination of my data is placed within a new theoretical framework designed to measure noble cause corruption, role theory (Cooper 2012, pp. 172–173). As seen from Klockers' work (1976) through to Porter and Warrender (2009), noble cause corruption has not evaded previous academic research. For Cooper, the problem is previous theoretical frameworks underpinning earlier research that is too wide to provide an understanding as to how and why noble cause corruption occurs and is applied by the police (Cooper 2012, pp. 171–172). This is not meant to devalue previous work on noble cause corruption as such work has been invaluable in building a knowledge base from which to provide a degree of understanding of noble cause corruption.

Role theory allows for a measurement of the power relationship between the police officer and the detainee during recruitment. The analysis discusses the "ends justifying the means" aspect of noble cause corruption leading to an important component of role theory, role conflict. Role conflict occurs because police officers are not only protectors of society, but also as agents of the state. As Cooper points out:

> As agents of the state, police are bound by procedural law to protect the civil rights of individuals. Line officers may see those guidelines as retarding their capacity to fulfill their role as protectors of the innocent (Cooper 2012, p. 170).

Role theory is applicable to counterterrorism investigations as compared with their police counterparts, counterterrorism detectives are under greater pressure to prevent rather than detect criminal-based activity. Why prevention is important can be explained within the political treatment of terrorism. Being an issue of national security it puts pressure on the police to align their efforts to government policy, a policy which emphasizes prevention to enable a state to show it can protect its citizens (Deflam 2009, p. 23). To compound this pressure, as terrorists see themselves as legitimate combatants in a political struggle where death of their victims is not perceived as murder but casualties of war, counterterrorism officers face a more committed suspect to their cause compared with their peers (Martin 2011, p. 14). From this perspective, a sliding scale of noble cause corruption is considered as practices are examined from a utilitarian perspective based on the level of coercion applied by the police.

Noble Cause Corruption

While economic police corruption (police misconduct for personal gain) may be declining, noble cause corruption is increasing (Cooper 2012, p. 169). Saying that individual officers care too much about protecting the wider community (Cooper 2012, p. 171), Cooper claims the heart of noble cause corruption lays in the role of the police safeguarding the innocent from evil (Cooper 2012, p. 173). In relation to my research, one evil that officers faced was the potential loss of innocent lives and an even greater number of severely injured casualties from just one terrorist attack. In justifying the use of noble cause corruption in counterterrorism investigations, Yoo states even if from time to time national security agencies are seen as bordering on the infringement of human rights, the state keeping them safe is what most citizens want (Yoo 2010, pp. 347–350). Here lays the nub of the issue: On one hand, police officers have to be seen as upholding the law equitably, protecting its moral foundations, while on the other hand there are occasions where the law or procedures are seen as fettering police actions. To protect the public, the police break the rules arguing the needs justify the means (Punch and Gilmour 2010, p. 10).

The genesis of noble cause corruption in policing can be traced to Klockers (1976) and Muir (1977). Basing the term from Clint Eastwood's popular detective *Dirty Harry* films, Klockers terms noble cause corruption as the "Dirty Harry Problem" where the police use "dirty means" to achieve legitimate ends (Klockers 1976, p. 121). Muir built on this theme stating that police officers have to develop two virtues, an intellectual virtue and a moral virtue. Elucidating the difference between the two, Muir states the intellectual virtue is where police officers grasp the nature of human suffering, with the moral virtue being where police officers have to resolve the contradiction of achieving just ends with coercive means (Muir 1977, pp. 3–4). Key to understanding the difference between these two virtues is the relationship between "means" and "ends" in policing (Miller 1999, p. 12). Caiden found that any form of corruption "… is offensive to any notion of public guardianship on which the edifice of democracy is built" (Caiden 1997, p. 2). Here is the caveat when justifying the utilitarian aspect of "noble": Being part of the public guardianship in a democratic society, the police can be seen as behaving outside the law. Under noble cause corruption this is more likely to be accepted within police ranks and wider society (Cooper 2012, p. 176) whereas economic police corruption is an anathema both outside and inside the police service (Westmarland 2005, p. 152; Porter and Warrender 2009, p. 94; Miller 1999, p. 12).

Research into police corruption has broken down economic police corruption into different categories of severity (Porter and Warrender 2009, p. 80; Westmarland 2005, pp. 148–149). There should also be different categories within noble cause corruption with a sliding scale of severity based on the use of coercion ranging from extreme violence used on a suspect at one end to a lesser forms of coercion such as obtaining information that may save lives and be accepted more approvingly by society. Crank et al.'s empirical study of noble cause corruption found it manifested in a number of police activities ranging from using deception to get suspects to reveal their guilt, providing false information to reporters and enticing potential informant wrong doing (Crank et al. 2007, pp. 105–106). The most severe and coercive category of noble cause corruption is "street justice," where unreasonable force is used against suspects (Westmarland 2005, p. 151). Street justice derives from police officers seeing themselves as protectors of society (Cooper 2012, p. 170) where the officers see their role as street cleansers (Crank and Caldero 2000, p. 35). This behavior led to Klockers labeling noble cause corruption as the "Dirty Harry Syndrome" (also used by Westmarland 2005, p. 162; Punch and Gilmour 2010, p. 10). Using the analogy to popular police dramas is useful in providing an instant pictorial understanding of why some police officers resort to this behavior. For example, in the United Kingdom, characters like DCI Gene Hunt in BBC television's *Life on Mars* and *Ashes to Ashes* are not only popular, but portray these characters' noble cause corruption in such a way viewers empathize with the respective officer's actions and integrity.

Noble cause corruption is more pervasive in police actions than simply adopting a street cleansing approach; it can cover all aspects of police discretion (Westmarland 2005, p. 151). Aligned to noble cause corruption is that law either assists policing or can be a barrier to it. Miller argues that noble cause corruption need not exist as criminal law processes should be sufficient and followed by police officers to the letter, saying:

> The moral rights enshrined in criminal law are those regarded as fundamental by the wider society. They constitute the basic moral norms [and rights] of the society (Miller 1999, p. 13).

If the moral goal of policing is the protection of citizens' rights, then police application of the law should provide sufficient safeguards without police officers resorting to noble cause corruption. The problem, as Cooper points out, is police officers are not simply protectors, they are also agents of the state and as such are bound by procedural law to protect civil rights of individuals (Cooper 2012, p. 170). This leads to a role conflict where police officers compliance with the law makes compliance as protector more difficult. The UK recently witnessed police officers circumventing a suspect's rights to have legal representation when being interviewed by the police.[*] Police officers interviewing suspects in their homes prior to taking them into custody was seen as immoral and the UK government amended the Police and Criminal Evidence Act's (PACE) Codes of Practice to now allow suspects to consult with a lawyer when attending a police station "or other location" such as a suspect's home.[†] As the presence of a lawyer can lead to suspects minimizing their responses to police questions, PACE was seen by the officers as a legal barrier to gaining admissions of guilt (Sanders et al. 2010, pp. 293–304). This can be understood by applying role theory. In essence, Cooper states noble cause corruption is an outcome of this role conflict, saying:

> ... the more strongly these two roles are simultaneously communicated and perceived by the police officer, the more likely they are to experience role conflict and hence behave according to noble cause corruption (Cooper 2012, p. 176).

Police officers enter the workforce with a desire to do good, an aspiration that guides their daily activity, but, as Cooper states, when confronted with procedural barrier (which can be a statutory obligation), "... some officers, compelled by their unquestionably good end, may cross a legal line" (Cooper 2012, p. 174). This can come about as corruption evolves due to group behavior rooted within established police practices (Porter and Warrender 2009,

---

[*] Section 58 Police and Criminal Evidence Act 1984.
[†] Police and Criminal Evidence Act Codes of Practice Code C, paragraph 3.21.

p. 81) and once "means justifying the end" principles are applied, most dubious actions can be justified in police cultural terms by the potential outcome (Westmarland 2005, p. 162). Role theory assists in analyzing my data from the informants as it can measure

1. The conflict that existed for the officers.
2. The scale of severity of coercion applied within noble cause corruption.
3. If the recruitment process would be an anathema or likely to be accepted by the wider society.
4. The integrity of the officers recruiting the informants.

Police Recruitment of Informants

Compared with other policing activities, there is little empirical work examining the police use of informants and what there is focuses mainly in nonterrorist investigations (Dunningham and Norris 1996; Innes 2000; Norris and Dunningham 2000; Rosenfeld et al. 2003; Miller 2011; Jones-Brown and Shane 2011). When compared with other areas of policing, Billingsley et al. explain the relative dearth of empirical studies into the police use of informants, saying:

> … the police have been reluctant to discuss the informer system, leaving it an un-researched area. Their reluctance is understandable, not least because protecting the informer's identity must be the foremost consideration. There is also the risk of having the police officer's own methods exposed and subjected to public scrutiny, and the accompanying risk of being shown to have compromised the informer, or behave in a way which invites criticism (Billingsley 2001, p. 5).

All the studies carried out on informants have led to a number of assertions, most surrounding corruption in the recruitment of informants. It is understandable why such assertions are made. Current informant studies reveal that most law-abiding citizens have no connection or contact with criminal activity. As a result, policing agencies have to use criminals to penetrate criminal circles to gain an intimate working knowledge of those they are targeting. One concern in using criminals is their commission of crimes while acting as informants (Colvin 1998, p. 38; Clark 2001, p. 38). This has courted controversy as informant handling by police officers carries a risk. That risk has been identified as a lack of integrity on the part of the police officers (Williamson and Bagshaw 2001, p. 50).

During the Irish Troubles, English Special Branch departments mainly recruited informants who were already active in terrorist cells (O'Callaghan 1998; Bamford 2005, p. 591) rather than placing agents into certain positions within terrorist organizations (McGartland 1997; Bamford 2005, p. 591; Hewitt 2010, p. 64), which was predominantly used by the RUC's Special Branch (Bamford 2005, p. 592). By the mid-80s, the RUC and British Army Intelligence ran joint operations handling informants with agents placed inside terrorist organizations (Taylor 1997, p. 288). Like any terrorist group or criminal gang, having informants placed inside their organization was one of the biggest dangers the Provisional IRA (PIRA) faced (Taylor 1997, p. 287), which, as Hewitt found, informants caused not only panic, but disillusion between PIRA members (Hewitt 2010, p. 124).

The traditional way of recruiting informants is with persons who are in police detention following their arrest or with every offender police officers meet. This method of informant recruitment has changed little over the years (South 2000, p. 69; Gill 2000, p. 187). From her research Turcotte also makes the point the police must ensure that relationships built up with informants are power-imbalanced in their favor (Turcotte 2008, p. 296). In 1976, the UK's Special Branch recruited the "paid-in-kind" informant who had been arrested and recruited during their suspect interview by the officers as officers had some form of hold over the informant including the threat of bringing charges for some minor offenses (Bunyan 1976, pp. 137–138). This method of informant recruitment has been criticized as being held in police custody is characterized by enforced dependency, frustration, isolation, and fear hence why it is not surprising that those detained in police custody are more likely to succumb to propositions to provide information (Dunninghan and Norris 1998, p. 21). This has been a global method of informant recruitment. In the Australia's New South Wales state's Independent Commission Against Corruption's 1993 discussion paper on police informants, while it mentions how police officers were encouraged to cultivate informants, it says there has been little guidance in applying the most appropriate ways of recruiting them (Independent Commission Against Corruption 1993, p. 20). Citing New South Wales detective training material, it says that every person arrested is a potential informant and they should be cultivated accordingly, adding:

> Never miss an opportunity to stop and speak to criminals … Always treat their womenfolk and families with the utmost respect and courtesy, particularly when searching their homes … conduct your interrogation in a proper manner. Then if you feel he is a potential informant be friendly towards him, try and oblige him with any small favor he may request … If he requests a packet of cigarettes, do so at your own expense. He may supply you with the correct identity of some person responsible for committing a crime and your small outlay will be repaid tenfold (Independent Commission Against Corruption 1993, p. 21).

While the language in this guidance indicates the social values of the day that may not be appropriate today, the message regarding recruitment still has not changed in today's policing environment.

Where a person under arrest in police detention is made an offer by the police of bail as an alternative to being remanded in custody, this choice is one of very restricted autonomy with an adverse consequence in the event of noncooperation. For Harfield, such an approach by the police is inherently "coercive in character" (Harfield 2012, p. 91). In such circumstances, how such offers are made is important as guidance from the independent prosecuting agency, such as the Crown Prosecution service in the United Kingdom and the District Attorney in the United States, should be sought. Inducements that cannot be realized should not be made to encourage persons to become informants, especially to those being recruited when detained in police custody.

Research Method

Research Subjects Interviewed and Sample Size

The 21 subjects who are no longer active informants were traced and consented to be interviewed. Nine were informants I handled between 1988 and 1993, during the Irish Troubles, and 12 were informants I handled in jihadist-based terror investigations between 1999 and 2007. Of this sample, 13 were recruited following their arrest. For this chapter, it is the data from the 13 subjects recruited following their arrest that have been examined.

Having only a few subjects, it can be argued there is a lack of representation of informants used in counterterrorism. Snell and Tombs addressed a similar issue when examining bereaved families from deaths in the workplace. Regarding the representativeness of their data they stated:

> Given both the nature of the research topic, which required a sensitive, personal, semi-structured interview type approach, and the problems of gaining access to the research population, we would argue that *any* data generated in this context should be treated as invaluable—and, that there is much to learn from it [original emphasis] (Snell and Tombs 2011, p. 212).

Rosenfeld et al.'s research into street informants only had a sample of 20 subjects and they felt this number was sufficiently comprehensive to encompass the diversity of views found among the population of street criminals (Rosenfeld et al. 2003, p. 293). Accepting this research cannot be a definitive panacea on the recruitment of informants in counterterrorism, the data obtained remains invaluable.

Research Method Used

Semi-structured interviews were used to obtain the data. A qualitative research method, the subject is interviewed on topic areas without being

interrupted (Bryman 2012, pp. 471–472). Only at the conclusion of the interviews would questions be put to clarify or expand on issues the subjects
raised (Bayerns and Roberson 2011, p. 112). Informing the interviewee of the
topic areas covered in the interview is important as it focuses the subject's
responses (Bayerns and Roberson 2011, p. 113). The interviews were tape
recorded along with handwritten notes recording times and topic areas covered by the interviewee. This was useful in the data analysis making it easier
to go straight to the subject area in the recordings.

While no set questions were used, the subjects were asked to talk about
the following topics:

1. How they were recruited
2. What methods were used by the officers to recruit them
3. Why they decided to become informants
4. How they felt during the process

As they had informed on terrorist cells, for their personal safety it was
important the subjects remained anonymous.

Turning Suspects into Informants

The police practice of "turning" (Turcotte 2008, p. 294) or "flipping" (Miller
2011, p. 212) suspects into informants following arrest is an area that has
courted academic and media controversy. Innes research found police policy documentation encouraged the recruitment of informants, reminding
officers that every person they dealt with, particularly offenders, should be
viewed as potential informants (2000, p. 367). He found a range of tactics
were used by officers to recruit informants "… according to the officer's
assessments of the individual concerned and what they believed would be the
most effective approach" (Innes 2000, pp. 367–368). These tactics and methods of informant recruitment are universal. For example, in Canada Turcotte
found police documentation encouraging officers to view every offender as a
potential informant. Interestingly, she found in the documentation the methods recommended to encourage offenders to inform was not to be through
physical coercion but through the use of mind games (Turcotte 2008, p. 296).
All the empirical work on informants found a variation of mind games were
used by the police to recruit informants ranging from

1. Exaggerating the offenses a suspect may be charged with
2. Threatening the potential of long prison sentences the suspect may
   receive should they be charged and tried for the offenses they were
   arrested for

3. Where there is more than one suspect, officers would imply to one that the other suspect is talking and about to make a deal
4. The financial implications of informing that can range from the officers saying how much an informant can earn, or, if the suspect does not inform, what they could lose if convicted. (Innes 2000, p. 368; Norris and Dunningham 2000, p. 387; Rosenfeld et al. 2003, p. 392; Leiberman 2007, p. 3; Turcotte 2008, p. 296; Jones-Brown and Shane 2011, p. 53; Miller 2011, p. 212)

Although Turcotte says none of the officers in her research sample used physical coercion, there appears to be little argument that the above tactics are coercive as they are aimed at intimidating a suspect in police custody.

Similar tactics were used with the subjects recruited following arrest in my research. At the time of his arrest, one of the Irish informants was living in England running a courier business. Friends from his days in Ireland paid him a visit and requested his business deliver packages for them. Due to his knowledge of their background, he suspected they were PIRA members. Fearing retribution from PIRA he agreed to do what they wanted. This brought him into the investigation and as a result he was arrested. The officers made him an offer that should he become an informant, the charges he was facing would be reviewed and potentially dropped. On his recruitment he said:

> I suspected AAAA and BBBB were IRA ... I was so scared of them I never asked what was in the packages, I knew it'd be IRA business, but I was frightened of them. When [the police] told me how I could help stop the IRA, I realised that losing my family and business was too much to give up. That's why I agreed to pass on information (Irish 1).

Two of the remaining five Irish informants recruited following their arrest were also born in Ireland and having had similar approaches from PIRA members to assist their activity, gave similar responses regarding their recruitment. The other two Irish informants recruited following arrest were British-born PIRA sympathizers. One had been fund-raising for PIRA and the other allowed her house to be used as a PIRA safe house. On his recruitment the fund-raiser said:

> It was after I'd been interrogated [by the police] I was sat in my cell when I realised how serious it was. The police said if I grassed on the IRA the charges I was facing could be dropped, if not the trial would be in the papers and I'd lose my job. I was young and I'd got caught up with XXX. I'd attend [names location], practice with the band, go marching and I enjoyed singing the rebel songs. Looking back it was stupid of me and when you're young, you don't appreciate the consequences (Irish 7).

The informant who allowed her house to be used by PIRA was English-born with Irish relatives. She allowed some of her extended Irish family and their friends to stay at her house. Initially, she thought it was innocent enough, but over time the visits became more frequent and the activities of her guests made her suspect some of her visitors were members of PIRA carrying out or planning attacks in the British mainland. She said:

> There were times I wanted to tell the police of my suspicions but I knew what the IRA did to those that grassed on them … When the police told me what [names individuals] did I felt sick knowing that by letting them stay at my house I'd helped this happen … When they said I could inform I had to think about it. What do you do? I didn't like what the IRA did, but [names individuals] were family. As I wasn't charged I kept a record of who stayed at my house and passed it on (Irish 4).

One of the jihadist informants was arrested and interviewed by police in relation to a minor offense under the UK's Terrorism Act 2000 (possessing a document of a kind likely to be useful to a person committing or preparing acts of terrorism).* Being an IT expert, this informant was duped by two targets from a jihadist terror group. He downloaded material from extremist jihadist websites. In these downloads, CTU officers suspected coded messages were being conveyed to operatives from a central source. During the suspect interview, it was becoming clear the suspect had no real idea of the consequences of his actions and an offer was made to him to become an informant. In the offer, he was told his case would be reviewed by the relevant agencies as there was a potential that he would be released on grounds of insufficient evidence to charge. It was put to him that should he agree to be an informant, this may help the charges being dropped. On his recruitment he said:

> Being young it was exciting at the time being an e-warrior … I didn't think using social media sites and having discussions on various websites [the police] would take it that seriously. Having my family home searched and being interviewed, reality kicked in big time … I was no jihadist … When I thought about the consequences, if I got charged the rest of my life would be fucked up. I had no choice but to help [the police] (Jihadist 1).

Most of the jihadist informants were arrested for possession of documents of a kind likely to be useful to a person committing or preparing acts of terrorism and they gave similar responses. One of the jihadist informants was arrested under different circumstances who on his recruitment said:

> It still comes as a shock to me that XXXX and YYYY were preparing terrorist attacks. You think you know someone well and then you find out what they've

---

* Section 58(1) Terrorism Act 2000.

really been up to. We'd been friends as kids and they never did anything that make you suspect they were AAAA. At the time I was arrested I was still in shock and I think I'd have done anything just to get out of the police station. Being arrested was close to ruining my life as I'd have been sacked at work, my family would most probably have disowned me ... When I agreed to inform my head was all over the place. I was vulnerable ... I thought the only way I could prove my innocence was to help the police (Jihadist 4).

Role Conflict and Police Officer Integrity

An important element in determining if noble cause corruption exists during informant recruitment is the coercive power used by the officers. Procedural guidelines are aimed at curtailing the use of coercion by police officers. In Canada, regulations were recently introduced through directives and guidelines regulating the use of informants (Turcotte 2008, p. 293). While no such statutory regulations appear to have been introduced in the United States (Jones-Brown and Shane 2011; Miller 2011, p. 204), the use of informants in the United Kingdom was governed by the Home Office Guidelines that have been replaced by Regulation of Investigatory Powers Act 2000 (RIPA). Under RIPA, informants are managed by a handler and a controller,[*] with the controller, who must be a rank higher that the handler,[†] having oversight of the use of the informant by the handler. Also in RIPA, risk assessments must be carried out prior to, during, and after their use with the assessment including the likely consequences should it become known a person was an informant.[‡]

What is not present in either RIPA or RIPA's associated Codes of Practice are guidelines as to how informants are recruited. The only reference to recruitment in both documents is where a person volunteers information. A volunteer uses free choice and, by definition, free choice must not involve *any* form of coercion. In the mind games cited above and my data, the action of the police officers is not procedurally illegal. As Miller points out, in relation to noble cause corruption police officers need to develop a habit to bend rules in the service of the greater moral good of justice (Miller 1999, p. 17). Looking at my data along with the previous studies' findings, the recruitment of informants' centers on police officer integrity and integrity implies honesty. Exaggerating, dropping, or lowering subsequent charges in return for agreeing to become an informant can be seen as morally wrong. With the example of the informant who was told if they did not inform their

---

[*] Section 29(5) RIPA and RIPA Codes of Practice, paragraph 6.7.
[†] Section 29(d)(a) and (b) RIPA and RIPA Codes of Practice, paragraph 6.9.
[‡] RIPA Codes of Practice, paragraph 6.4.

subsequent trial would "be in the papers" is not corruption per se, but is coercion as advantage is taken of suspects in custody who are vulnerable to noble cause corruption. The same could be said regarding the recruitment of the informant who said he was vulnerable and would do anything to prove his innocence. Not knowing what is happening to them makes it an intimidating environment for suspects as they are relatively powerless in police custody (Sanders and Young 2012, p. 851).

When confronted with procedural barriers, if officers feel compelled to cross a line to achieve the "good end" and compromise their integrity then we have a role conflict under role theory (Cooper 2012, p. 174). Applying role theory, we are seeing police officers adopting the utilitarian principle where the means justify the ends to achieve the greater good. Counterterrorism investigating officers are under pressure to protect the wider community by preventing terrorist acts and the subsequent devastation such acts cause. This explains why in this role conflict officers feel compelled to resort to noble cause corruption (Cooper 2012, p. 176). In understanding the context of this dilemma faced by officers, it is the utilitarian notion where the good of the individual suspect is balanced against good of the community to be protected from harm (Williamson and Bagshaw 2001, p. 56). In such cases, the public are prepared to turn a blind eye to a minor infringement of police integrity (Williamson and Bagshaw 2001, p. 59).

It is important to determine where the loss of integrity in these circumstances fits with the role conflict. Cooper identified four role conflicts:

1. Intrasender—conflicts between police officers and supervisor, where the supervisor expects the officer to behave by the book
2. Intersender—where supervisors expect officers to get the bad guys off the street but public prosecutor demands the police stay within the boundaries of the law
3. Interrole—where there is a lack of connection with family and associates outside the police service who are sensitive to constitutional requisites and question police actions, but the police are aware of public perception of their dual roles as protectors and agents of the state
4. Person role conflict—the relationship between the means and the end where the police see themselves as protectors to protect the innocent and offer constitutional protections to the bad guy (Cooper 2012, p. 175)

The two role conflicts that would apply to the officers' loss of integrity when taking advantage of a suspect's vulnerability are the Intersender and person-role conflicts.

Regarding the Intersender role conflict, investigations in organized and serious crime investigations (including terrorism) involve a number of stakeholders including the public prosecutor such as the District Attorney in the United States, the Examining Magistrate in most European countries (where even the EU is proposing the creation of Public Prosecutor's Office) (Peers 2011, pp. 855–860) and the Crown Prosecution Service in the United Kingdom (Sanders et al. 2010, pp. 423–428). Public prosecutors expect the police to operate within the respective state's rules of evidence to ensure any evidence obtained remains admissible. This can cause conflict within other categories of noble cause corruption, certainly at the more severe scale of categories of noble cause corruption. If any form of dishonesty, including loss of police officer integrity when recruiting a suspect as an informant, has the potential for the public prosecutor to withdraw any future evidence obtained from that informant for fear of questionable police tactics being revealed that may cause a court to render that evidence as inadmissible.

The most applicable category of role conflict in the recruitment of informants is the person role conflict. In my data when the offer to inform was made to them the subjects raised their feeling of powerlessness and vulnerability while detained at the police station. While no overt coercion was used, such as physical violence, mind games were used as the police officers exploited that vulnerability. This can amount to a loss of integrity as when the officers give the suspect a stark choice to become an informant and have their potential charges dropped or refuse to cooperate and they will be charged. In doing so, the officer can be accused of exploiting the detained person's vulnerability. Although this police behavior may be at a lower end of the scale of severity, nevertheless, it is a category of noble cause corruption because when presented with role conflict the police have a higher likelihood of engaging in noble cause corruption (Cooper 2012, p. 176). Cooper says this test implies two important components:

1. The police subjectively feel they are to be protectors, which the officers in my research felt seeing themselves protecting the wider public from acts of terrorism.
2. The police subjectively feel they are expected to act as agents of the state, in which the officers in my research paradoxically may feel that technically they have not infringed any rules or laws when recruiting the informants who were under arrest, but will be aware of the loss of integrity as they take advantage of the suspect's vulnerability (Cooper 2012, p. 176).

Cooper adds that

One may also posit and test that the more strongly these two roles are simultaneously communicated and perceived by the police officer, the more likely they are to experience role conflict and hence behave according to noble cause corruption (Cooper 2012, p. 176).

Conclusion

Within the wider study of police corruption, when examining noble cause corruption one can see differing categories of police behavior that ranges from very severe to less severe forms of coercion. This range should cover a variety of police officer behavior from the severest use of coercion, such as excessive violence, tampering with evidence down to loss of officer integrity. In relation to my research, it was not in breaking any law or procedural rules where the loss of integrity occurred, it was in the use of mind games on vulnerable suspects in police custody.

Cooper's role theory was a useful theoretical framework to provide an understanding of the circumstances and occasions when noble cause corruption occurs. The role conflict aspect of the theory, where officers see themselves as protectors and state agents, provides an insight into how pervasive noble cause corruption is in policing. Applying role theory demonstrates there should be different categories of noble cause corruption and not to see it solely in light of Klocker's "Dirty Harry Problem," where excessive violence is used on suspects to protect society from criminality. Role theory allows us to consider less severe but more subtle forms of categories of noble cause corruption carried out by police officers on the basis they are protecting society. The less severe categories of noble cause corruption could receive legitimacy from the wider public as they condone police action, such as recruiting informants, as the police seek to obtain high-quality intelligence to prevent acts of terrorism.

What also comes out when applying role theory to my data is that officers are not so much bending procedural rules (as the only rules present are departmental police policies encouraging recruitment suspects as informants) but how officers balance the utilitarian notion of the needs of the wider society outweighing the needs of the individual suspect regarding what they could be charged with. This challenges the integrity of police officers recruiting informants, an integrity issue that can have society's approval. Cooper warns that even though in such circumstances, noble as that cost is, the public legitimacy could result in the police introducing other less noble forms of corruption (Cooper 2012, p. 177). In conclusion, this assertion may be questionable as the stakes in preventing harm coming to members of society from terrorist attacks is paramount. This is one of the occasions in police work when the ends do justify the means and for the majority of counter-terrorism officers this may be the limit they go to in noble cause corruption.

Handling Informants
8

Introduction

Once recruited, officers have to handle informants and this takes them into an environment that is a potential ethical minefield. In part, this is due to the fact that most informants are still active in terrorist or criminal activity. The officer handling the informant will know this and the question is to what level can the informant be permitted to continue with their activity? The informant cannot suddenly disassociate themselves from their circles and stop their practices as they may point the finger of suspicion from their associates that the person is an informant.

This can be dangerous to that individual. This chapter examines the law and policy relating to handling informants, focusing mainly on the United Kingdom, Australia, and the United States. As we have seen in other areas, there are inconsistencies between how the respective states' govern the handling of informants. The UK's handling is governed by legislation whereas in Australia it is a policy. In the United States, there is a policy that federal agencies must follow but this is not the case with all the policing agencies in the United States, where some states and counties have no policy at all. This leads onto an examination of the ethical issues in handling informants where a case study of how informants were handled during the 1968–1997 Irish Troubles illustrates the problems that occur when the handling becomes unethical. The chapter concludes by discussing the evidence of informants in criminal trials where again we see a disparity between the states as to how that is carried out.

Law or Policy in Handling Informants?

When examining the process of how police officers handle informants, there is no consistency in protocols and procedures between nation states. Some like the United Kingdom have mandatory statutory guidelines that must be followed, while other nation states vary between mandatory or recommended policy guidelines, with some have no guidance at all. In some nation states, the format of guidelines can change as seen in the United Kingdom where prior to the police use of informants being governed by the RIPA and its accompanying Codes of Practice. Like most other states the use of informants was governed by a policy document under the former Home Office

Guidelines. This section will examine the impact of legislation and policy in the police handling of informants.

UK's Regulation of Investigatory Powers Act

In essence, RIPA tightened up the procedures governing the recruitment and use of informants that RIPA refers to as Covert Human Intelligence Sources.[*] RIPA was introduced to replace the Home Office policy. This came about as a result of decisions by the ECtHR in cases like *Khan v UK*.[†] The facts of *Khan* were concerned with the use of covert surveillance by the police. Khan claimed the surveillance was illegal as the authority granted to the police was under a policy guidance not an act prescribed by law. The ECtHR held a Home Office policy document is not an act prescribed by law (a statute) which is required under the limitations given in article 8 European Convention on Human Rights (right to privacy) for the state to interfere with this right. As a result, RIPA significantly changed the law governing the police use of surveillance in the United Kingdom. RIPA defines an informant as one who covertly establishes or maintains a personal or other relationship with a target (person or organization) to obtain information or gain access to another person to gain information to be passed on to the state agencies.[‡] Another key change on informant handling is the accompanying Codes of Practice that provides guidance to the police in applying RIPA when handling informants. While a breach of the Codes of Practice will not always amount to unlawful action by a police officer, such a breach is likely to result in any information obtained by an informant during an investigation that could be used as evidence in a criminal trial being rendered inadmissible. One significant change in RIPA and the act's accompanying Codes of Practice is that informants are managed by a handler[§] and a controller.[¶] The controller has to be a rank above that of the handler and their role is to maintain a general oversight in the use of the informant by the handler.[**] Under RIPA, a risk assessment is carried out prior to, during, and at the end of the use of the informant regarding the tasking they are asked to do and the likely consequences should it become known that the person was an informant.[††]

---

[*] Section 26(1)(c) RIPA.
[†] (2000) 8 EHRC 310.
[‡] Section 26(8) RIPA.
[§] Section 29(5)(a) RIPA and paragraph 6.7 Codes of Practice: Covert Human Intelligence Sources.
[¶] Section 29(5)(b) RIPA and paragraph 6.9 Codes of Practice: Covert Human Intelligence Sources.
[**] Paragraph 6.8 Codes of Practice: Covert Human Intelligence Sources.
[††] Paragraph 6.14 Codes of Practice: Covert Human Intelligence Sources.

Under the previous Home Office guidelines risk assessments were carried out, but recording how they were managed was not as rigorous as RIPA. Under RIPA, the handler must continually report to the controller.* These reports include informing the controller when and where any meetings or contact will be made with the informant, the conduct of the informant, and the safety and welfare of the informant.† Under RIPA, it is not acceptable for the handler to meet the informant on their own without the knowledge of their supervisor or line manager acting as a controller and RIPA encourages the handler to be accompanied by a colleague during any meetings with the informant. This is to provide corroboration that the handler was acting ethically with the informant.

Policies on the Use of Informants in Other States

Australia

Concerned with corruption undermining the use of informants, in criminal investigations Australian state governments have considered introducing policies regarding the use of informants. In 1993, the New South Wales' Independent Commission Against Corruption put forward recommendations regarding the recruitment and handling of informants which included the following:

1. When recruiting informants an assessment is made of the potential informants through an evaluation of the information likely to be supplied and the characteristics of the individual.
2. A preregistration assessment stage of the informant be introduced that includes consideration of the informant's motives or suspected motives, informants' personality/psychological makeup, drug use, police's previous experiences with the informant, anticipated dangers, or potential problems in the handling of this informant and the nature or quality of the information the informant is likely to pass on.
3. Police officers be trained in the handling of informants, police officers instructed regarding the consequences in developing informant relationships, and introducing procedures in managing pole officer or informant relationships.
4. Introduce mechanisms of accountability that involves notifying supervisors of meetings with informants, completing an informant

---

* Section 29(5)(b) RIPA.
† Paragraph 6.15 Codes of Practice: Covert Human Intelligence Sources.

contract or informant information report, involve police supervisors in the handling of informants and employ informant case officers (Independent Commission Against Corruption 1993, pp. 81–83).

Many of these recommendations echo concerns in the recruitment and handling of informants around the world and some of these concerns were behind the introduction of the statutory provisions in the UK's RIPA legislation. While acknowledging the distinct benefits derived from the police use of informants in criminal investigations, Western Australia Parliament's Corruption and Crime Commission 2011 report into corruption risks of controlled operations and informants identified the risks informant use poses to law enforcement. As a result, the Commission recommended developing and implementing "… robust internal policies and procedures for mitigating risks inherent to its own investigations" (Western Australia Parliament Joint Standing Committee on the Corruption and crime Commission 2011, p. 28). From both the 1993 New South Wales report to the Western Australian Parliament's report, no policy on police procedure in dealing with informants has been formalized and introduced as mandatory for officers to follow.

Although no specific policy has been introduced regarding informant use by the police, New South Wales' Parliament has introduced the Law Enforcement (Controlled Operations) Act 1997 where a controlled operation is one conducted for the purpose of obtaining evidence or frustrating or arresting persons involved in criminal activity or corrupt activity.[*] A police officer can apply for the controlled operation in which the application outlines the nature of the activity that is being investigated[†] and to be authorized by a chief executive officer[‡] (that includes the Commissioner of the New South Wales Police).[§] The act is clear in what activities are not permitted in the authorization and they include

1. Inducing or encouraging another to engage in criminal activity or corrupt conduct.
2. Engaging in conduct that is likely to endanger the health or safety of another participant or the result in serious loss or damage to property.
3. Engaging in conduct that involves the commission of sexual offenses.[¶]

Under the act a civilian participant, which would include an informant, cannot be authorized to participate in a controlled operation unless the chief

---

[*] Section 3(1) Law Enforcement (Controlled Operations) Act 1997.
[†] Section 5 Law Enforcement (Controlled Operations) Act 1997.
[‡] Section 6 Law Enforcement (Controlled Operations) Act 1997.
[§] Section 3(1) Law Enforcement (Controlled Operations) Act 1997.
[¶] Section 7(1) Law Enforcement (Controlled Operations) Act 1997.

executive officer is satisfied that it is impracticable for an officer to participate in that aspect of the operation and it is also impracticable for that civilian participant to participate without having to engage in that activity.* While there would appear to be a degree of statutory control, unlike the UK's RIPA, the act itself lacks specifics in how informants should be handled. As it is not solely focused on handling informants, the act is more concerned with preventing any form of corrupt activities by police officers during criminal investigations.

United States

The 2006 Attorney General's Guidelines Regarding the Use of Confidential Informants are mandatory but only apply to US federal agencies such as the FBI or the Drug Enforcement Agency and do not apply to US police departments at state, county, or municipal level. As with other nation states, we see a similarity of conditions and protocols that officers must follow regarding the use of informants in criminal investigations. Among the factors officers have to take into account in determining if a person is suitable to become an informant includes the person's age, the person's motivation in providing information, the risk that person might adversely affect a criminal investigation, that person's reliability and truthfulness, and their prior criminal record (2006, pp. 8–9). The guidelines state that approval of using a person as a high level informant is required. High level informants are those who are part of an enterprise that has national or international sphere of activities. The activities have to be of a high significance to the federal agencies' objectives or where the informant would be involved in serious criminal activity, corruption, or violence (2006, p. 3). The approval must be granted by the Confidential Informants Review Committee (Attorney General's Guidelines 2006, p. 13).

In handling the informant, the officer must not impede or interfere with any investigation or arrest of the informant and the officer cannot reveal to the informant information relating to other investigations being conducted against the informant. Also, the agent cannot exchange gifts or receive anything of more than a nominal value from the informant, nor can the officer socialize with the informant except where it is necessary for operational reason, (2006, p. 17). The officer cannot authorize the informant to engage in any activity that constitutes a misdemeanor or a felony otherwise than the activity authorized (2006, p. 19). Due mainly to concerns over corruption and informants committing crime while being handled during investigations, we see similarities in the policy and procedure recommended in using informants where a constant theme running through a number of national states' policies is strict control, recoding of informant usage and accountability.

---

* Section 7(3) Law Enforcement (Controlled Operations) Act 1997.

In 2005, the FBI examined the Agency's application of the 2002 Guidelines and reported that out of 120 confidential informant files examined, they found Guideline deficiencies in 104 (87%) of the files examined. The deficiencies they found included failure of officer's evaluation on suitability of a person to be an informant, officers to give the informant the required instructions, to obtain a proper authority to permit an informant to engage in illegal activities, and to report unauthorized illegal activity by informants (2005, paragraph VI). Concerns over how the guidelines were being adhered to since that report was published have not abated. In August 2013, Congressman Stephen Lynch (2013) (representing the 8th District of Massachusetts) wrote to the Attorney General of the US Department of Justice requesting that the guidelines be revised to enhance the accountability and transparency in the FBI's use of informants and to protect the public against authorized and unauthorized informant crime. Congressman Lynch's concern was that in 2011, the FBI approved of 5658 instances of illegal activity by informants.* The focus of his concern was the US congressional scrutiny of and the accountability of Federal agencies, in particular the FBI's authorizing of person's becoming informants. As a result, he forwarded a Bill, the "Confidential Informant Accountability Act 2013," in the House of Representatives. If enacted, the Bill would require a report from the Federal Agencies governed by the Attorney General's Informant Guidelines revealing the total number of crimes authorized and the category of crime, the amount of drugs involved if it is a drug crime, the amount of money if the crime was a theft or robbery, and if the crime was authorized or unauthorized along with informing the state each crime took place in.

In another study on the use of informants in the state of New Jersey, Jones-Brown and Shane found that written policies regarding the use of informants existing at state, county, and municipal levels was problematic as at state level they found the use of informant policies were disjointed and spread through various documents. The county policies differ from each other and in some case that difference was substantial as written policies did not exist in the entire municipal police departments. This is contrary to the Commission on Accreditation of Law Enforcement Agencies recommendations (the accrediting body for US police agencies). They also found that among those police departments that had policies governing the use of informants, police officers were not uniformly aware of the existence of the policies and neither were they trained in them leaving what they said as "… room for intentional and unintentional violations" (Jones-Brown and Shane 2011, p. 4).

What is important, especially in police jurisdictions where there is little or no mandatory guidance in the police use of informants, is that officers

---

* The document can be retrieved from http://www.documentcloud.org/documents/742049-fbi-oia-report.html [date accessed May 27, 2014].

follow good practice that has been adopted where the procedures in using informants are more tightly controlled. This includes the following:

1. Having an officer of a higher rank of the officer handling the informant to act as a controller that the controller can oversee proceedings and guide and support the handling officer.
2. A risk assessment is carried out that assesses the risk to the informant of the activity they will be expected to carry out, the potential risk of unacceptable criminal activity the informant may carry out and, based on the informants behavior and connections, the potential traps that could lead to corrupt activity between the informants and officers handling them. This risk assessment should be ongoing and carried out by the controlling officer while the informant is deployed.
3. That all contact with the informant and what information they pass on to the handling officer is recorded and retained.
4. The handling officer is accompanied by a second officer to corroborate what is said during contact with the informant.

All these points are related to protecting not just the informant while active in the field, but also the officer handling that informant as the next section will explain why such concern exists in using informants in criminal investigations.

Ethical Issues in Handling Informants

Motives and Incentives to Inform

Previous studies on informants show that incentives and motivation to inform range from receiving money for information passed on, revenge, taking out criminal competition to looking for a favor from the police officer handling them (Billingsley et al. 2001, p. 86). Rosenfeld et al. state the incentives and motivation to inform include fear (of the police), greed, revenge, altruism, a reduced jail term and even includes the need for self-esteem (Rosenfeld et al. 2003, p. 292). Miller's research found that the financial motivation of being paid to inform was the second most common motivation of his sample to inform, with the first most common being the reduction in sentence or reduced charges (Miller 2011, pp. 211–221).

Miller identified four classifications of motivation for a person to become an informant:

1. Those who are "hammered" into compliance—these are individuals who have been "turned" or "flipped" following their arrest and have only agreed to inform due to legal duress, that duress being how the

pending criminal charge will be dealt with should the person agree to comply with the officer's request to inform.

2. The bounty-hunter—motivated by money this category of informant works on a contingency fee basis that can be problematic as the fee may only be payable on the successful prosecution of the individual they are informing on. The potential danger with this category of motivation as in their desire for money, the informant could potentially fabricate situations, give false testimony, or even plant evidence to ensure a successful prosecution.

3. Vengeful informants—this is a motivation driven by revenge and could be other criminals desirous of removing competition, a "friend" responding to rumors or scorned partners in intimate relationships with the individual they are informing on.

4. Police Buff—they tend to be eccentric citizens and police fans who may have on occasion useful information, but who generally have poor quality information as they are not usually submerged in criminal subcultures (Miller 2011, pp. 214–215).

From the studies carried out, the motivation factor that appears to cause most concern is the informant looking for a favor from the police officer. The criminal informant could be looking for the handler to turn a blind eye to their criminality while passing on information regarding the "bigger criminal" (Colvin 1998, p. 41). This relationship between the handler and the informant has been regarded as a form of police corruption with the potential to lead to payments being made by immune criminals to police officers (Sanders et al. 2010, p. 328). For Clark, this is the reversal of the informant and handler roles where criminals actively recruit potentially corrupt officers, protecting the officer from exposure and rewards the officer with money commensurate with the value of intelligence provided (Clark 2001, p. 41). As Leiberman states, it is an imperative that officers understand the motivation of informants who come forward with information (Leiberman 2007, p. 2).

Informants: The Necessary Evil

It is recognized by both practitioners and academics that the use of informants is central and an important source of information in criminal investigations (Bean and Billingsley 2001, p. 25; Leiberman 2007, p. 1; Miller 2011, p. 203). The most effective informant is the person who has contact or involvement with criminals and Greer's categorization of informants is still a useful model to use. Greer states the categories of informant hinge on two variables, one being the relationship between informants and the people on whom they inform, with the second being the relationship with the police to whom the informant supplies their information (Greer 1995, p. 510). He categorizes informants as

1. "Casual observer"—who is an "outsider" with no connection or relationship with the person about whom they pass information onto. The casual observer has simply observed an incident and bring it to the attention of the police.
2. "One-off accomplice witness"—who is an "insider" as they have some connection or relationship with the person on whom they are passing information onto the police. They are passing information onto the police out of contrition or because of the possibility of lesser charges.
3. "Supergrass"—who not only has a connection or relationship with the person on whom they are passing information onto the police, but they also have inside information on the crimes being planned or committed by that person and the supergrass informs the police of multiple incidents of crime (Greer 1995, pp. 11–12).

While witnesses who have no connection with criminals that pass on information are of course important sources in criminal investigations, it is the supergrass category of informants who are necessary to cultivate if police officers want to gain that valuable inside information. As Leiberman points out, the use of confidential informants can lead investigators to their key targets as they are insiders who have the ability to go places and speak with people who are inaccessible to the police (Leiberman 2007, p. 1). To gather such information entails police officers not only having to handle informants who are criminals because they are more effective in gathering the required information (Miller 2011, p. 206), but the officers also have to handle criminal's morals and values that potentially leads to police corruption and unethical behavior (Crous 2009, p. 117).

Ethical Handling of Informants

In handling informants, there is a degree of deception by the officer where the deception includes placing a person who is an informant into a criminal circle to gain the criminal target's trust. As this deception is concerned with being effective in proactive policing where the aim is to prevent serious crime being committed, this deception can be justified on the grounds of the role of the informant being essential to be effective in carrying out this task during the criminal investigation (Williamson and Bagshaw 2001, pp. 55–57). Williamson and Bagshaw term this justification as "ends-based thinking" where the need to tackle high crime rates and serious crime justifies the deception in police dealings. The dealings they refer to include forfeiting the right to fair treatment to criminals indulging in crime (Williamson and Bagshaw 2001, p. 57). Adopting this approach to crime control involves a moral justification by the police in their use of immoral methods. Harfield points out the dilemma for operational police officers in handling informants (especially those who are active criminals) is that they can only truly confirm another is committing crime through the use of informants especially if it is to ascertain if that crime is of sufficient seriousness (examples he includes are drug dealing, human trafficking, pedophilia-based sexual crimes) (Harfield 2012, pp. 79–80). In balancing moral rights between informant use and victims of crime Harfield says:

> The moral rights of victims/potential victims to be protected from serious crimes or to have such a crime investigated and prosecuted as fully as possible must, in the circumstances, outweigh the suspect's moral rights to privacy (Harfield 2012, p. 80).

Even where an officer warns the informant only to play a minor role, that officer cannot take into account the possibility of the informant feeling it necessary to play a more active role, and as a result the handling officer does not know the true extent of the informant's involvement in planning a crime and the degree to which they were the primary instigator (Dunningham and Norris 1998, p. 22). This raises an important issue that in the desire to obtain information, to what degree does the officer allow their informant to engage in criminality to obtain that information? For Harfield, this is an important question for an officer to consider as the more involved the informant becomes in criminality there is a correlative increase in the moral wrongs committed by the informant that compounds the cumulative moral harm (Harfield 2012, p. 81). As he says:

> Assuming that the given law is not itself immoral, committing crime is itself a moral harm. This in turn gives rise to a further moral harm: committing crime in order to prosecute crime undermines the very purpose of the criminal justice system and the integrity of its actors and agencies (Harfield 2012, p. 82).

The 1968–1997 Irish Troubles: A Case Study in Unethical Police Handling of Informants

A good example of how this can escalate was seen during the 1968–1997 Irish Troubles in Northern Ireland, where republican terrorist groups such as the PIRA, mainly Roman Catholic, wanted independence from British rule and loyalist terror groups such as the Ulster Defence Association (UDA) and the

Ulster Volunteer Force (UVF), mainly Protestant, carried out a campaign to remain under British rule. This was a vicious terrorist campaign that was fought on two fronts. The PIRA deployed their England Department's Active Service Units (ASU) on the British mainland where their activities were policed by the UK's secret service MI5 and the UK's police department Special Branch's CTU. In Northern Ireland British Army Intelligence, MI5 and the police, the former Royal Ulster Constabulary (RUC), policed the activities of PIRA and the Loyalist groups. Crucial to preventing acts of terrorism was the use of informants who were active within these terrorist groups. Rather than recruiting and then placing informants into certain positions within terrorist organizations (McGartland 1997; Bamford 2005, p. 591; Hewitt 2010, p. 64), on the British mainland one method of informant recruitment by the English Special Branch CTU's was through recruiting those already active in or who had a connection with PIRA terrorist cells (O'Callaghan 1998; Bamford 2005, p. 591). The main reason why English Special Branch CTU's had to adopt this approach is they found it difficult to place agents in the PIRA's England Department's ASU's as the ASU's based in England contained no more than four members and consequently were difficult to penetrate. As Sarma points out, PIRA's "… England Department was an example of the effectiveness of the ASU format and the internal security it provided" (Sarma 2005, p. 171). As a result, English Special Branch CTU's had to rely on informants who had a peripheral connection with operatives in PIRA's England Department and who were willing to come forward as volunteers or had been turned by CTU officers following their arrest and detention in police custody.

This was not the case for the RUC in Northern Ireland. It is important to differentiate the informant handling practices adopted by the RUC's Special Branch and English Special Branch during the Troubles, which was such a violent conflict it has been described as the UK's Vietnam (Ryder 1989, p. 6). The RUC recruited and placed individuals as informants into Loyalist groups where some RUC Special Branch officers were accused in the complicity of those informants' actions in killing not just members of PIRA, but also lawyers whose main clients were republicans and Irish Catholics that were suspected of connections with PIRA's republican cause (Punch 2012, pp. 121–135). At that time, the UK's Home Office Guidelines on the use of informants was the only policy English and Northern Irish Special Branch CTU's had to follow. The Guidelines stated the police should never use an informant to encourage another to commit a crime, police officers should not counsel, incite or procure the commission of a crime and protecting informants does not grant the informant immunity from arrest or prosecution for the crime they fully participate in (Police Ombudsman for Northern Ireland 2007, paragraph 31.5). While there is no empirical evidence that English Special Branch CTU's followed the informant handling guidelines during the Troubles (which can be due to lack of access granted by the respective agencies to empirical research), there is evidence from the 2007 Ballast Report that they did follow the guidelines (Police Ombudsman for Northern Ireland 2007, paragraph 31.3). In contrast, a number of Reports carried out following the Troubles, from the 2003 Stevens Report (Punch 2012, pp. 123–124), the 2004 Corey Report (Moran 2010, p. 20; Punch 2012, pp. 136–138) to the Ballast Report (Police Ombudsman for Northern Ireland 2007, paragraph 31.2), along with empirical work reveals the RUC Special Branch did not abide by the Home Office guidelines (Bamford 2005, pp. 600–603; Moran 2010, pp. 19–20; Sarma 2005, p. 168; Punch 2012, p. 120) and the officers were associated with the unauthorized killings.

Placing a degree of context into this example, Clark points out corruption in and around the use of informants is not rampant and neither is it out of control (Clark 2001, p. 49), but the behavior of some of the RUC officers at that time is a classic example of those rare occasions where standards fall, supervision fails, and officers become vulnerable to temptation where "… under such circumstances the dangers of [informants] and police officers becoming corrupt are high" (Clark 2001, p. 38). In addition to this, ethically such behavior undermines the trust on which social interaction is based (Harfield 2012, p. 92). Even with the pressure police officers face in their desire of getting a result in the end-based thinking during an investigation, this reason cannot be used to condone unethical handling of informants.

Evidence of Informants

There are occasions where the information passed on by informants becomes evidence in criminal trials. This in itself has courted controversy on two counts. First, regarding arrangements for reducing the potential sentence an informant may face for their involvement in the criminal activity they informed on. Second, regarding the anonymity of informants who are a witness in criminal trials. Here, we will look at some examples of how some nation states jurisdictions have dealt with this issue.

Immunity from Prosecution/Reduction in Sentence

The UK's Serious Organized Crime and Police Act 2005 (SOCPA)

Sections 71 and 72 of SOCPA introduced statutory guidance for the prosecution to introduce evidence from an informant in a criminal trial. One reason being the use of informants is the most economical investigative method of piercing the shield of criminal activity (Colvin 1998, p. 38; Williamson and Bagshaw 2001, p. 55; Sanders et al. 2010, p. 326). This can range from a reduction in the length of a possible custodial sentence to the informant being immune from prosecution.[*] However, conditions are placed on this immunity as it must be appropriate to do so[†] and is only granted by a specified prosecutor like the Director of Public Prosecutions,[‡] who will give the offender a written notice to this affect laying out the conditions of the immunity.[§] While this immunity is an incentive to tackle organized crime, this power is wide and can be applied to lesser offenses (Owen et al. 2005, p. 48). The aim of this statutory provision was to clarify and strengthen the common law provisions concerned with encouraging criminals assisting law enforcement agencies by passing on information and evidence against other criminals (Corker et al. 2009, p. 261). Since the commencement of sections 71 and 72 of SOCPA, Corker et al. found that due to the complexities of using the statutory provisions, prosecutors were disinclined toward using these provisions, staying with the common law provisions instead where it is the court that makes decisions regarding immunity (Corker et al. 2009, p. 262).

The US New Jersey Brimage Guidelines

In *State v Brimage*,[¶] the Supreme Court of New Jersey was asked to consider through a negotiated plea agreement to waive a mandatory minimum sentence under section 12 Comprehensive Drug Reform Act 1987. To ensure a degree of uniformity, the Court ordered the New Jersey Attorney General to review new plea offer guidelines that all 25 New Jersey counties had to follow where these guidelines include minimum and standard sentences and eliminate the provisions that encourage inter-county disparity. The guidelines had to specify permissible range of offers for particular crimes and be explicit regarding bases for upward and downward departures. The Court added that the New Jersey Attorney General could also provide for differences in treatment among various offenders based on specific factors of flexibility among the counties, adding that in all plea offers the individual characteristics of the crime and the defendant, such as whether the defendant is a first- or second-time offender, must be considered. Also, the prosecutors must state on the record their reasons for choosing to waive or not to waive the mandatory period of parole ineligibility and if the prosecutor

[*] Section 71 Serious Organised Crime and Police Act 2005.
[†] Section 71(1) Serious Organised Crime and Police Act 2005.
[‡] Section 71(4) Serious Organised Crime and Police Act 2005.
[§] Section 71(1)–71(3) Serious Organised Crime and Police Act 2005.
[¶] (1998) 706 A.2d 1096.

departs from the guidelines they must give reasons why they are departing and state them clearly on record.*

Informant Witness Anonymity in Criminal Trials

The UK's Coroners and Justice Act of 2009

Sections 86–97 of the Coroners and Justice Act 2 of 2009 make provisions regarding the anonymity of witnesses in criminal trials. The UK Parliament introduced these provisions following a House of Lords decision in *R v Davies*[†] where seven witnesses to a murder feared for their lives, including three who identified Davis as the gunman. At Davis' trial, the judge ordered that the witnesses gave evidence under a pseudonym, their addresses and personal details that might identify them were withheld from the court, the witnesses gave evidence behind a screen so they could only be seen by the judge and the jury and the witness' natural voices were subject to mechanical distortion to Davis and his counsel to prevent recognition.[‡] Davis' appeal was that he was denied the right to face his accuser, a long-established principle of the English common law. The House agreed with Davis and allowed his appeal. In the decision, Lord Mance said that

> … any further relaxation of the basic common law principle requiring witnesses on issue of dispute to be identified and cross-examined with knowledge of their identity and permitting the defence to know and put to witnesses … relevant questions about their identity is one for Parliament to endorse and delimit, not for the court to create.

This is what the UK Parliament did where to protect the safety of a witness or another person or to prevent serious damage to property or to prevent real harm to the public interest,[§] the prosecution can apply for a "witness anonymity order" where

1. The witness' name and other identifying details can be withheld or removed from materials disclosed to any party in the criminal proceedings.
2. The witness may use a pseudonym.
3. The witness is not asked questions of any specified description that might lead to the identification of the witness.

---

* (1998) 706 A.2d 1096, III paragraph C.
† [2008] UKHL 36.
‡ [2008] UKHL 36, paragraph 3.
§ Section 88(3) Coroners and Justice Act 2009.

4. The witness is screened (except to the judge and jury).
5. The witness' voice is subjected to modulation.[*]

On an application, the prosecutor must inform the court of the identity of the witness but is not required to provide information that might lead to the witness' identity or provide information that might lead to the witness being identified to any other party in the proceedings of their legal representatives.[†] The act also allows defendants to make such an application in relation to any witnesses they wish to call where again they must inform the court of the identity of the witness, and this includes the prosecutor but not any other defendant or their legal representative.[‡] As would be expected, there are conditions attached to the application of a "witness anonymity order" that includes where the credibility of the witness is relevant and needs to be assessed, where the witness might be the sole or decisive evidence implicating the defendant, and whether the witness' evidence can only be properly tested if their identity is disclosed.[§] While the 2009 Act's provisions are written to cover a number of categories of witnesses, it is clear that this will include informants' evidence that could be submitted in UK criminal trials.

Canada's Confidential Informant Privilege

While having no statutory provisions through its common law, Canada has developed legal procedures for dealing with informant privilege and revealing the identity of an informant at criminal trials. In summary, there is a duty not just on the police but also the Crown prosecutors and the courts not to release any information that risks revealing the identity of a police informant.[¶] This principle has been recognized for some time in Canada and is seen as being of fundamental importance to the workings of the criminal justice system.[**] The rationale behind this is to protect informants from the risk of retribution was recognized in *R v Barros* to encourage cooperation from future informants where the court said that

> … the privilege encourages other potential [informants] to come forward with some assurance of protection form reprisal … The obligation to protect confidential sources clearly goes beyond a rule of evidence and is not limited to the courtroom.[††]

---

[*] Section 86(2) Coroners and Justice Act 2009.
[†] Section 87(2) Coroners and Justice Act 2009.
[‡] Section 87(3) Coroners and Justice Act 2009.
[§] Section 89(2) Coroners and Justice Act 2009.
[¶] *Named Person v Vancouver Sun* (2007) 224 C.C.C. 1 (3d) (S.C.C.), paragraph 17.
[**] *R v Leipert* (1997) 112 C.C.C. (3d) 385 (S.C.C.), paragraph 10.
[††] *R v Barros* (2011) 273 C.C.C. (3d) 129 (S.C.C.), paragraph 30.

One important principle in this privilege is that the Crown prosecutors cannot rely on material that is withheld under informant privilege to help prove the guilt of a defendant. As Mister Justice Fish held in *R v Basi*, the prosecution cannot introduce withheld information as evidence at a trial without first providing that evidence to the defense.[*] The only occasion the defense can challenge informant privilege is when the defendant can show their innocence is at stake.[†]

Not every nation state has similar provisions related to informant immunity and offers of reduction in sentencing regarding informants during criminal trials. Especially for informants who are classed as confidential informants (those active within criminal circles involved in serious and organized criminal activity) revealing their details in an open court imperils the personal safety of the informant and potentially their family members. Regarding the use of informants in criminal investigations, one constant theme is the importance of the information they pass on. Unless there are sufficient safeguards in place one can see why officers are reluctant to pass on informants' personal details, especially when that information becomes evidence to be used in a criminal trial against the investigation's main criminal target.

Conclusion

This chapter reveals how state officials are concerned about the potential for corrupt activity between police officers and their informants. The corruption ranges from how much the handling officer allow their informant to carry on with their nefarious activity to officers being paid by terrorists or criminals to in effect become informants to that terror or organized crime group. This will always be an issue when reliance is placed on gathering intelligence or information from persons involved in such activity. As reliable informants tend to provide the best source of intelligence, this will be an issue that will not disappear overnight. As we have seen, one possible way of resolving this is to have a dedicated informant handling unit that is detached from the investigating officer as this can remove the officers' temptation to allow for unethical behavior to get a result in that investigation.

There are occasions when what the informant passes on to the officer has the potential to be evidence in a criminal trial. It may be the key evidence that could secure a conviction. This poses another dilemma in revealing the identity of the informant. As seen in a number of jurisdictions, be it through statutory law, case law, or policy, measures are in place to prevent

---

[*] *R v Basi* (2009) 248 C.C.C. 257 (S.C.C.), paragraph 51.
[†] *R v Basi* (2009) 248 C.C.C. 257 (S.C.C.), paragraph 40.

any potential defendant from finding out the identity of the informant. This is important for two reasons. One for health and safety reasons, as informants can receive violent retribution. For informants in terrorism cases that violent retribution can lead to their death. The second reason in protecting the informant's identity is to ensure that informant can continue in that role. As discussed, there is an issue regarding due process in trials as defendants have the right to face their accuser. One example where a compromise can be achieved without affecting the due process is seen in the example of the United Kingdom introducing legislation that still ensures there is a fair trial for defendants.

Conclusion

Three constant themes emerge from the various terrorism studies contained in this book. Those are issues concerned with preventing acts of terrorism, balancing the interests of national security and an individual's rights, and improving the compatibility between investigation procedures between states.

Preventing Acts of Terrorism

Among the issues coming out of this study, one paramount theme emerging in all the states examined is the desire to prevent acts of terrorism from occurring. This is seen in the policies issued by governments and the statutory provisions they have put in place related to terrorism. These provisions include wider powers of entry to premises, search and seizure of items given to counterterrorism officers and the creation of offenses related to prevention that allow those officers to arrest suspects before they can unleash the carnage resulting from an act of terrorism. That carnage can be the number of deaths in one attack. In the 9/11 attack on the United States, 2977 victims were killed and the 7/7 London bombing incurred 52 deaths. More recently in December 2013, thirty-four victims were killed in two separate attacks by Caucasian-based separatists in Volgograd, Russia. In addition to these attacks, 2013 saw low-level terrorist attacks such as that seen in Boston, April 2013. The death rate in these types of attacks may be lower compared with those seen in sophisticated high level attacks such as 9/11 and 7/7, as seen in the Boston attack where three victims were killed, however it is still as divesting as the attack left 264 injured, many of whom were permanently disabled. Another low-level attack that caused concern around the world was the killing of an off-duty British Army soldier, Lee Rigby, outside Woolwich barracks in London in June 2013. Lee Rigby was knocked down on a weekday afternoon by a car driven by two jihadist terrorists, who then got out of the car and hacked Lee Rigby to death in front of passers-by. It does not matter how many victims are killed, even where there is a solitary victim such as Lee Rigby, the terror effect this puts into the minds of people can be devastating.

As pointed out throughout this book regarding terrorist attacks, what is alarming for many is that there is no direct connection between the attacker and their victim. In most cases, they are people who are going about their daily business, be it work- or leisure-based activities that many of us perform day in and day out. This is another category of carnage an act of terrorism can cause as it places fear into people who suddenly feel vulnerable to an attack. The results of this fear is that some people may change their daily practices because of that vulnerability, which can include using some forms of public transport or avoiding some geographical areas all together. In addition to preventing deaths and injuries incurred through terrorist attacks, it is this part of the terror effect that states also want to prevent. To achieve this, counterterrorism investigators require wide powers under the rule of law to interfere with the lives of targets suspected to be involved in acts of terrorism, even those who are on the fringe of such activity. This interference ranges from carrying out surveillance on targets to having the ability to arrest a person at an early stage in the preparation of an act of terrorism. To cover a number of actions motivated by a variety of causes explains why the legal definitions of terrorism, such as those in the United Kingdom and Canada, are wide. In addition to this, we have seen an expansion in the number of statutory preventative measures that have been introduced to enable counterterrorism officers to act at an early stage of an act of terrorism, especially where the act is still being planned or prepared.

Balancing the Interests of National Security and an Individual's Rights or Liberties

Another issue that comes out of the study in this book is regarding the wide legal definition of terrorism and the increase in statutory preventative offenses and powers granted to counterterrorism investigators. As seen in the examination of the legal provisions, concerns have been raised regarding the intrusive nature of the powers and how activities that at one time would not be associated with acts of terrorism now come under that scrutiny of counterterrorism agencies' investigations. As seen with quasi-criminal measures, and the asset freezing orders in particular, the courts have ensured that an individual's rights and liberties are protected. The UK's TPIM orders is an example of this where due to the courts' decisions the UK government has had to amend the law on a number of occasions to ensure that individual rights and liberties are protected and not unduly interfered with. Balancing the interests of national security and an individual's rights is an onerous task performed by the courts and in doing so they will make decisions that will come down in favor of the interests of national security. As seen with the *Miranda* case in the United Kingdom, where the Schedule 7 Terrorism Act 2000 stop and search power at ports and border controls was used on David Miranda, the partner of *The Guardian* journalist who received secret documentation from former NSA employee Edward Snowden has courted a degree of controversy. Key to this was whether Miranda was carrying journalistic material. When the court decided this was not the case the proponents who espouse the importance of individual liberty were clearly disappointed. This was demonstrated by the exaggerated claims these proponents made. An example of this was discussed in Chapter 3 with Atkinson's claim that the *Miranda* decision would fetter the freedom of the media. Atkinson claimed that in writing articles with the intent of influencing a government both the journalists and their employers could be prosecuted under terrorism-related legislation. As the court in *Miranda* and in similar cases in all states' jurisdictions make clear in their decisions, there are times when we have to accept that in relation to investigating terrorist activity it would not be in the national interest to find against the state. The national interest is not solely about protecting the actions of the state, but includes keeping the majority of its citizens safe from a terrorist attack.

Another example of how the courts juggled the interest of national security and individual liberty examined in Chapter 3 was on the issue of on intelligence exchange in the *In Re Sealed* and *Clapper* cases. In both of these cases, the US courts held that what is of paramount importance is the state's ability to obtain valuable intelligence that can keep citizens safe and the state agencies' ability to identify potential targets of a criminal prosecutions in terrorism investigations. Both of these cases were concerned with the Foreign Intelligence Surveillance Act powers. A third case related to the act was *Klayman*. As discussed in Chapter 3, by considering the strength of individual applicants' claims on a case by case basis, we see in *Klayman* the courts consider not deciding always in favor of the interests of national security and with that the actions of the state. By not always rubber stamping state's action, this reinforces how within the separation of powers the courts demonstrate their independence for the executive. This is seen in *Klayman* where Justice Leon held that he was not convinced the removal of the applicants from a database would degrade the overall program. As the interests of national security and individual rights are not exclusive, but inclusive, the courts have consistently shown they will protect an individual's rights where it is deemed necessary and equitable to do so.

Improving the Compatibility of Terrorism Investigation Procedures between States

Especially where an international terrorist threat requires international co-operation by various states' counterterrorism agencies, compatibility in the law and evidence gathering process is important, especially where there is the potential for evidence obtained in one state to be used in a trial or court procedure in another. Although this study has shown there is a degree of compatibility in the law, ranging from the legal definition of terrorism to certain statutory preventative measures, there are differences that exist. While there is no one legal definition of terrorism in the United States, there are statutory provisions that define international terrorism in the US Code 18 that is similar to those in the United Kingdom, Canada, and Australia that will provide a degree of compatibility. An example of where compatibility between the states is present is seen in Chapter 1 in the study on the evidence amounting to a religious cause motivating an act of terrorism. Another example of compatibility of the law between states is seen in Chapter 4 in relation to the funding of terrorism and the asset freezing measures imposed on individuals.

Where there is a degree of concern, there is lack of compatibility in the provisions governing the use of informants in counterterrorism investigations. While, as Chapter 7 revealed, there is a similarity in how informants are recruited, it is the law or in some cases, especially in the United States, the lack of law governing the handling and use of informants that has the potential to be problematic in regard to international cooperation. As Chapter 8 shows, the United Kingdom is the only state that has statutory provisions in all aspects of handling of informants and how the information they obtain can be used as evidence in criminal trials, but this is not the case in every state. In the United States, there are some policing agencies where there is not even a policy guiding the use of informants. This raises questions on the reliability of the information or intelligence the informant passes on that could have repercussions where, for example, that intelligence is key to potential extradition procedures between states. While it is understandable in a federal state that the federal government would not want to be seen as dictating to its state governments, it is submitted that minimum statutory guidelines should be introduced for all US policing agencies involved in counterterrorism. It should be a statute governing the use of informants, not a policy. As shown in Chapter 8, the application of the US Attorney General's guidelines regarding the use of confidential informants appear to be ineffective as the FBI were found to be up to 87% deficient in their application of the guidelines. A statute is more likely to ensure the governance of informant use controls, especially where the sanction for not following the statutory control can be the inadmissibility of evidence that can potentially result in the prosecution having to withdraw their case in a criminal trial to disciplinary action being taken against officers who do not adhere to the statute's provisions.

Summary

What the research in this book reveals is that countering terrorist activity is not an easy task. For both governments and investigating officers, there is the constant pressure to prevent terrorist acts from occurring. This explains

why we have witnessed a plethora of terrorism-related legislation being introduced, especially in Western states that are main targets of international terrorist groups. The pressure of prevention has the potential for investigators to
take short cuts or turn a blind eye to the requirements of statutory and policy
governance of their actions. Where that action is governed by policy guidelines only, there is a greater opportunity for investigators to breach those
guidelines compared with statutory guidelines. Another pressure facing
police officers investigating terrorism is in respecting an individual's rights,
more so as their respective states has introduced legislation granting them
wider powers to intrude into the privacy of citizens, ranging from conducting surveillance into their private and family life to monitoring a person's
finances. These are issues that led to Edward Snowden whistle blowing on the
activities of the NSA and GCHQ in relation to Operation PRISM. He claimed
the surveillance was illegal as the NSA conducted most of its surveillance
without a relevant FISA authority or by using GCHQ's services the United
States could circumvent the US legal requirements to conduct surveillance
on electronic sources. The courts have not found it an easy task to ensure
fairness as they balance the needs of national security with an individual's
rights, but of all the criminal activity carried out it is acts of terrorism that
are the worst forms of the use of violence. With the devastating results that
emanate from acts of terrorism, as is stated in this book, detention is temporary, the loss of life is permanent. This point should not be lost on those who
consistently critique the state's responses to terrorism and the actions of its
counterterrorism officers.

Bibliography

Aas, K.F., 2007. *Globalisation and Crime*. London: Sage.

Adams, G., 1989. Presidential address to Sinn Fein's January 1989 Ard Fheis. *An Phoblacht/Republican News*, February 2, 1989.

Adams, G., 1990. *Cage Eleven*. Dingle: Brandon Book Publishers.

Adams, G., 1996. *Before the Dawn*. London: Heinemann.

Adams, G., 2003. *A Farther Shore: Ireland's Long Road to Peace*. New York: Random House.

Alston, P., and Weiler, J.H.H., 1999. An "ever closer union" in need of a human rights policy: The European Union and human rights. In Alston, P. et al. (editors), *The EU and Human Rights*. Oxford: Oxford University Press, pp. 3–68.

American Civil Liberties Union, 2007. ACLU Fact Sheet on the "Police America Act." Retrieved from https://www.aclu.org/national-security/aclu-fact-sheet-%E2%80%9Cpolice-america-act [accessed September 5, 2013].

Anderson, D., 2012. *The Terrorism Acts in 2011*. London: The Stationary Office.

Anderson, D., 2013. *The Terrorism Acts in 2012*. London: The Stationery Office.

Anderson, D., 2014. *The Terrorism Acts in 2013*. London: The Stationery Office.

Anderson, M., 1998. European frontiers at the end of the twentieth century. In Anderson, M., and Eberhard, B. (editors), *The Frontiers of Europe*. London: Pinter, 1–100.

Anderson, M., and Eberhard, B., 1998. *The Frontiers of Europe*. London: Pinter.

Argomaniz, J., 2012. *The EU and Counter-Terrorism*. London: Routledge.

Arreguin-Toft, I., 2002. Tunnel at the end of the light: A critique of US counter-terrorist grand strategy. *Cambridge Review of International Affairs* 15(3), 549–563.

Attorney General's Guidelines Regarding the Use of Confidential Informants, 2006. Retrieved from https://fas.org/irp/agency/doj/fbi/chs-guidelines.pdf [accessed August 8, 2014].

Audit Commission, 1993. *Tackling Crime Effectively Management Handbook*, vol. 2. London: Audit Commission.

Baker, C., 1998. Membership categorization and interview accounts. In Silverman, D. (editor), *Qualitative Research: Theory, Method and Practice*. London: Sage, 130–143.

Balzacq, T., Bigo, D., Carrera, S., and Guild, E., 2006. Security and the two-level game. *CEPS Working Document* No. 234/January 2006.

Bamford, B., 2004. The United Kingdom's "War against Terrorism." *Terrorism and Political Violence* 16(4), 737–756.

Bamford, B.W.C., 2005. The role and effectiveness of intelligence in Northern Ireland. *Intelligence and National Security* 20(4), 581–607.

Barnett, H., 2013. *Constitutional and Administrative Law* (10th edition). Abingdon: Routledge.

Bayerns, G.J., and Roberson, C., 2011. *Criminal Justice Research Methods: Theory and Practice*. Boca Raton, FL: CRC Press.

BBC, 2010. Real IRA admits to border killing. Retrieved from http://news.bbc.co.uk/1/ hi/northern_ireland/foyle_and_west/8535731.stm [accessed January 30, 2013].

BBC, 2012. BBC spotlight: Irish Republicans and the drugs war. Transmitted October 30, 2012 from http://www.youtube.com/watch?v=mVYcacfwook [accessed January 29, 2013].

BBC News, 2014. Police fail to seize terror inmate Munir Farooqi's home. May 23, 2014. Retrieved from http://www.bbc.co.uk/news/uk-england-manchester-27540945 [accessed July 7, 2014].

Bean, P., and Billingsley, R., 2001. Drugs, crime and informers. In Billingsley, R., Menitz, T., and Bean, P. (editors), Informers: Policing, Policy, Practice. Cullompton: Willan Publishing, pp. 25–37.

Bell, S. 2013. Canada pushed EU to add Hezbollah to list of banned terrorist organisations official says national post. July 31, 2013. Retrieved from http://news. nationalpost.com/2013/07/24/canada-pushed-eu-to-add-hezbollah-to-list-of-banned-terrorist-organizations-official-says/ [accessed October 20, 2013].

Berenskoetter, F., 2012. Mapping the field of UK–EU policing. Journal of Common Market Studies 50(1), 37–53.

Bergeron, J., 2013. Transnational organised crime and international security. The Rusi Journal 158(2), 6–9.

Bigo, D. et al. 2013. Open season for data dishing on the web. CEPA Policy Brief No. 293, June 18, 2013.

Billingsley, R., Menitz, T., and Bean, P. (editors), 2001. Informers: Policing, Policy, Practice. Cullompton: Willan Publishing.

Bogusz, B., and King, M., 2003. Controlling drug trafficking in Central Europe: The impact of EU policies in the Czech Republic, Hungary and Lithuania. In Edwards, A., and Gill, P. (editors), Transnational Organised Crime: Perspectives on Global Security. London: Routledge, pp. 143–156.

Brodeur, J.P., 2005. Cops and spooks: The uneasy partnership. In Newburn, T. (editor), Policing: Key Readings. Cullompton: Willan Publishing, pp. 797–812.

Brodeur, J.P., 2007. High and low policing in post-9/11 times. Policing 1(1), 70–79.

Bryman, A., 2012. Social Research Methods (4th edition). Oxford: Oxford University Press.

Bunyan, T., 1976. The History and Practice of the Political Police in Britain. London: Quartet Books.

Bures, O., 2008. Europol's fledgling counterterrorism role. Terrorism and Political Violence 20(4), 498–517.

Burkinshaw, P., 2003. European Public Law. London: Butterworths.

Caiden, G.E., 1997. Undermining good governance: Corruption and democracy. Asian Journal of Political Science 2(5), 1–22.

Cape, E., 2012. Police station and practice update. Legal Action 24–29.

Carpenter, J.S., Levitt, M., and Jacobson, M., 2009. Confronting the ideology of radical extremism. Journal of National Security Law and Policy 3, 301–327.

Cini, M., 2003. European Union Politics. Oxford: Oxford University Press.

Clark, R., 2001. Informer and corruption. In Billingsley, R., Menitz, T., and Bean, P. (editors), Informers: Policing, Policy, Practice. Cullompton: Willan Publishing, pp. 38–49.

Clarke, R., and Lee, S., 2008. The PIRA, D-Company and the Crime-Terror Nexus. Terrorism and Political Violence 20(3), 376–395.

Cochrane, F., 2013. Not so extraordinary: The democratisation of UK counterinsurgency strategy. *Critical Studies on Terrorism* 6(1) 29–49.

Cohen, S., 1985. *Visions of Social Control*. London: Sage.

Colvin, M., 1998. *Under Surveillance: Covert Policing and Human Rights Standards*. London: Justice.

Commission (EC), 2007. *Report from the Commission Based on Art 11 of the Council Framework Decision of 13 June 2002 on Combating Terrorism*. COM(2007) 681, Brussels. November 6.

Commission of the European Communities, 2005a. *Proposal for a Council Framework Decision on the Exchange of Information under the Principle of Availability*. COM(2005)490 Final 12.10.2005. Brussels: EU Commission.

Commission of the European Communities, 2005b. *Proposal for a Framework Decision on Exchange of Information under the Principle of Availability*. Memorandum MEMO/05/367. Brussels: EU Commission.

Commission of the European Communities, 2005c. *Communication from the Commission to the Council and the European Parliament*. COM(2005)124 Final 06.04.2005. Brussels: EU Commission.

Commission of the European Communities, 2005d. *Communication from the Commission to the Council and the European Parliament—The Hague Programme: Ten Priorities for the Next Five Years, a Partnership for Renewal*. Brussels: EU Commission.

Commission of the European Communities, 2005e. *Communication for the Commission to the Council and the European Parliament: Developing a Strategic Concept on Tackling Organised Crime*. COM(2005)232 Final 02.06.2005. Brussels: EU Commission.

Commission of the European Communities, 2005f. *Communication of the Commission to the Council and the European Parliament: Establishing a Framework Programme on "Security and Safeguarding Liberties" for the Period 2007–2013*. Retrieved from http://europa.eu.in/council [extracted December 10, 2005].

Commonwealth of Australia, 2012. National Counter-terrorism Plan. Retrieved from www.nationalsecurity.gov.au/.../national-counter-terrorism-plan-2012.pd... [accessed August 8, 2014].

Coogan, T.P., 1995. *The Troubles: Ireland's Ordeal 1965–1956 and the Search for Peace*. London: Hutchinson.

Cooper, J.A., 2012. Noble cause corruption as a consequence of role conflict in the police organisation. *Policing and Society* 22(2), 169–184.

Cope, N., 2008. Crime analysis: Principles and practice. In Newburn, T. (editor), *Handbook of Policing*. Cullompton: Willan Publishing, pp. 404–429.

Corker, D., Tombs, G., and Chisholm, T., 2009. Sections 71 and 72 of the Serious Organised Crime and Police Act 2005: Wither the common law? *Criminal Law Review* 261–271.

Council of Europe, 2004. *Combating Organised Crime: Best Practice Surveys of the Council of Europe*. Strasbourg: Council of Europe Publishing.

Council of Europe, 2005a. *Council of Europe Convention on Action Against Trafficking in Human Beings and its Explanatory Report*. Strasbourg: Council of Europe Publishing.

Council of Europe, 2005b. *Special Investigation Techniques in Relation to Serious Crimes Including Acts of Terrorism: Recommendation Rec(2005)10 and Explanatory Memorandum*. Strasbourg: Council of Europe Publishing.

Council of the European Communities, 2005. *Communication from the Commission to the Council and the European Parliament.* COM(2005)124, Brussels, April 6.

Council of the European Union, 2004. *EU Drugs Strategy (2005–2012).* Brussels, 15074/04.

Council of the European Union, 2005. The European Union Counter-Terrorism Strategy. 14469/4/05, November 30, 2005.

Council of the European Union, 2006. *Press Release: Justice and Home Affairs.* (April 2006) 8402/06 (Presse 106).

Crank, J., Flaherty, D., and Giacommazzi, A., 2007. The noble cause: An empirical assessment. *Policing and Society* 35, 103–116.

Crank, J.D., and Caldero, D.S., 2000. *Police Ethics: Noble Cause Corruption.* Burlington: Anderson Publishing.

Crawford, A., 2002. *Crime and Insecurity: The Governance of Safety in Europe.* Cullompton: Willan Publishing.

Crous, C., 2009. Human intelligence sources: Challenges in policy development. *Security Challenges* 5(3), 117–127.

Danziger, Y., 2012. Changes in methods of freezing funds of terrorist organisations since 9/11: A comparative analysis. *Journal of Money Laundering Control* 15(2), 210–236.

DeBreadun, D., 2012. McGuiness outlines SF vision. *The Irish Times*, May 25.

Deflam, M., 2006. Europol and the policing of international terrorism: Counter-terrorism in a global perspective. *Justice Quarterly* 23(3), 336–335.

Deflam, M., 2009. *The Policing of Terrorism: Organizational and Global Perspectives.* London: Routledge.

Den Boer, M., Hillebrand, C., and Nolke, A., 2008. Legitimacy under pressure: The European web of counterterrorism networks. *Journal of Common Market Studies* 46(1), 101–124.

Department of Work and Pensions, 2011. Family Resources Survey. Retrieved from http://www.research.dwp.gov.uk/asd/frs/[accessed March 31, 2012].

Dillon, M., 1994. *25 Years of Terror: The IRA's War against the British.* London: Bantam.

Dixon, D., 1997. *Law in Policing: Legal Rules and Police Practices: Legal Regulation and Police Practices.* Oxford: Oxford University Press.

Donohue, L.K., 2008. *The Cost of Counterterrorism: Power, Politics and Liberty.* Cambridge: Cambridge University Press.

Douglas, R., 2010. Must terrorists act for a cause? The motivational requirement in definitions of terrorism in the United Kingdom, Canada, New Zealand and Australia. *Commonwealth Law Bulletin* 36(2), 295–312.

Douglas-Scott, S., 2002. *Constitutional Law of the European Union.* Harlow: Pearson Education Ltd.

Dunningham, C., and Norris, C., 1996. A risky business: The recruitment and running of informers by English police officers. *Police Studies* 19(2), 1–25.

Dunningham, C., and Norris, C., 1998. Some ethical dilemmas in the handling of police informers. *Public Money and Management* (1891) 18(1), 21–25.

Edwards, A., and Gill, P. (editors), 2003. *Transnational Organised Crime: Perspectives on Global Security.* London: Routledge.

Ekblom, P., 2003. Organised crime and the conjunction of criminal opportunity framework. In Edwards, A., and Gill, P. (editors), *Transnational Organised Crime: Perspectives on Global Security.* London: Routledge, pp. 241–263.

Elvins, M., 2003. Europe's response to transnational organised crime. In Edwards, A., and Gill, P. (editors), *Transnational Organised Crime: Perspectives on Global Security.* London: Routledge, pp. 28–41.

English, R., 2009. *Terrorism: How to Respond.* Oxford: Oxford University Press.

Ericson, R.V., and Haggerty, K.D., 1997. *Policing the Risk Society.* Oxford: Oxford University Press.

EU Commission, 2005. Communication from the Commission to the Council and the European Parliament: Developing a strategic concept on tackling organised crime. Brussels, COM (2005) 232 Final.

EU Council, 2002. Council decision of February 28, 2002: Setting up Eurojust with a view to reinforcing the fight against serious crime. *Official Journal of the European Communities,* June 3, 2002, L63/1.

EU Council, 2003. 2889th Council Meeting—Justice and Home Affairs, Brussels, February 27–28, 2003. 6162/03 (Presse 42).

EU Council, 2004. 2579th Council Meeting—Justice and Home Affairs, Luxembourg, April 20, 2004. 8694/04 (Presse 123).

EU Council, 2005a. 2642nd Council Meeting—Justice and Home Affairs, Brussels, February 24, 2005. 6228/05 (Presse 28).

EU Council, 2005b. Council Meeting—Justice and Home Affairs, Brussels, December 12, 2005. 12645/05 (Presse 247).

EU Council, 2005c. EU Drugs Action Plan (2005–2008). *Official Journal of the European Union* C168/01 08.07.2005.

EU Presidency, 2004. *Presidency Conclusions—Brusssels, 4/5 November 2004.* Document 14292/04.

Europol, 2006a. *The Threat Form OC.* The Hague: Europol.

Europol, 2006b. *Financial and Property Crimes.* The Hague: Europol.

Europol, 2012. *EU Terrorism Situation and Trend Report TE-SAT 2012.* Hague: Europol.

Evans, J., 2012. The Olympics and beyond. MI5. Retrieved from https://www.mi5.gov.uk/home/about-us/who-we-are/staff-and-management/director-general/speeches-by-the-director-general/the-olympics-and-beyond.html [accessed August 21, 2013].

Felsen, D., and Kalaitzidis, A., 2005. A historical overview of transnational crime. In Reichel, P. (editor), *Handbook of Transnational Crime and Justice.* London: Sage, pp. 3–19.

Fenwick, H., 2008. Proactive counter-terrorist strategies in conflict with human rights. *International Review of Law, Computers and Technology* 22(3), 259–270.

Finckenauer, J.O., and Albenese, J., 2005. Organised crime in North America. In Reichel, R. (editor), *Handbook of Transnational Crime and Justice.* London: Sage, pp. 439–456.

Foucault, M., 1978. *Discipline and Punish.* London: Penguin Books.

Garland, D., 2001. *The Culture of Control: Crime and Social Order in Contemporary Society.* Oxford: Oxford University Press.

Gearty, C., 2013. *Liberty and Security.* Cambridge: Polity Press.

Genson, R., 1998. The Schengen agreements—police cooperation and security aspects. In Cullen, P.J., and Gilmore, W.C. (editors), *Crime Sans Frontieres: International and European Legal Approaches.* Edinburgh: Edinburgh University Press.

Gill, P., 1994. *Policing Politics: Security Intelligence and the Liberal State.* London: Frank Cass.

Gill, P., 2000. *Rounding Up the Usual Suspects: Developments in Contemporary Law Enforcement Intelligence.* Aldershot: Ashgate.

Githens-Mazer, J., 2008. Causes of jihadi terrorism: Beyond paintballing and social exclusion. *Criminal Justice Matters* 73(1), 26–28.

Government of Canada, 2013. Building resilience against terrorism. Retrieved from http://www.publicsafety.gc.ca/cnt/rsrcs/pblctns/rslnc-gnst-trrrsm/index-eng. aspx [accessed August 7, 2014].

Grabbe, H., 2002. *Justice and Home Affairs: Faster Decisions, Secure Rights.* London: Centre for European Reform.

Greenberg, M.R., Wechsler, W.F., and Wolosky, L.S., 2002. *Terrorist Financing: Report of an Independent Task Force Sponsored by the Council on Foreign Relations.* New York: Council on Foreign Relations.

Greenwald, G., 2013. NSA collecting phone records of millions of Verizon customers daily. *The Guardian*, June 6, 2013. Retrieved from http://www.theguardian. com/world/2013/jun/06/nsa-phone-records-verizon-court-order   [accessed September 1, 2013].

Greenwald, G., 2014. *No Place to Hide.* New York: Metropolitan Books.

Greer, S., 1995. Towards a sociological model of police informants. *British Journal of Sociology* 46(3), 509–527.

Hall, S., Jefferson, T., and Clark, T., 1978. *Policing the Crisis.* London: Macmillan.

Hansard, 2011. HC Vol. 529, col. 75, June 7, 2011, Yvette Cooper.

Harden., T., 2000. *Bandit Country: The IRA and South Armagh.* London: Hodder and Stoughton.

Harfield, C., 2012. Police informers and professional ethics. *Criminal Justice Ethics* 31(2), 73–95.

Hayes, B., 2002. *The Activities and Development of Europol: Towards an Unaccountable FBI in Europe.* London: Statewatch.

Hewitt, S., 2008. *The British War on Terror.* London: Continuum Books.

Hewitt, S., 2010. *Snitch: A History of the Modern Intelligence Informer.* London: Continuum Books.

Hesterman, J.L., 2013. *The Terrorist-Criminal Nexus.* Boca Raton: CRC Press.

Hill, C., 2005. Measuring transnational crime. In Rachel, R. (editor), *Handbook of Transnational Crime and Justice.* London: Sage, pp. 47–64.

HM Government, 2011. *CONTEST: The United Kingdom's Strategy for Countering Terrorism.* London: The Stationery Office.

HM Treasury, 2007. *The Financial Challenge to Crime and Terrorism.* London: HMSO.

Holdaway, S., 1983. *Inside the British Police.* Oxford: Blackwell.

Hopkins, N., 2013. UK gathering secret intelligence via covert NSA operation. *The Guardian*, June 7, 2013. Retrieved from http://www.theguardian.com/ technology/
2013/jun/07/uk-gathering-secret-intelligence-nsa-prism [accessed September 2, 2013].

Hopkins, N., and Ackermenn, S., 2013. Flexible laws and weak oversight give GCHQ room for manoeuvre. *The Guardian,* August 2, 2013. Retrieved from http://www. theguardian.com/uk-news/2013/aug/02/gchq-laws-oversight-nsa [accessed September 2, 2013].

Hopkins, N., and Borger, J., 2013. Exclusive: NSA p[pays £100m in secret funding for GCHQ. *The Guardian,* August 1, 2013. Retrieved from http://www.theguardian.

com/uk-news/2013/aug/01/nsa-paid-gchq-spying-edward-snowden [accessed September 2, 2013].

Hopkins, N., Borger, J., and Harding, L., 2013. GCHQ: Inside the top secret world of Britain's biggest spy agency. *The Guardian*, August 2, 2013. Retrieved from http://www.theguardian.com/world/interactive/2013/aug/01/gchq-spy-agency-nsa-edward-snowden [accessed September 2, 2013].

Horgan, J., 2009. *Walking Away from Terrorism*. London: Routledge.

Hutson, R., Long, T., and Page, M., 2009. Pathways to violent radicalisation in the Middle East: A model for future studies of transnational jihad. *Rusi Journal* 154(2), 18–26.

Independent Commission Against Corruption, 1993. *Policy Informants: A Discussion Paper*. Sydney, New South Wales: Independent Commission Against Corruption.

Innes, M., 2000. "Professionalising" the role of police informant. *Policing and Society* 9(4), 357–384.

Innes, M., and Thiel, D., 2008. Policing terror. In Newburn, T. (editor), *Handbook of Policing* (2nd edition). Cullompton: Willan Publishing, pp. 553–579.

International Commission of Jurists (ICJ), 2009. *Assessing Damage, Urging Action*. Geneva: ICR.

Irish Independent, 2012. The truth about Alan Ryan and his funeral. *Irish Independent*, September 15, 2012. Retrieved from http://www.independent.ie/national-news/the-truth-about-alan-ryan-and-his-funeral-3229680.html [accessed January 30, 2013].

Joffe, G., 2008. The European Union, democracy and counter-terrorism in the Maghreb. *Journal of Common Market Studies* 46(1), 147–171.

Jones-Brown, D., and Shane, J., 2011. *An Exploratory Study of the Use of Confidential Informants in New Jersey*. Newark: American Civil Liberties Union of New Jersey.

Kaczorowska, A., 2011. *European Union Law* (2nd edition). London: Routledge.

Kaunert, C., 2010. Europol and EU counterterrorism: International security actorness in the external dimension. *Studies in Conflict and Terrorism* 33(7), 652–671.

Keohane, D., 2008. The absent friend: EU foreign policy and counter-terrorism. *Journal of Common Market Studies* 46(1), 125–146.

Kirby, A., 2007. London bombers as self-starters: A case study in indigenous radicalisation and the emergence of autonomous cliques. *Studies in Conflict and Terrorism* 30(Winter 2007), 415–428.

Klockers, C.B., 1976. The dirty Harry problem. In Blomburg, A.S., and Neiderhoffer, E. (editors), *The Ambivalent Force: Perspectives on the Police*. New York: Holt Reinhart & Winston, pp. 52–69.

Laqueur, W., 1987. *The Age of Terrorism*. London: Little, Brown and Company.

Lee, R., 2002. *Terrorist Financing: The US and International Response Report for Congress*. Washington: Congressional Research Service.

Leiberman, B., 2007. Ethical issues in the use of confidential informants for narcotic operations. *The Police Chief* 74(6), 1–5.

Lenaerts, K., and Nuffel, P., 2005. Community law. In Bray, R. (editor), *Constitutional Law of the European Union* (2006 reprint). London: Sweet and Maxwell, pp. 129–152.

Leveson, 2012. *The Right Honourable Lord Justice, An Inquiry into the Culture, Practice and Ethics of the Press*, Vol. 1. London: The Stationery Office.

Lewis, N., 2005. Expanding surveillance: Connecting biometric information systems to international police cooperation. In Zureil, E., and Salter, M.B. (editors),

Global Surveillance and Policing: Borders, Security, Identity. Cullompton: Willan Publishing, pp. 77–101.

Liebling, A., and Stanko, B., 2001. Allegiance and ambivalence: Some dilemmas in researching disorder and violence. *British Journal of Criminology* 41, 421–430.

Liu, E.C., 2013. *Reauthorization of the FISA Amendments Act.* CRS Report for Congress 7-5700.

Loader, I., 2002. Policing, securitization and democratization in Europe. *Criminal Justice: The International Journal of Policy and Practice* 2(2), 125–153.

Loader, I., and Walker, C., 2007. *Civilizing Security.* Cambridge: Cambridge University Press.

Lord Macdonald, 2011. *Review of Counter Terrorism and Security Powers.* Cm.8003.

Lowe, D., 2010. Spooking the spooks: Researching National Security Agencies. In Roberson, C., and Das, D. (editors), *Police Without Borders.* London: Routledge, pp. 217–240.

Lynch, S., 2013. Congressman Lynch urges Attorney General Holder to strengthen guidelines on FBI confidential informants, August 23, 2013. Retrieved from http://lynch.house.gov/press-release/congressman-lynch-urges-attorney-general-holder-strengthen-guidelines-fbi-confidential [accessed May 27, 2014].

MacAskell, E., Borger, J., Davies, N., and Ball, J., 2013. GCHQ taps fibre-optic cables for secret access to world's communications. *The Guardian*, June 21, 2013. Retrieved from http://www.theguardian.com/uk/2013/jun/21/gchq-cables-secret-world-communications-nsa [accessed September 1, 2013].

MacDonald, S., 2008. MI5 targets dissidents as Irish terror threat grows. *The Guardian.* Retrieved from http://www.theguardian.com/uk/2008/jul/28/northernireland.uksecurity [accessed May 6, 2015].

Mackay, J., 1996. *Michael Collins: A Life.* Edinburgh: Mainstream Publishing.

Martin, G., 2011. *Essentials of Terrorism: Concepts and Controversies* (2nd edition). London: Sage.

Martin, K., 2004. Domestic intelligence and civil liberties. *SAIS Review of International Affairs* 24(1), 7–21.

Martin, M., 2013. *Understanding Terrorism: Challenges, Perspectives, and Issues* (4th edition). London: Sage.

McBarnett, D.J., 1992. It's not what you do but the way that you do it: Tax evasion, tax avoidance and the boundaries of deviance. In Downes, D. (editor), *Unravelling Criminal Justice.* London: Macmillan, pp. 178–201.

McCann, E., 2012. The detention of IRA veteran Marian Price harks back to internment. *The Guardian.*

McGartland, M., 1997. *Fifty Dead Men Walking.* London: Blake Publishing.

McLaughlin, E., 2007. *The New Policing.* London: Sage.

Middleton, B., 2013. Terrorism prevention and investigation measures: Constitutional evolution, not revolution? *Journal of Criminal Law* 77(6), 562–582.

Miller, J.M., 2011. Becoming an informant. *Justice Quarterly* 26(2), 203–220.

Miller, S., 1999. Noble cause corruption in policing. *African Security Review* 3(8), 12–22.

Moran, J., 2010. Evaluating special branch and the use of informant intelligence in Northern Ireland. *Intelligence and National Security* 25(1), 1–23.

Moriarty, G., 2012. Now is the time to "forge new friendships." *The Irish Times.*

Muir, W.K., 1977. *Police: Street Corner Politicians.* Chicago: The University of Chicago Press.

Muller-Wille, B., 2008. The effect of international terrorism on EU intelligence co-operation. *Journal of Common Market Studies* 46(1), 49–73.

Munro, V.E., 2006. Stopping traffic? A comparative study of responses to the trafficking in women for prostitution. *British Journal of Criminology* 46, 318–333.

Murphy, C.C., 2012. *EU Counter-Terrorism Law: Pre-Emption and the Rule of Law*. Oxford: Hart Publishing.

Mythen, G., and Walklate, S., 2006. Criminology and terrorism: Which thesis risk society or governmentality? *British Journal of Criminology* 46(3), 379–398.

National Strategy for Counter-Terrorism, 2011. Fact sheet. Retrieved from http://www.whitehouse.gov/the-press-office/2011/06/29/fact-sheet-national-strategy-counterterrorism [accessed September 2, 2013].

Newburn, T., 2006. Contrast in intolerance. In Newburn, T., and Rock, P. (editors), *The Politics of Crime Control*. Oxford: Oxford University Press, pp. 227–270.

Nolan, P., 2012. *Northern Ireland Peace Monitoring Report*. Belfast: Community Relations Council.

Norris, C., and Dunningham, C., 2000. Subterranean blues: Conflict as an unfinished consequence of the police use of informers. *Policing and Society* 9(3), 385–402.

O'Callaghan, S., 1998. *The Informer*. London: Bantam Press.

O'Carroll, L., and Norton-Taylor, R., 2013. David Miranda detention prompts outcry over "gross misuse" of terror laws. *The Guardian*, August 19, 2013. Retrieved from http://www.theguardian.com/world/2013/aug/19/david-miranda-detention-outcry-terrorism-laws [accessed September 2, 2013].

O'Connor, E., 2002. *James Larkin*. Cork: Cork University Press.

Oltermann, P., 2013. Britain accused of trying to impede EU data protection law. *The Guardian*, September 27, 2013. Retrieved from http://www.theguardian.com/technology/2013/sep/27/britain-eu-data-protection-law [accessed September 27, 2013].

OT Institute for Safety, Security, and Crisis Management, 2008. *Radicalisation, Recruitment and the EU Counter-Radicalisation Strategy*. Brussels: European Commission.

Owen, T., Bailin, A., Knowles, J.B., Macdonald, A., Ryder, M., Sayers, D., and Tomlinson, H., 2005. *Blackstone's Guide to the Serious Organised Crime and Police Act 2005*. Oxford: Oxford University Press.

Palmer, P., 2012. Dealing with the exceptional: Pre-crime anti-terrorism policy and practice. *Policing and Society* 22(4), 519–537.

Pantucci, R., 2010. A contest to democracy? How the UK has responded to the current terrorist threat. *Democratization* 17(2), 251–271.

Parker, A., 2013. MI5 security service director general's speech at RUSI. Retrieved from https://www.mi5.gov.uk/home/about-us/who-we-are/staff-and-management/director-general/speeches-by-the-director-general/director-generals-speech-at-rusi-2013.html [accessed March 1, 2014].

Parmar, A., 2011. Stop and search in London: Counter-terrorist or counter-productive? *Policing and Society* 21(4), 369–382.

Paul, R., 2013. Protect America for the Protect America Act. Retrieved from http://antiwar.com/paul/?articleid=12295 [accessed September 5, 2013].

Peers, S., 2011. EU *Justice and Home Affairs Law* (3rd edition). Oxford: Oxford University Press.

Pious, R.M., 2006. *The War in Terrorism and the Rule of Law.* Los Angeles, CA: Roxbury Publishing Company.

Police Ombudsman for Northern Ireland, 2007. *Investigate Report (Ballast Report).* Belfast: Information Directorate.

Porter, L.E., and Warrender, C., 2009. A multivariate model of police deviance: Examining the nature of corruption, crime and misconduct. *Policing and Society* 19(1), 79–99.

Punch, M., 2012. *State Violence, Collusion and the Troubles: Counter Insurgency, Government Deviance and Northern Ireland.* London: Pluto Press.

Punch, M., and Gilmour, S., 2010. Police corruption: Apples, barrels, and orchards. *Criminal Justice Matters* 79(1), 10–12.

Ratcliffe, J., 2008. *Intelligence-Led Policing.* Cullompton: Willan Publishing.

Rawlinson, R., 2003. Bad boys in the Baltics. In Edwards, A., and Gill, P. (editors), *Transnational Organised Crime: Perspectives on Global Security.* London: Routledge, pp. 131–142.

Rees, G.W., and Webber, M., 2002. Fighting organised crime: The European Union and internal security. In Crawford, A. (editor), *Crime and Insecurity: The Governance of Safety in Europe.* Cullompton: Willan Publishing, pp. 77–101.

Reiner, R., 1992. Policing a postmodern society. *The Modern Law Review* 55(6), 761–781.

Reiner, R., 2000. *The Politics of the Police* (3rd edition). Oxford: Oxford University Press.

Reiner, R., 2010. *The Politics of the Police* (4th edition). Oxford: Oxford University Press.

Rifkin, J., 2004. *The European Dream: How Europe's Vision of the Future is Quietly Eclipsing the American Dream.* Cambridge: Polity Press.

Robson, S., and Roberts, H., 2013. IRA militant on run from Italian police for alleged involvement in mafia money laundering scheme as luxury properties worth £390 million are seized. *Daily Mail.* Retrieved from http://www.dailymail.co.uk/news/article-2288630/Police-seize-resorts-Italy-IRA-militant-run-alleged-involvement-mafia-money-laundering-scheme.html [accessed May 6, 2015].

Rosenfeld, R., Jacobs, B.A., and Wright, R., 2003. Snitching and the code of the street. *British Journal of Criminology* 43(2), 291–309.

Rossington, B., 2012. Scouse/IRA gang ran massive drug trade across the UK, Bebington boxer Brett Flounery trial told. *Liverpool Echo,* January 28, 2012. Retrieved from http://www.liverpoolecho.co.uk/liverpool-news/local-news/2012/01/28/scouse-ira-gang-ran-massive-drug-trade-across-the-uk-bebington-boxer-brett-flournoy-murder-trial-told-100252-30214775/[accessed January 30, 2013].

Rusbridger, A., 2013. David Miranda, schedule 7 and the danger that all reporters now face. *The Guardian,* August 19, 2013. Retrieved from http://www.theguardian.com/commentisfree/2013/aug/19/david-miranda-schedule7-danger-reporters [accessed September 2, 2013].

Ryder, C., 1989. *The RUC: A Force Under Fire.* London: Methuen.

Ryder, N., 2007. A false sense of security? An analysis of legislative approaches towards the prevention of terrorist finance in the United States and the United Kingdom. *Journal of Business Law* 821–850.

Saar, J., 2004. Crime, crime control, and criminology in post-communist Estonia. *European Journal of Criminology* 1(4), 505–531.

Sageman, M., 2008. *Leaderless Jihad: Terror Networks in the Twenty-First Century.* Philadelphia, PA: University of Philadelphia Press.

Sanders, A., and Young, R., 2012. From suspect to trial. In Maguire, M. et al. (editors), *The Oxford Handbook of Criminology.* Oxford: Oxford University Press, pp. 838–865.

Sanders, A., Young, R., and Burton, M., 2010. *Criminal Justice* (4th edition). Oxford: Oxford University Press.

Sarma, K., 2005. Informers and the battle against Republican terrorism: A review of 30 years of conflict. *Police Practice and Research* 6(2), 165–180.

Saul, B., 2010. *Defining Terrorism in International Law.* Oxford: Oxford University Press.

Seib, P., 2012. Public diplomacy versus terrorism. In Freedman, D., and Kishan Thussu, D. (editors), *Media and Terrorism* 14(3), 63–76.

Sedgwick, M., 2004. Al Qaeda and the nature of religious terrorism. *Terrorism and Political Violence* 16(4), 795–814.

Shelley, L., and Picarelli, J.T., 2002. Methods not motives: Implications of the convergence of international organised crime and terrorism. *Police Practice and Research* 3(4), 305–318.

Sheptycki, J., 2007. High policing in the security control society. *Policing* 1(1), 25–37.

Silke, A., 2008. Holy warriors: Exploring the psychological processes of Jihadi radicalisation. *European Journal of Criminology* 5(1), 99–123.

Sledge, M., 2013. Supreme Court's *Clapper v. Amnesty International* decision could affect indefinite detention lawsuit. *Huffington Post*, February 27, 2013. Retrieved from http://www.huffingtonpost.com/2013/02/27/clapper-v-amnesty-international_n_2769294.html [accessed September 5, 2013].

Snell, K., and Tombs, S., 2011. How do you get your voice heard when no-one will let you? Victimisation at work. *Criminology and Criminal Justice* 11(3), 207–223.

Social Research Association's Ethical Guidelines, 2003. Available from www.the-sra.org.uk [accessed January 11, 2012].

South, N., 2000. Informers, agents and accountability: Some matters arising from the use of human information sources by the Police and the Security Service. In Billingsley, R., Menitz, T., and Bean, P. (editors), *Informers: Policing, Policy, Practice.* Cullompton: Willan Publishing, pp. 67–80.

Sparrow, A., Gabbat, A., and Quinn, B., 2013. Reactions to the detention of David Miranda at Heathrow Airport—as it happened. *The Guardian*, August 20, 2013. Retrieved from http://www.theguardian.com/politics/blog/2013/aug/19/glenn-greenwald-partner-detained-live-reaction [accessed September 3, 2013].

Staniforth, A., 2010. *Blackstone's Counter-terrorism Handbook* (2nd edition). Oxford: Oxford University Press.

Stuttmoeller, M. et al., 2011. Radicalisation and risk assessment. In Kennedy, L.W., and McGarrell, E.F. (editors), *Crime and Terrorism Risk: Studies in Criminology and Criminal Justice.* London: Routledge, pp. 78–96.

Surtees, R., 2008. Traffickers and trafficking in Southern and Eastern Europe: Considering the other side of human trafficking. *European Journal of Criminology* 5(1), 39–68.

Taylor, P., 1997. *Provos: The IRA and Sinn Fein.* London: Bloomsbury.

The European Parliament, 2005. The Hague Programme—Ten priorities for the next five years—a partnership for European renewal. Brussels, COM2005.

The Poverty Site, 2011. Annual survey of hours and earnings 2010. Retrieved from www.poverty.org.uk [accessed March 31, 2012].

The White House Blog, 2011. National strategy for counterterrorism, June 2011. Retrieved from http://www.whitehouse.gov/blog/2011/06/29/national-strategy-counterterrorism%20 [accessed August 29, 2013].

Tuman, J.S., 2010. *Communicating Terror: The Rhetorical Dimensions of Terrorism* (2nd edition). London: Sage.

Tupman, W.A., 1998. Where has all the money gone? The IRAS as a profit-making concern. *Journal of Money Laundering Control* 1(4), 303–311.

Turcotte, M., 2008. Shifts in police informants negotiations. *Global Crime* 9(11), 291–305.

United Nations General Assembly, 2001. Resolution 55/25: United Nations Convention Against Transnational Organised Crime. A/Res/55/2.

US Attorney General's Guidelines Regarding the Use of Confidential Informants. 2006. Retrieved from https://www.fas.org/irp/agency/doj/fbi/dojguidelines.pdf [accessed May 27, 2014].

Valino, A. et al., 2010. The economics of terrorism: An overview and applied studies. In Buesa, M., and Baumert, T. (editors), *The Economic Repercussions of Terrorism*. Oxford: Oxford University Press, pp. 3–36.

Van Cleef, C.R., 2003. USA Patriot Act: Statutory analysis and regulatory implementation. *Journal of Financial Crime* 11(1), 73–102.

Vaughan, B., and Kilcommins, S., 2008. *Terrorism, Rights and the Rule of Law.* Cullompton: Willan Publishing.

Vermeulen, F., 2014. Suspect communities—targeting violent extremism at the local level. *Terrorism and Political Violence* 26(2), 286–306.

Vertigans, S., 2011. *The Sociology of Terrorism: People, Places and Processes.* London: Routledge.

Waddington, P.A.J., 1999. Police (Canteen) sub-culture: An appreciation. *British Journal of Criminology* 39(2), 287–309.

Walker, C., 2007. The legal definition of "terrorism" in United Kingdom law and beyond. *Public Law* 331–352.

Walker, C., 2009. *Blackstone's Guide to the Anti-Terrorism Legislation* (2nd edition). Oxford: Oxford University Press.

Walker, C., 2012. The Terrorism Prevention and Investigation Measures Act 2011: One thing but not much the other? *Criminal Law Review* 6, 421–438.

Walkers, A., 2008. Democracy's double edge: Police and procedure in the United States. In Haberfeld, M.R., and Ibrahim, C. (editors), *Comparative Policing: The Struggle for Democratization*. London: Sage, pp. 325–340.

Wannenburg, G., 2003. Links between organised crime and Al Qaeda. *South African Journal of International Affairs* 10(2), 77–90.

Watt, N., 2013. Prism scandal: European commission to seek privacy guarantees from US. *The Guardian*, June 10, 2013. Retrieved from http://www.theguardian.com/world/2013/jun/10/prism-european-commissions-privacy-guarantees [accessed September 1, 2013].

Weinberg, L. et al. 2004. The challenges of conceptualising terrorism. *Terrorism and Political Violence* 16(4), 777–794.

Weiss, M.A., 2005. *Terrorist Financing: US Agency Efforts and Inter-Agency Coordination.* Congressional Research Service: The Library of Congress.

Western Australia Parliament Joint Standing Committee on the Corruption and Crime Commissionm, 2011. *Corruptions Risks of Controlled Operations and*

Informants. Report No. 15 in the 38th Parliament. Perth: Legislative Assembly, Parliament of Western Australia.

Westmarland, L., 2005. Police ethics and integrity: Breaking the blue code of silence. *Policing and Society* 15(2), 145–165.

Whitman, J.Q., 2004. The two western cultures of privacy: Dignity versus liberty 113. *Yale Law Journal* 1151–1221.

Whittaker, D., 2012. *The Terrorism Reader* (4th edition). London: Routledge.

Williamson, T., and Bagshaw, P., 2001. The ethics of informer handling. In Billingsley, R. Menitz, T., and Bean, P. (editors), *Informers: Policing, Policy, Practice.* Cullompton: Willan Publishing, pp. 50–66.

Wyn Rees, G., and Webber, M., 2002. Fighting organised crime: The European Union and internal security. In Crawford, A. (editor), *Crime and Insecurity: The Governance of Safety in Europe.* Cullompton: Willan Publishing.

Yoo, J., 2010. Counterterrorism and the constitution: Does providing security require a trade-off with civil liberties? In Gottlieb, S. (editor), *Debating Terrorism and Counterterrorism: Conflicting Perspective on Causes, Contexts and Responses.* Washington: CQ Press, pp. 336–352.

Index